Laws against Marijuana

Laws
against
Marijuana

The Price We Pay

ARTHUR D. HELLMAN

University of Illinois Press
URBANA CHICAGO LONDON

To my mother and father

LIBRARY OF CONGRESS CATALOGING IN PUBLICATION DATA

Hellman, Arthur D 1942–
    Laws against marijuana.

    Includes bibliographical references and index.
    1. Marihuana—Law and legislation—United States.
I. Title.
KF3891.M2H4   344'.73'0545   74-34150
ISBN 0-252-00438-8

Contents

Preface

In an era when readers are calling upon publishers to practice literary birth control, a heavy burden of justification rests upon anyone who would send yet another book into the world. Especially is this so when his brainchild appears to closely resemble earlier arrivals in the literary maternity ward. Doctors, lawyers, and even other law professors have had their say about marijuana; is there really a need for further exploration of the subject?

To begin with, this is not a book about marijuana; it is a book about the marijuana laws. I am not arguing that the use of marijuana is desirable or even that it is harmless. I am arguing, rather, that in the light of what is known and what is likely to be learned about the drug, society is injured far more seriously by law enforcement efforts aimed at stamping out marijuana use than it is by marijuana itself.

It is difficult to write about marijuana without becoming embroiled in discussions of the drug's effects on users or of the validity and application of John Stuart Mill's strictures against society's attempting to protect individuals from their own folly. I have not entirely avoided these issues in the pages that follow. Nevertheless, this book is addressed to the reader who is not persuaded by claims of the benefits to be obtained from marijuana smoking and who believes that neither philosophical nor constitutional principles disable society from imposing criminal sanctions on the use and distribution of marijuana. I hope to persuade this reader that whatever consequences he might apprehend from the widespread use of marijuana, the greater threat to the values he cherishes as an American citizen is posed by the marijuana *laws*.

In March, 1972, a presidential commission headed by former Pennsylvania Governor Raymond Shafer recommended a sharply limited decriminalization of marijuana: the possession and distribution of small amounts in the home would no longer be unlawful, but most of the other prohibitions in current statutes would be retained. Even these mild reforms were rejected by the administration that chartered the commission, but the commission's report remains an important document deserving of detailed analysis. I suggest that if the commission is correct in its diagnosis (and other studies strongly indicate that it is), then the appropriate cure is total decriminalization accompanied by the enactment of a licensing system similar to that used for alcohol, not the continued "partial prohibition" urged by the commission.

The heart of this book is a study of the practices used by the police in enforcing laws against marijuana. The conclusion is that *any* attempt to deal with marijuana through the criminal process will require the police to resort to techniques which approach the limits of constitutional guarantees and which conflict most strongly with the values of privacy, spontaneity, and individual dignity. The halfway measures proposed by the Shafer commission would thus do little to mitigate the worst consequences of the present laws.

The reader who has never used marijuana and who feels no temptation to do so may think that the police practices of snooping, surveillance, and harassment—described in detail in the following pages—have nothing to do with his life. Unfortunately, as I will try to show, it is not so easy to escape the consequences of these practices. This is so for two independent reasons. First, the tactics used by the police to enforce marijuana laws are those which inevitably intrude on the privacy and security of the innocent as well as the guilty. Second, the effects of these practices are felt not only by their victims but also by society as a whole: every citizen has an interest in preserving the rule of law and the integrity of those who enforce it.

In a sense it would be accurate to say that I have written another book about the marijuana laws because the earlier ones have failed. The laws remain on the books, and the Law is the loser. I hope to persuade the reader that whatever harm he may attribute to the use of marijuana, the criminal process is an undesirable way of attempting to prevent it.

Washington, D.C.   ARTHUR D. HELLMAN
April, 1974

Acknowledgments

For assistance and counsel in the writing of this book, I owe a great deal to many people. Dean John E. Cribbet of the University of Illinois College of Law encouraged me in many ways and made it possible for me to obtain financial support for research. Professor Wayne LaFave, also of the University of Illinois College of Law, read a late draft of the manuscript and offered many valuable suggestions. Robert Finch, now of the Illinois bar, provided useful insights as well as assistance in research.

I am also grateful, for particularly valuable help, to Dean Howard Sacks and Professor Robert Bard of the University of Connecticut School of Law; Dean Douglas R. Heidenreich of William Mitchell College of Law; John Burnes; Peter Carey; and Michael Gordon.

Finally, Richard Wentworth and Noel Parsons of the University of Illinois Press have provided counsel and encouragement in addition to thoughtful and thorough editing. I am in their debt.

Note on Citations

Anyone who has read Frank Sullivan's classic parody "A Garland of Ibids for Van Wyck Brooks" [1] will think twice before weighting his prose with sheaves of *supra's*, columns of *ibid.*'s, and other indicia of scholarly respectability. The instinct of a lawyer, on the other hand, is to attach footnotes to his sentences the way a bird fastens twigs to her nest (and, I suppose, for essentially the same reason). As a writer who is both a member of the bar and a Sullivan fan,[2] I have tried to steer a middle course between the shoals of pedantry on the one side and the shallows of irresponsibility on the other.

The reason for including citations is, of course, to identify the authorities on which a writer's assertions rest so that the curious reader can follow up points that interest him or simply verify the author's use of his sources. In writing the footnotes to this volume I have attempted to provide in a convenient form all of the information needed by the reader who wishes to pursue further inquiries, without unduly disfiguring the page for the reader who prefers to concentrate on the text. Thus, successive quotations from the same work are cited in a single footnote unless the text requires separate citations. In Part Two a single footnote is used for most of the cases discussed except when reference is made to scattered pages of a lengthy opinion.

[1] Frank Sullivan, "A Garland of Ibids for Van Wyck Brooks," in *A Subtreasury of American Humor,* ed. E. B. White and Katherine White (New York, 1941), 263.

[2] *Cf. ibid.,* 266.

References to nonlegal sources are in reasonably conventional form (except for the introductory signals, discussed below), but it may be useful to say a few words about the references to legal materials. The legal materials cited are principally of two kinds: legal periodicals and appellate case reports. To anyone coming upon them for the first time, citations to legal materials may appear somewhat arcane, but their basic form is simple enough: each "cite" directs the reader to a particular series of books and identifies the particular volume and page (or pages) where the reference is to be found. It is all very logical, with one exception: the name of the series is bracketed between the number of the volume and the number of the page. Thus, a citation to "60 *Geo. L. J.* 507 (1971)" directs the reader to volume 60, page 507, of the *Georgetown Law Journal.* (The name of the series is ordinarily abbreviated, and all initial citations in each chapter include the date of publication.) Finally, where two or more page numbers are given, the first indicates the page where the article or case begins, and the others indicate the particular page or pages quoted from or referred to in the text. Case reports are somewhat more complicated, in part because most cases are to be found in more than one series of reports— an official report and one or more unofficial reports. Moreover, the official citation usually indicates the court of decision, but sometimes it does not. Once again, however, the basic patterns are essentially simple.

United States Supreme Court cases are cited only to the official report. For example, Cohen v. California, 403 U.S. 15 (1971) will be found in volume 403 of the *United States Reports* at page 15. For very recent cases, the unofficial *Supreme Court Reporter* citation is given, as: United States v. Robinson, 94 S. Ct. 467 (1973).

Cases in the United States Courts of Appeals are cited to the *Federal Reporter* (usually the second series), while cases in the district courts are cited to the *Federal Supplement,* with the particular circuit or district indicated in parentheses following the page number. For example, United States v. Giordano, 469 F.2d 522 (4th Cir. 1972) identifies a case decided by the Fourth Circuit Court of Appeals in 1972; the report of the case begins at page 522 of the *Federal Reporter, Second Series,* volume 469. Johnson v. Beto, 337 F. Supp. 1371 (S.D. Tex. 1972) identifies a case decided by the United States District Court for the Southern District of Texas; the report begins at page 1371 of the *Federal Supplement,* volume 337.

State court cases are cited first to the official report, if one exists, and then to the unofficial report (or reports) in one (or two) of the regional reporters published by the West Publishing Company, a private but bibliographically ubiquitous enterprise. For example, State v. Curtis, 290 Minn. 429, 190 N.W.2d 636 (1971) is reported officially on page 429 of the *Minnesota Reports,* volume 290; it will also be found at page 636 of the *Northwestern Reporter, Second Series,* volume 190. If no official report is available, only the unofficial citation is given, with the jurisdiction identified in parentheses along with the date of decision. For example, State v. Monteith, 477 P.2d 224 (Ore. App. 1970) identifies a 1970 decision of the Oregon Court of Appeals; it will be found at page 224 of the *Pacific Reporter, Second Series,* volume 477.

Finally, there remain the signals used to introduce many of the citations. These signals (*"cf.,"* "see," "but see," and so forth) were developed by the legal periodicals "to indicate the purpose for which an authority is cited, or the degree of support the authority gives to a proposition." [3] The *Uniform System of Citation* gives the following exegesis for the signals used in this volume:

Signal	*Significance*
[none]	Cited authority directly supports statement in text.
e.g.,	There are other examples, but citation to them would not be helpful.
see	Cited authority constitutes basic source material supporting an opinion or conclusion of either law or fact drawn in a textual statement. It indicates that the asserted opinion or conclusion will be suggested by an examination of the cited authority rather than that the opinion or conclusion is stated by the cited authority.
cf.	Cited authority supports a statement, opinion, or conclusion of law different from that in text but sufficiently analogous to lend some support to the text.
But see	Cited authority strongly suggests a contrary proposition. . . .

---

[3] Harvard Law Review Association, *A Uniform System of Citation,* 11th ed. (Cambridge, Mass., 1967), 86.

| But *cf.* | Cited authority supports a position different from the statement in text, but sufficiently analogous to it to suggest a contrary conclusion. |
| See generally
See also | Cited authority is broader in scope than, or develops a question analogous to, discussion in text without lending support to proposition asserted, but can profitably be compared with it.[4] |

The subtle distinctions among some of these signals have baffled more than one writer, and law review editors have been known to argue far into the night over whether a citation should be preceded by "But see" or "But *cf.*" The reader need not bother with these niceties if he prefers not to; the signals are there (used properly, I hope) for anyone who wishes to make use of them.

[4] *Ibid.,* 86–88.

PART ONE

I

Arguments against
the Marijuana Laws

At least four distinct kinds of arguments may be made to support the repeal of criminal sanctions against the use and distribution of marijuana. These arguments may be summarized briefly as follows:

(1) Criminal sanctions against marijuana use and distribution should be repealed because the use of marijuana is or may be beneficial to the user and thus to society.

(2) Criminal sanctions against the use and distribution of marijuana should be repealed because society has no warrant to interfere with the liberty of the individual to do as he likes simply to protect him from harm to himself.

(3) Criminal sanctions against the use and distribution of marijuana should be repealed because they are unconstitutional.

(4) Laws against the use and distribution of marijuana should be repealed because the costs to society of attempting to enforce them far exceed any benefits to be gained from dealing with the phenomenon of marijuana use through the criminal process.

For the purpose of this volume I am willing to assume that the reader has rejected the first three arguments but is open to persuasion by the fourth and narrowest. The limited compass of the position advocated here can be best appreciated after a review of the broader arguments.

BENEFIT

The argument that marijuana is or may be beneficial to the user and thus to society usually rests on one of two possible bases: the hedonistic or the pharmacological.

What I have termed the *hedonistic* argument derives from the philosophy expressed in the pre-Christian era by the Greek thinker Aristippus and in the nineteenth century by Walter Pater. In the widely read conclusion to his study of the Renaissance, Pater wrote: "Not the fruit of experience, but experience itself, is the end. A counted number of pulses only is given to us of a variegated, dramatic life. How may we see in them all that is to be seen in them by the finest senses? . . . To burn always with this hard, gemlike flame, to maintain this ecstasy, is success in life. . . . [W]e have an interval, and then our place knows us no more. [O]ur one chance lies in expanding that interval, in getting as many pulsations as possible into the given time." [1] It may be that many of Pater's enthusiastic readers misunderstood and even vulgarized his message, but the attitude he was thought to express continues to find followers and to serve as a counterweight to the dominant Anglo-American work ethic.

One need not accept a hedonistic philosophy with all of its ramifications in order to urge that marijuana should be decriminalized because it gives pleasure to the user. It is enough that the drug produces agreeable sensations or increases perception without causing harmful effects. Many advocates have written about marijuana as an aid to perception and creativeness. Typical is this comment by the poet Allen Ginsberg: "Although most scientific authors who present their reputable evidence for the harmlessness of marijuana make no claim for its surprising *usefulness,* I do make that claim: Marijuana is a useful catalyst for specific optical and aural esthetic perceptions. I apprehended the structure of certain pieces of jazz and classical music in a new manner under the influence of marijuana, and these apprehensions have remained valid in years of normal consciousness." Ginsberg concludes by urging the legalization of marijuana "as a catalyst to self-awareness." [2] Similar arguments have been made by Timothy Leary. His second "Commandment for the Nuclear Age" proclaims, "Thou Shalt Not Prevent Thy Fellow Man from Altering His Own Consciousness." For Leary, marijuana "and other stimulants of sensory awareness are like corrective lenses; they bring visions into sharper focus." [3] The novelist

[1] Walter Pater, *The Renaissance* (New York, Modern Library ed., n.d.), 197.

[2] Allen Ginsberg, "First Manifesto to End the Bringdown," in *The Marihuana Papers,* ed. David Solomon (New York, Signet ed., 1968), 244, 248.

[3] The first commandment is "Thou Shalt Not Alter the Consciousness of Thy Fellow Man" (Timothy Leary, "The Politics, Ethics and Meaning of Marijuana," in *ibid.,* 130, 139).

William Burroughs has written along similar lines: "[C]annabis is very useful to the artist, activating trains of association that would otherwise be inaccessible. . . . Cannabis serves as a guide to psychic areas which can then be re-entered without it. . . . [C]annabis and the other hallucinogens provide a key to the creative process. . . ." [4] Even the National Commission on Marihuana and Drug Abuse, which concludes by recommending a program for discouraging the use of marijuana, concedes that "[f]or most marijuana users who continue to use the drug, the experience is overwhelmingly pleasurable." [5]

Arguments based on the pleasure-giving qualities of marijuana are not likely to influence legislators to decriminalize the drug and indeed might have a negative effect. As Dr. Lester Grinspoon has pointed out, "Marijuana is considered to be used 'just for fun,' and therefore is in conflict with powerful vestiges of the Protestant ethic, which demands self-control—except at specially prescribed times, when the restraints are lowered briefly—hard work, rationality, order, moderation, and future-oriented planning. Drug use is viewed by adherents to this ethic as just one more manifestation of a growing interest in sensual gratification, both esthetic and hedonistic." [6] An American audience is more likely to be impressed by pragmatic arguments claiming medical effectiveness. Such arguments have been made and are supported by clinical reports to an extent that will surprise those who think of marijuana solely as an intoxicant. (Indeed, one authority was struck by the fact that "so many of the early medical reports on cannabis fail to mention the plant's intoxicating properties.") [7]

Dr. Solomon Snyder, professor of psychiatry and pharmacology at Johns Hopkins School of Medicine, and Grinspoon, who is an associate clinical professor of psychiatry at Harvard Medical School, have described in detail the many medicinal applications which nineteenth-century physicians found for marijuana. *Cannabis* was used extensively and with apparent success to treat a wide variety of ailments, "from migraines and excessive menstrual bleeding to

[4] William Burroughs, "Points of Distinction between Sedative and Consciousness-Expanding Drugs," in *ibid.,* 445–46.

[5] National Commission on Marihuana and Drug Abuse, *Marihuana: A Signal of Misunderstanding* (Washington, D.C., 1972), 58 [hereinafter cited as *Signal of Misunderstanding*].

[6] Lester Grinspoon, *Marihuana Reconsidered* (New York, Bantam ed., 1971), 373.

[7] Solomon Snyder, "What We Have Forgotten about Pot—A Pharmacologist's History," *N.Y. Times Magazine,* Dec. 13, 1970, p. 124.

ulcers, epilepsy and even tooth decay." [8] It may also be effective in helping patients to withdraw from the use of addictive drugs and in treating various psychiatric illnesses.[9] Other studies have raised the possibility that *Cannabis* may have antibacterial properties.[10] More recently, researchers have reported that marijuana smoking may prevent glaucoma by reducing fluid pressure in the eyes.[11]

Grinspoon concludes that although the Marijuana Tax Act of 1937 precluded further research, "a spate of papers published prior to that time have established for [marijuana] a compelling potential as a medicinally useful substance. . . . With the relaxation of the restrictions on research and the chemical manipulation of the various cannabinol derivatives, this potential will doubtless eventually be realized." [12] His optimism is echoed by Snyder, who predicts that "the latter part of this century will witness the revival of cannabis in new forms as a valuable therapeutic agent." [13]

INDIVIDUAL LIBERTY

The argument that sanctions against marijuana should be repealed because society has no warrant to interfere with the liberty of the individual to do as he likes simply to protect him from harm to himself rests on two premises. The major premise is the jurisprudential proposition, stated in classic form by John Stuart Mill, that "the only purpose for which power can be rightfully exercised over any member of a civilized community, against his will, is to prevent harm to others. His own good, either physical or moral, is not a sufficient warrant." [14] The minor premise is the assertion that if the use of marijuana has any harmful consequences at all, they are visited only upon the user. The argument has been stated concisely by Dr. Thomas Szasz: "In an open society, it is none of the government's business what idea a man puts into his mind; likewise, it should be none of the government's business what drug he puts into his body." [15]

Mill's admirers acknowledge that the "harm to others" formula

---

[8] *Ibid.*, 26.
[9] *Ibid.*, 122; Grinspoon, *supra* note 6, at 248–49.
[10] Grinspoon, *supra* note 6, at 247–48.
[11] *N.Y. Times*, July 28, 1972, p. 35, col. 4.
[12] Grinspoon, *supra* note 6, at 242–43.
[13] Snyder, *supra* note 7, at 125.
[14] John Stuart Mill, *On Liberty* (London, Blackwell ed., 1948), 8.
[15] Thomas Szasz, "The Ethics of Addiction," *Harper's*, April, 1972, p. 75.

"solves very little. . . . The question is not one of whether or not there will be harm done; it is one of the remoteness and probability of the harm." [16] Nevertheless, as Herbert Packer has stated, the formula is useful because it "forces an inquiry into precisely what bad effects are feared if the conduct in question is not suppressed by the criminal law." [17] Norval Morris and Gordon Hawkins have sought to frame the inquiry in somewhat more specific terms: "For the criminal law at least, man has an inalienable right to go to hell in his own fashion, provided that he does not *directly* injure the *person or property* of another on the way." [18] The approach advocated by Morris and Hawkins is usually termed *utilitarianism*. Utilitarianism has been defined by a modern writer as "the theory that the social good is nothing more than maximization of the aggregated welfare of the individual members of society. A utilitarian will tend to consider as costs and benefits of penal laws only those consequences which involve harm and the prevention of harm to specific individuals." [19] This, of course, is an expanded version of the celebrated dictum of Jeremy Bentham, the founder of the utilitarian school of philosophy: "The greatest happiness of the greatest number is the foundation of morals and legislation." Today, however, the term is somewhat misleading, since many of the contemporary disciples of Mill and Bentham, such as Herbert Packer, Morris, and Hawkins, rely essentially on cost-benefit arguments rather than on theories of moral philosophy. In order to distinguish between the two lines of argument I refer to the position epitomized by Szasz as the "ethic of individualism"—a phrase which he himself uses.

The advantage (or disadvantage, depending on one's point of view) [20] of the ethic of individualism is that it permits the legislator to ignore arguments based upon the supposed intangible effects of marijuana use on society in general. Such arguments can never be proved or disproved, for they depend on the values accepted by the individual. It is sometimes said, for example, that marijuana use leads to idleness, dropping out, underachievement, and rejection of

[16] Herbert Packer, *The Limits of the Criminal Sanction* (Stanford, Calif., 1968), 266.

[17] *Ibid.*, 267.

[18] Norval Morris and Gordon Hawkins, *The Honest Politician's Guide to Crime Control* (Chicago, 1970), 2 [emphasis added].

[19] Schneyer, "Problems in the Cost-Benefit Analysis of Marijuana Legislation," 24 *Stan. L. Rev.* 200 (1971).

[20] *Cf.* Barrett, book review in 44 *S. Cal. L. Rev.* 517 (1971).

the work ethic.[21] Even if such charges should be substantiated, the question would remain whether dropping out, rejection of the work ethic, and similar consequences can be considered harmful to society. As Lester Grinspoon has written, "Suppose . . . that the use of marijuana does promote the development of what has been called the 'antimotivational syndrome,' and that the widespread existence of this will change the lifestyle of our society. Even under these circumstances, whether such a change would constitute a 'harm' is basically a value judgment about what kind of a society is both possible and ideal." [22] Under the approach of Morris and Hawkins, harm of this kind, however disturbing it might be to some people, would be irrelevant to the formulation of the criminal law.

Advocates of the individualistic ethic would make the point more generally: it is impossible to say that the use of marijuana is harmful to society without relying on considerations which are none of the law's business. Harm to the user—whatever it might be—is irrelevant. Equally irrelevant are any consequences which do not involve harm to specific individuals or which are injurious only if one accepts an organic theory of society.[23]

It may be suggested, however, that dropping out and similar conduct may cause harm to individuals that is neither intangible nor defined in moral terms. The harm may be indirect and difficult to trace, but that would not make it less real. For example, if large numbers of young people were to repudiate the professional or technical jobs for which they have been trained, or if they were to lose interest in material acquisitions and achievements, society would suffer a significant economic loss, and that loss would be reflected in higher taxes, lower earnings, and perhaps a lower standard of living for many individuals.

An individualist would probably respond to this argument by saying that the causal relationship between the conduct to be prohibited and the harm that is feared is simply too attenuated to justify invoking the criminal law in order to avoid the harm. Criminalization is a very crude and awkward tool for dealing with economic or social problems. Conclusions about the origins of behavior like dropping out or underachievement must rest to a large extent on speculation. In a democratic society dedicated to the pursuit of happiness, among other things, a burden rests on the government to

---

[21] *Cf. Signal of Misunderstanding,* 97–101.
[22] Grinspoon, *supra* note 6, at 407.
[23] *Cf.* Schneyer, *supra* note 19, at 215; Barrett, *supra* note 20, at 520–21.

justify restrictions on individual freedom in the name of social good, and that burden is not met by speculative arguments about economic losses.

CONSTITUTIONALITY

In dealing with the constitutionality of sanctions against marijuana we are dealing not with a single argument but with several kinds of arguments directed primarily to laws against possession or use. The narrowest argument is that lengthy sentences of imprisonment for possession of marijuana violate the constitutional ban on cruel and unusual punishment. The argument is narrow in several respects. It addresses itself, for the most part, only to laws regulating possession and not to laws regulating sale or distribution. It does not call into question the substantive validity of the statutory ban—only the penalties inflicted for violation. And in some jurisdictions the argument has been made obsolete by legislatures which have reduced penalties for simple possession. Nevertheless, the argument remains important in the many jurisdictions where more stringent penalty schemes remain in force.

In Michigan, five of the six justices who joined in reversing the conviction of the radical poet John Sinclair agreed that a minimum sentence of nine and one-half years for possession of two marijuana cigarettes constituted cruel and unusual punishment.[24] Justice Brennan, writing the principal opinion on that issue, laid no emphasis on the miniscule quantity of marijuana involved in the particular case. He argued first that contrary to some earlier decisions the supreme court may find a punishment to be cruel and unusual even though it is within the range permitted by statute. He continued: "Where a minimum sentence is imposed which is demonstrably and grossly excessive, in the light of the depravity of the criminal as shown in the commission of the act and in light of the usual and customary disposition of those convicted of like conduct, such minimum sentence violates the constitutional prohibition against the inflicting of cruel or unusual punishment, and is illegal and void." [25]

Three justices on the Michigan court also accepted a broader

[24] People v. Sinclair, 387 Mich. 91, 194 N.W.2d 878 (1972). The court was unanimous in reversing the judgment; Black, J., took no part. Although some members of the court preferred to rest the decision on broader constitutional grounds, all but one agreed that the sentence constituted cruel and unusual punishment.
[25] 387 Mich. at 153, 194 N.W.2d at 906.

argument, holding that the statutory classification of marijuana along with "hard drug" narcotics violated the Equal Protection clause because the classification was unreasonable.[26] Justice Swainson, in a lengthy opinion, reviewed much of the recent literature on marijuana as well as the findings of the trial court in a companion Michigan case, *People* v. *Lorentzen*.[27] Although Justice Swainson does not describe the manner in which evidence was taken at Lorentzen's trial, the trial must have been conducted very much like a legislative hearing. In the appellate court, scholarly works, commission reports, and the *Lorentzen* findings were cited in support of the conclusion that "based on current scientific knowledge, marijuana is not a narcotic drug." [28] The Illinois court had earlier reached the same conclusion without citations.[29]

The equal protection argument may appeal to judges who believe that the Fourteenth Amendment does not enact John Stuart Mill's *On Liberty* any more than it does Herbert Spencer's *Social Statics*. Unfortunately, as Justice Black (among others) has pointed out, "substantive" equal protection involves the judiciary in second-guessing the legislature in a way that differs little from the bad old days of substantive due process.[30] The similarity becomes apparent when one looks at the "Stipulated Findings of Fact" in the *Lorentzen* case, cited by Justice Swainson in *Sinclair*.[31] One need not accept any clear-cut distinction between "legislative" and "adjudicative" facts in order to agree that these "findings of fact" resemble the report of a legislative committee much more than they resemble the findings ordinarily expected of a judge.

I do not mean to suggest that substantive equal protection has no place in constitutional law. I do suggest that Justice Swainson, in

[26] T. M. Kavanagh, C.J., and Williams and Swainson, JJ., agreed explicitly with this position. Brennan and Adams, JJ., concurred solely on the cruel and unusual punishment ground discussed above. T. G. Kavanagh, J., accepting a much broader argument, appeared to reject the equal protection claim.

[27] 387 Mich. 167, 194 N.W.2d 827 (1972).

[28] 387 Mich. at 115, 194 N.W.2d at 887.

[29] People v. McCabe, 49 Ill. 2d 338, 275 N.E.2d 407 (1971). Other courts have rejected the equal protection holdings of *McCabe* and *Sinclair*. See State v. Wadsworth, 109 Ariz. 59, 505 P.2d 230 (1973); Boswell v. State, 276 So. 2d 592 (Ala. 1973); Egan v. Sheriff, 503 P.2d 16 (Nev. 1972).

[30] See Harper v. Virginia Bd. of Elections, 383 U.S. 663, 676–77 (1966) (dissenting opinion); Karst, "Invidious Discrimination: Justice Douglas and the Return of the 'Natural-Law-Due-Process Formula,'" 16 *U.C.L.A. L. Rev.* 716, 738–39 (1969).

[31] 387 Mich. at 105 n. 14, 106 n. 16, 107 n. 18, 108 n. 27, 114 n. 35, 194 N.W.2d at 882, 883, 884, 886.

arguing that the legislature acted arbitrarily in classifying marijuana as a narcotic, is making a judgment that is not very different in kind from the broader conclusions reached by Justice T. G. Kavanagh.

It is Justice Kavanagh who, in a remarkable opinion, finds that the Constitution *does* enact Mill's *On Liberty.* The opinion is remarkable both for its conclusion and for the way in which it is reached. The major premise is that "an individual is free to do whatever he pleases, so long as he does not interfere with the rights of his neighbor or of society." [32] The only authority cited for this proposition is John Stuart Mill. Kavanagh does not even state the minor premise of the syllogism; he simply assumes that the private use of marijuana has no effect on other individuals or on society. Nor does he explain how this premise, which is implicit in his conclusion, can be reconciled with his warning that it is not the prerogative of a court to substitute its assessment of the data upon which laws are based for that of the legislature. Rather, Kavanagh marches forward to his conclusion: the law prohibiting the private possession of marijuana "is an impermissible intrusion on the fundamental rights to liberty and the pursuit of happiness, and is an unwarranted interference with the right to possess and use private property."

It is unfortunate that Kavanagh was content to rest his conclusion on little more than an *ipse dixit,* for the position he takes does find some support in American jurisprudence. The Kentucky court in 1909 (admittedly the heyday of substantive due process) held that the legislature could not constitutionally abridge the right to use liquor for one's own comfort "if the use is without *direct* injury to the public." [33] The court cited Blackstone, Cooley, Mill, and cases from West Virginia and North Carolina.[34] (The two earlier cases reached similar conclusions on the basis of less extensive analysis.) In more recent years, several courts have struck down laws requiring motorcyclists to wear protective helmets. Some of these decisions have rested on the proposition that the legislature cannot constitutionally prohibit conduct that is harmful only to the actor. Although these decisions represent the minority view, they indicate that Kavanagh is not alone in his approach.[35]

[32] 387 Mich. at 133, 194 N.W.2d at 896.

[33] Commonwealth v. Campbell, 133 Ky. 50, 63, 117 S.W. 383, 387 (1909) [emphasis added].

[34] State v. Gilman, 33 W. Va. 146, 10 S.E. 283 (1889); State v. Williams, 146 N.C. 618, 61 S.E. 61 (1908).

[35] The cases are collected in Annot., 32 A.L.R.3d 1270 (1970).

Kavanagh could also have cited Packer's recent article calling for a new look at substantive due process. Packer suggests that courts should ask "the (discredited) question of whether there is a 'rational basis' for the use of the criminal sanction in such areas as getting abortions, selling pornography, engaging in gambling, engaging in deviant sexual behavior, and trafficking in marijuana." If the court can find no "rational basis" for the legislation, the legislation would be held unconstitutional.[36]

Two aspects of Packer's analysis bear with special force on the plethora of opinions in the *Sinclair* case. First, Packer suggests that many recent cases which the United States Supreme Court purported to decide on equal protection grounds really raised issues of substantive due process. The same comment may be made about Swainson's classification rationale in *Sinclair*. Second, Packer addresses himself briefly to the question of how an advocate would prove the arbitrariness and, therefore, under his rationale, the unconstitutionality of a law. By far the best device, he states, is that of introducing evidence at the trial. This is the course that was followed in *Lorentzen,* the companion case to *Sinclair*. It thus seems that the Michigan court could have written an opinion closely tracking Packer's prescription by adopting the harm-to-others rationale of Justice Kavanagh and supporting the decision with the data cited by Justice Swainson in his equal protection opinion.

The court could also have struck down the law without relying on Mill at all; it could have argued instead that the private use of marijuana falls within the right of privacy adumbrated by the United States Supreme Court's decisions in *Griswold* v. *Connecticut* and *Stanley* v. *Georgia*.[37] Certainly those cases do not compel this conclusion; *Griswold* repeatedly emphasized the sanctity of the marital relationship, while the *Stanley* opinion laid heavy stress on the protection of free speech. Nevertheless, as Packer has suggested, these decisions "may have laid the foundation for invalidating criminal laws proscribing the possession of marijuana." [38] In *Griswold* the Court pointed out that the Connecticut law prohibiting the use of contraceptives could not be enforced without "allow[ing] the

[36] Packer, "The Aims of the Criminal Law Revisited: A Plea for a New Look at 'Substantive Due Process,' " 44 *S. Cal. L. Rev.* 490, 493 (1971).

[37] Griswold v. Connecticut, 381 U.S. 479 (1965); Stanley v. Georgia, 394 U.S. 557 (1969). *Griswold* held that the state could not prevent the use of contraceptives by married couples. *Stanley* struck down a law prohibiting the mere private possession of obscene matter.

[38] Packer, *supra* note 36, at 496.

police to search the sacred precincts of marital bedrooms. . . ."[39] If laws against the possession of marijuana cannot be enforced without unconstitutional searches, as Part Two of this volume suggests, similar reasoning would suggest that these laws, too, should be struck down. In *Stanley* the Court canvassed the various purposes that have been advanced for obscenity laws and found that these could not justify the state in regulating what a man may read or observe in his own home. The Court disclaimed any intention to curtail the power of governments to make possession of "other items, such as narcotics, firearms, or stolen goods, a crime,"[40] but two years later the Court seemed to indicate that *Stanley* did, after all, involve protection of privacy as much as it did free speech.[41]

In any event, it can be argued that *Stanley* and *Griswold* in conjunction support the proposition that marijuana possession laws are unconstitutional. The argument is the following: the threat to Fourth Amendment values which the Court emphasized in *Griswold* is analogous to the First Amendment concerns emphasized in *Stanley*. The Court in *Stanley* found that state interests which arguably justified restrictions on the *distribution* of obscenity could not constitutionally support restrictions on *possession* because such restrictions conflicted with the mandate of the First Amendment. The next step is to say that state interests which might justify prohibiting the distribution of marijuana cannot support a ban on private possession because the latter prohibition cannot be enforced without doing violence to the command of the Fourth Amendment. This minor premise would, of course, require proof, but in theory the Court might be persuaded of what is noticed judicially in *Griswold*.[42]

Other constitutional arguments can be made, but in an era of retrenchment on the Supreme Court their chances for acceptance are dim indeed.[43]

[39] 381 U.S. at 485.

[40] 394 U.S. at 568 n. 11.

[41] United States v. Reidel, 402 U.S. 351, 356 (1971).

[42] I do not suggest that the present court is likely to accept this reasoning; but *cf.* Eisenstadt v. Baird, 405 U.S. 438 (1972); Roe v. Wade, 410 U.S. 113 (1973).

[43] It could be argued, for example, that some use of marijuana falls within the "free exercise of religion" protected by the First Amendment or that the use of marijuana for political purposes may be considered symbolic "speech," also protected by the First Amendment. See, *e.g.*, Weiss and Wizner, "Pot, Prayer, Politics and Privacy: The Right to Cut Your Own Throat in Your Own Way," 54 *Iowa L. Rev.* 709 (1969).

COST-BENEFIT ANALYSIS

The argument I am making in this book is that laws against the use and distribution of marijuana should be repealed because the costs to society of attempting to enforce them far exceed any benefits to be gained from dealing with the phenomenon of marijuana use *through the criminal process.* In other words, I am writing for the reader who is not persuaded by claims for the benefits of marijuana and who believes that neither of the other arguments given above in this chapter disables society from imposing criminal sanctions on the use and distribution of marijuana. Even accepting all of these assumptions, I suggest, the rational legislator would vote to repeal our marijuana laws.

The argument, then, is cast in terms of a cost-benefit analysis similar to that employed by John Kaplan in *Marijuana: The New Prohibition.*[44] In a review of Kaplan's book, Theodore Schneyer praised Kaplan's analysis but found a need for further clarification and refinement.[45] I do not claim that the analysis here will meet all of Schneyer's strictures. I do suggest some considerations—some peculiar to the marijuana laws, some not—which I believe blunt the force of his criticisms.

The legislative processes that bring about the passage or repeal of criminal laws have received little scholarly attention,[46] but most observers would probably agree with Schneyer that legal costs— "negative effects which are borne by the legal system"—are "externalities of legal policy-making: legislators rarely take them into consideration and are not held accountable [to their constituents] for them." [47] Indeed, the same may be said for all kinds of social costs and often for enforcement costs. But it is precisely for this reason that there is value in bringing these costs to the attention of legislators and their constituents, even without meticulous analysis that would satisfy an economist. Unless the legislator is persuaded of the significance of such costs, he can be expected to vote on a proposed revision of the criminal law solely on the basis of whether he and his constituents approve or disapprove of the conduct in-

[44] John Kaplan, *Marijuana: The New Prohibition* (New York, Pocket Books ed., 1971).

[45] Schneyer, *supra* note 19.

[46] See Heinz, Gettleman, and Suskin, "Legislative Politics and the Criminal Law," 64 *Nw. U. L. Rev.* 277 (1969).

[47] Schneyer, *supra* note 19, at 203.

volved.[48] Unfortunately, the desirability of criminalizing conduct depends on many other considerations as well.

Proposals for reform of the marijuana laws may present an especially acute dilemma for the conscientious legislator. It has been shown that a large majority of the American public clings to beliefs about marijuana that have been discredited with virtual unanimity by responsible studies.[49] In order to remain in office, therefore, the legislator will feel strong pressure to cast his votes in accordance with those erroneous beliefs.[50] If he is to do otherwise, he must be convinced—and he must convince his constituents—that the issue is not simply whether marijuana is good or bad, but rather what happens when the government attempts to enforce a ban on its use and distribution. This volume attempts to answer that question.

[48] *Cf.* Packer, *supra* note 16, at 271–72. "Politicians rely heavily on the criminal law and like to invoke criminal sanctions in connection with most social problems, if only to indicate their moral fervor and political virtue. They take little interest in the consequences of the invocation" (Morris and Hawkins, *supra* note 18, at 2).

[49] See *infra* pp. 34–37.

[50] *Cf.* Boyko and Rotberg, "Constitutional Objections to California's Marijuana Possession Statute," 14 *U.C.L.A. L. Rev.* 773 (1967).

II

Costs and Benefits

Herbert Packer has reminded us that "[t]he prudent legislator, faced with . . . the question of whether to continue applying the criminal sanction to a certain kind of conduct, will ask himself what other means of control are available." [1] Costs and benefits cannot be described in the abstract.[2] The costs and benefits of "total prohibition"—the description given by the National Commission on Marihuana and Drug Abuse (the Shafer commission) to our present approach to marijuana [3]—must be described by reference to the costs and benefits of other proposed or plausible approaches. In this book I advocate the use of what Professor John Kaplan of the Stanford University School of Law terms the "licensing model" (referred to by the Shafer commission as "regulation").[4] In discussing the costs of our present approach I shall emphasize those costs that would not be incurred if a regulatory scheme were substituted for total prohibition. I shall also attempt to evaluate the difference in costs between total prohibition and the "partial prohibition" preferred by the commission (referred to by Kaplan as the "vice model").[5] Similar comparisons will be made with respect to benefits.

Of course, no one expects a legislator to weigh costs and benefits

[1] Herbert Packer, *The Limits of the Criminal Sanction,* 251.
[2] I have used the term *described* instead of *calculated* in effort to emphasize the lack of precision inherent in the analysis.
[3] See *infra* pp. 26–27.
[4] John Kaplan, *Marijuana: The New Prohibition,* 346–60; National Commission on Marihuana and Drug Abuse, *Marihuana: A Signal of Misunderstanding,* 146 [hereinafter cited as *Signal of Misunderstanding*].
[5] *Signal of Misunderstanding,* 150; Kaplan, *supra.* note 4, at 329–44.

with the precision of a chemist titrating a solution, but his constituents may reasonably ask that he use the right scale—or, to change the metaphor, that he put the equation in proper form. Admittedly, both sides of the equation include elements that must remain somewhat speculative. Nevertheless, to ignore those elements is to risk making a judgment that is at best ill informed and at worst hopelessly distorted.

HARM AND DETERRENCE

We may begin with the benefit side of the ledger. Theodore Schneyer states, "In gauging the extent to which the manifest purpose of the marijuana laws—to deter consumption—has been accomplished, the critical question is this: without the laws, how much more marijuana use would occur?" [6] This is accurate as far as it goes, but it implies that the purpose of the laws (or the reason for retaining them) is simply to deter consumption for deterrence's sake. If, on the other hand, the purpose is to prevent the harm which is thought to result from consumption, then the critical question for the rational legislator is not "Without the laws, how much more marijuana use would occur?" but "Without the laws, how much more harm resulting from the use of marijuana would occur?" [7]

Paradoxical as it may seem, the more refined formulation may in some respects be easier to answer than the question posed by Schneyer. As Schneyer points out, measuring the effectiveness of a law in terms of the extent to which it deters the forbidden conduct is extremely difficult. With the revised formulation, it is not necessary to measure *all* deterrence; the inquiry focuses only on the instances of deterrence which prevent the specific evils that the laws are aimed at preventing. [8]

[6] Schneyer, "Problems in the Cost-Benefit Analysis of Marijuana Legislation," 24 *Stan. L. Rev.* 200, 201 (1971).

[7] The use of the term "the laws" in both formulations is of course a great oversimplification. A law prescribing a minimum penalty of five years' imprisonment will, one supposes, have a very different deterrent effect from that of a law prescribing a penalty of seven days' imprisonment. (For reasons to be discussed later, see *infra* p. 193, the more stringent penalty may not necessarily have a greater deterrent effect.) Even identical laws may have different deterrent effects as a result of different patterns of enforcement. These variables must be taken into account whether Schneyer's formulation or mine is used.

[8] Schneyer acknowledges the possibility of this kind of analysis but finds that it involves "a kind of bootstrapping": "One approach would be to consider enforcement costs in light of the manifest purpose of the marijuana laws and per-

This distinction loses its force if the use of marijuana is itself considered to be an evil, regardless of the circumstances or the consequences of its use. With the exception of one consideration, however,[9] recent studies suggest that a rational legislator would be hard put to conclude that *any* use of marijuana is harmful. On the contrary, the harm which he might seek to prevent results from a particular kind of use, and that kind of use is probably the least likely to be deterred by laws.

The National Commission on Marihuana and Drug Abuse divided marijuana users into five categories, but in assessing the harm likely to result from use, the commission reduced these categories to two groups. In one group are the experimental, intermittent, and moderate users. In the other group are the heavy and very heavy users.[10] As to the first group, the commission concluded that "experimental or intermittent use of [marijuana] carries minimal risk to the public health."[11] This finding is supported by virtually every major study that has been published.[12] To the prudent legislator, then, the benefits to society of deterring experimental or intermittent use of marijuana must be considered minimal.[13]

The commission finds a more serious threat in the heavy use of marijuana, though even here the commission's conclusion can be termed tentative: "On the basis of past studies, the chronic, heavy use of marijuana seems to constitute a high-risk behavior, particularly among predisposed adolescents."[14] Because these studies are

haps the degree to which that purpose is effectuated. . . . [But] the analyst's ultimate conclusion will tend to reflect only his assessment of the desirability of the purpose of the legislation rather than the aggregate desirability of its real consequences" (Schneyer, *supra* note 6, at 203 n. 13). But surely it is possible to assess the degree to which laws effectuate their purpose without assessing the desirability of that purpose. In any event, the problem disappears when the analyst is also the legislator.

[9] See the discussion of the symbolic function of marijuana laws, *infra* pp. 21–26.
[10] *Signal of Misunderstanding,* 36–41.
[11] *Ibid.,* 91.
[12] Lester Grinspoon, *Marihuana Reconsidered,* 256–323; Kaplan, *supra* note 4, at 147–208; Michael Schofield, *The Strange Case of Pot* (London, Penguin ed., 1971), 40–41 (summarizing earlier studies).
[13] I have omitted the commission's caveat that "social influences might cause those who would not otherwise use the drug to be exposed to this minimal risk and the potential escalation of drug-using patterns" (*Signal of Misunderstanding,* 91). The meaning of this statement is not clear. The report repudiates the argument that the use of marijuana leads, in any causal sense, to the use of "harder" drugs (*ibid.,* 87–89). If the commission is concerned about "escalation" to heavier use of marijuana itself, there is strong reason to doubt that the law makes much difference in this regard. See *infra* p. 21.
[14] *Signal of Misunderstanding,* 87.

fragmentary and often conflicting, it is difficult to extract from the commission's report a clear picture of the risks involved. A close reading of the report suggests several possible ways in which the heavy use of marijuana may create public health problems.[15]

First, the commission states that "the chronic, heavy use of marijuana may jeopardize social and economic adjustments of the *adolescent.*"[16] Kaplan agrees: "Adolescence is a period of painful adjustment and of developing a whole new set of responses to the challenges of maturity. Use of a drug that allows one to avoid these problems can leave the adolescent half grown up and without sufficient 'coping mechanisms.' "[17] Evidence that heavy marijuana use has resulted in maladjusted or half-grown-up adolescents is, of course, difficult to obtain. Apart from the illegality of marijuana, which probably tends to inhibit candid reporting by physicians or their young patients, it will usually be impossible to isolate a single causative factor in a case of "maladjustment" or "inability to cope." It cannot be said, therefore, that the commission is wrong in concluding that the chronic, heavy use of marijuana by adolescents poses a threat to public health in the sense in which the commission uses the term.

Second, the commission expresses its concern that the "small minority of heavy, long-term marijuana users" may be exposed to a risk of "impaired general functioning in contemporary America."[18] What the commission means by "impaired general functioning" is not clear. The report refers to "clinical findings of impaired psychological function, carefully documented by medical specialists,"[19] but this assertion seems difficult to reconcile with the Task Force Report on which it presumably is based. Indeed, the Task Force presents much evidence suggesting that the heavy use of marijuana does *not*

---

[15] See *ibid.,* 8: "The Commission broadly defines public health concerns as all health problems which affect people en masse and are thereby difficult to treat on a traditional physician-to-patient basis. This category would include social and economic dependence and incapacity." In discussing the risks which the commission associates with the heavy use of marijuana, I have not attempted to separate those involving consequences solely to the user and those involving consequences to society. For reasons given earlier (*supra* pp. 6–9) I have assumed that both kinds of harm are properly the concern of the law. Those who accept the ethic of individualism as a philosophy of government will find virtually all "public health concerns," except those involving physical contagion and the like, to be outside the purview of the criminal law.

[16] *Signal of Misunderstanding,* 87 [emphasis added].

[17] Kaplan, *supra* note 4, at 174.

[18] *Signal of Misunderstanding,* 91.

[19] *Ibid.,* 90.

ordinarily result in impaired general functioning: "Objective studies of chronic, heavy smokers of potent preparations have not causally linked this drug with the amotivational syndrome which has been described by many clinicians. Almost all chronic, heavy smokers are indistinguishable from their peers in the lower socio-economic strata of their respective societies in social behavior, work performance, mental status and overall life style." [20] This is not to say that the risk is chimerical, but rather that the commission appears to have greatly exaggerated its significance.

Finally, the commission expresses the fear that heavy users "constitute a source of contagion within American society. They actively proselytize others into a drug-oriented way of life." [21] Even if the commission's assumptions about the proselytizing activities of heavy users are accurate (a dubious proposition),[22] several questions must be answered before it can be concluded that this proselytizing presents a significant danger to society. Do those who are proselytized become heavy users themselves, or do they use marijuana only on a casual or intermittent basis? For how long are they drawn into a "drug-oriented way of life"? Does a drug-oriented way of life necessarily preclude more socially productive activities? (A study conducted in Boston for the commission suggests that it does not.) [23]

Other researchers have found even the commission's conclusions, tentative and qualified though they are, to be unduly pessimistic. Dr. Lester Grinspoon said of the commission's report: "So much of the rationale for recommending the policy that they finally arrive at is based on their concern for the heavy user, one would suppose that they had presented compelling evidence that the pot-head very seriously jeopardizes his mental and physical well-being. In fact, they do little more than raise the question that there are some uncertainties about the consequences of long-term heavy use." [24] But even if further research should confirm the commission's worst fears about the consequences of heavy use, those findings would not

[20] *Signal of Misunderstanding, Appendix,* 58. See also *ibid.,* 24 (long-term ganja smokers in Jamaica show no decreased ability to perform usual activities), and *ibid.,* 55 (no gross behavioral deviations in long-term Greek hashish users).

[21] *Signal of Misunderstanding,* 82.

[22] See Erich Goode, The *Marijuana Smokers* (New York, 1970), 244 ("even the police realize that drug sellers need not proselytize potential users, that friends introduce friends to a drug"); *N.Y. Times,* Feb. 17, 1971, p. 20, col. 3 (quoting dealer, "Where do people get the idea we have to push grass? . . . I have to turn guys away.").

[23] *Signal of Misunderstanding, Appendix,* 68–249.

[24] Lester Grinspoon, "A Critique of *Marihuana: A Signal of Misunderstanding,*" *The Leaflet,* May–June, 1972, p. 5.

necessarily mean that society benefits from the marijuana laws. The prudent legislator would then have to ask: To what extent do the laws *deter* heavy use?

Obviously, this question can never be answered with precision, but two important considerations suggest great skepticism about the role of law. First, those persons who are so strongly drawn to marijuana that they will use it to excess are those who are least likely to be deterred by legal sanctions. Excessive use of any drug indicates a certain instability, or at least heedlessness. A person who is willing to experiment with his mental or physical health in that way is not likely to refrain from doing so simply because the particular drug is illegal as well as dangerous. Nor will the more tangible consequences of illegality affect his decision significantly; in most of the population centers of the country marijuana is easy enough to obtain, while for anyone who is reasonably careful the risk of being apprehended is very small.[25]

A second consideration is suggested by the commission itself. Positing that "a preference for individual productivity underlies this society's opposition to indiscriminate drug use," the commission cites "the fact that so few of the 24 million Americans who have tried marijuana . . . have used it irresponsibly"[26] as evidence of the extent to which the users have internalized that value. One may quarrel with the commission's identification of "a preference for individual productivity" as the principal value that inhibits Americans from using drugs indiscriminately, but certainly such values exist. And to the extent that these values are internalized (as the commission agrees they are), laws serve as no more than a reinforcement. In other words, the vast majority of Americans do not need laws to tell them not to use marijuana to excess.[27] The small minority whose internalized values do not inhibit such conduct are unlikely to be deterred by external legal sanctions either, for reasons I have just stated.

SYMBOLIC FUNCTIONS OF THE MARIJUANA LAWS

At least one critic has faulted John Kaplan for not including in his cost-benefit analysis "the possible symbolic functions" of the mari-

[25] *Cf.* Kaplan, *supra* note 4, at 339–40.

[26] *Signal of Misunderstanding,* 170–71.

[27] Indeed, it has been suggested that many, perhaps most, Americans would not be interested in using marijuana at all even if it were legal: "Most Americans have already found their drug of choice—alcohol—and there is more conditioning involved in such preferences than most people realize" (Joel Fort, "Pot: A Rational Approach," *Playboy,* Oct., 1969, p. 227).

juana laws.[28] Kaplan devotes the first chapter of his book to demonstrating that "the symbolic aspect of the law is of major significance," [29] but thereafter he does not consider the possible benefits to society of this symbolic function. Both Kaplan and the reviewer draw upon the analysis of Prohibition found in Joseph Gusfield's already-classic study *Symbolic Crusade*. I suggest that if one analyzes the symbolic functioning of the marijuana laws within the framework suggested by Gusfield, the net benefit that emerges is minimal at best.

Gusfield distinguishes between the instrumental and the symbolic functions of law. Law functions as an instrument when it influences behavior through enforcement. This, of course, is the function ordinarily envisioned for law by the common man, and distinguished writers have argued that it is the only function which the criminal law, at least, may legitimately perform. But it has long been recognized that law can also perform symbolic functions. "Symbolic aspects of the law," Gusfield writes, "do not depend on enforcement for their effect. . . . The symbolic act 'invites consideration rather than overt reaction.' " Law functions as a symbol when it "affects the designation of public norms" by "designating the content of public morality. . . . Law can thus be seen as symbolizing the public affirmation of social ideals and norms as well as a means of direct social control." [30]

Law in its symbolic aspects can provide two kinds of benefits for society. First, even when a law is not enforced, society may benefit from a phenomenon which Robin M. Williams, Jr., has labeled the "patterned evasion of norms." [31] Second, apart from patterned evasion, "the passage of legislation, the acts of officials, and decisions of judges" may have significance as "gestures of public affirmation."

"Patterned evasion" refers to a particular kind of inconsistency between a social norm (which may be a law) and actual behavior. It exists when a pattern of behavior "occurs in a recurrent socially organized manner and is seldom punished" in spite of the fact that "the written, publicly stated norms of the society call for punish-

---

28 Schneyer, *supra* note 6, at 215.

29 Kaplan, *supra* note 4, at 18.

30 Joseph Gusfield, *Symbolic Crusade: Status Politics and the American Temperance Movement* (Urbana, Ill., 1963). This summary of Gusfield's analysis draws upon both the book (principally chapter 5) and Gusfield's later article, "Moral Passage: The Symbolic Process in Public Designations of Deviance," 15 *Social Problems* 175 (1967).

31 See generally Robin M. Williams, Jr., *American Society: A Sociological Approach* (3d ed., New York, 1970), 413–19. Gusfield refers to an earlier edition of the work.

ment and proscribe the behavior." Gusfield suggests that such systematic evasion may function "to minimize conflicts between cultures by utilizing law to proclaim one set of norms as public morality and to use another set of norms in actually controlling that behavior. . . . Those groups who adhere to the public norm see it upheld at the public level while those whose cultural norms are offended are able to pursue the behavior they find legitimate." [32]

Certainly it is arguable, as Theodore Schneyer suggests in his review of Kaplan's book, that such conflict reduction may constitute a social benefit. Unfortunately, it is difficult to apply this argument to the marijuana laws. Schneyer recognizes that "the older and younger generations whose conflict is symbolized by the marijuana issue may be forced to confront one another's values and behavior so openly and frequently that the laws do not serve to reduce the level of conflict between them." [33] In view of the high emotional and rhetorical level of the marijuana debate, this is probably an understatement. Indeed, it is not even clear that patterned evasion is now occurring with respect to the marijuana laws. While it may be true that those groups who support the prohibition against marijuana see that norm upheld at the public level, it is difficult to believe either that they do not recognize that the law is being widely violated or that they are content with a law that is largely unenforced. At the same time, it would be at least an exaggeration to say that those who want to smoke marijuana "are able to pursue the behavior they find legitimate." As a practical matter this is probably true in most of the population centers of the country, but it does not mean that the law has no restrictive consequences for the user: he cannot smoke in public, he may fear apprehension, and his relationships with parents or nonsmoking friends may be tainted.[34] It is worth noting that in the 1970 edition of *American Society* Williams does not include marijuana use in his "more-or-less random listing" of examples of patterned evasion. (He does refer to Prohibition and to organized gambling.) [35]

---

[32] Gusfield, *Symbolic Crusade, supra* note 30, at 115. This definition differs somewhat from the one found in Gusfield's 1967 article, and both in turn are different from Williams' definition. Williams emphasizes the significance of public as opposed to concealed violations: *"Public* violation . . . is often felt to require punishment, even when private evasion and violation are prevalent and widely recognized" (Williams, *supra* note 31, at 419 [emphasis in original]). In some areas of the country this is an apt characterization of marijuana law enforcement.

[33] Schneyer, *supra* note 6, at 213.

[34] See *infra* pp. 74–79.

[35] Williams, *supra* note 31, at 421. The argument here is not meant to suggest that patterned evasion can never exist. At least some of the examples cited by

Far from reducing conflicts between social groups, the symbolic aspects of the marijuana laws may well exacerbate existing conflicts. Gusfield points out that different forms of deviance from the public norm have different effects on the symbolic character of the norm itself. When the deviant is neither repentant nor sick but instead "accepts his behavior as proper and derogates the public norm as illegitimate," he is perceived by supporters of the norm as an enemy. "When the deviant and the designator perceive each other as enemies, and the designator's power is superior to that of the deviant, we have domination without a corresponding legitimacy. . . . The struggle over the symbol of social power and status is focused on the question of the maintenance or change of the legal norm."

Gusfield's description of the "enemy deviant" corresponds closely with what observers have reported about marijuana users. Kaplan notes that the marijuana laws "are not only widely violated, but . . . they are not even considered morally binding by those who have violated them." [36] Erich Goode has found that marijuana users "are, to a considerable degree, isolated from the dominant American ideology on pot and deeply involved in their own subculture's conception of it as harmless and beneficial." [37] On the other side, those who support the laws see the growing acceptance of marijuana as, in Gusfield's words, "a threat to the social dominance symbolized in the affirmation of the norm." Marijuana is regarded as a symbol of radicalism, permissiveness, lack of respect for authority, and unconventional life-styles. It therefore becomes important to discredit the attitudes of the marijuana subculture and to reaffirm the legal norm. To paraphrase Gusfield, the maintenance of a norm that defines marijuana use as deviant behavior symbolizes the maintenance of the social and political superiority of the "silent majority," "Middle America," or whatever term one prefers.[38] The result is a struggle that intensifies divisions within society rather than a patterned evasion that minimizes conflicts.

Gusfield suggests that laws may have significance as "gestures of

Williams appear to fit the description, as, for example, "[l]egal rules regarding divorce vs. court practice."

[36] Kaplan, *supra* note 4, at 34.

[37] Goode, *supra* note 22, at 289.

[38] The Shafer commission indirectly acknowledged this attitude when it expressed the fear that if marijuana were decriminalized, supporters of the present law "might lose respect for a policy-making establishment which appeared to bend so easily to the wishes of a 'lawless' and highly vocal minority" (*Signal of Misunderstanding,* 133; see *infra* pp. 177–78).

public affirmation" apart from the phenomenon of patterned evasion. "First, the act of public affirmation of a norm often persuades
listeners that behavior and norm are consistent." This is probably
true of the marijuana laws just as it was true of Prohibition, in spite
of the widespread violation of both.[39] When wishful thinking ex-
tends even to a national commission,[40] it is hardly surprising that
reaffirmation quiets and comforts less sophisticated persons. Nevertheless, as Gallup polls and *Playboy* surveys reveal ever-widening
violation,[41] the gesture of public affirmation provided by the laws
will become increasingly hollow even to their most ardent votaries.

"Second, public affirmation of a moral norm directs the major
institutions of the society to its support." Increasingly, however, the
major institutions of society are drawing away from support of the
marijuana laws. In the tristate New York area, most colleges are
"virtual sanctuaries" for marijuana users, and administrators at
many schools ignore all but large-scale dealing.[42] According to the
Shafer commission, a major midwestern university apparently permits students to have up to a week's supply of the drug.[43] Drug
education programs that treat marijuana as a serious health menace
are in disrepute.[44] Several religious leaders and groups have spoken
out against current marijuana legislation.[45] Even law enforcement
officials have called for the decriminalization of marijuana use.[46]

Third, "[t]he fact of affirmation through acts of law and government expresses the public worth of one set of norms, of one subcul-

[39] Andrew Sinclair, *Era of Excess* (New York, Harper Colophon ed. 1964),
p. 182.
[40] See *infra* pp. 170–74.
[41] See *infra* pp. 170–71.
[42] *N.Y. Times*, Nov. 20, 1972, p. 1, col. 5.
[43] *Signal of Misunderstanding*, 118.
[44] Richard H. DeLone, "The Ups and Downs of Drug-Abuse Education,"
Saturday Review, Nov. 11, 1972, pp. 27–32.
[45] *N.Y. Times*, May 23, 1970, p. 15, col. 3 (Presbyterian Church report asks
that all penalties for marijuana use be reduced to misdemeanors); *ibid.*, Apr. 17,
1972, p. 17, col. 1 (Episcopal dean expresses disappointment that the commission
favored "decriminalization" but stopped short of legalization); *ibid.*, Apr. 28, 1972,
p. 36, col. 1 (general conference of the United Methodist Church urges reform
of the laws controlling marijuana).
[46] E.g., *N.Y. Times*, Nov. 8, 1970, § 1, p. 84, col. 4 (Eugene Gold, Brooklyn
District Attorney, calls for legalization of individual possession and use); *ibid.*,
Feb. 11, 1972, p. 19, col. 2 (John Finlater, former deputy director of the Bureau
of Narcotics and Dangerous Drugs, joins National Organization for the Reform of
the Marijuana Laws [NORML], stating "We must stop sending people to jail for
smoking marijuana"). For a summary of more recent statements by law enforcement officials, generally supporting decriminalization of marijuana use, see *N.Y.
Times*, Dec. 8, 1974, § 4, p. 11, col. 1.

ture vis-a-vis those of others. . . . Accordingly it enhances the social status of groups carrying the affirmed culture and degrades groups carrying that which is condemned as deviant." It is by no means clear that Gusfield regards this consequence as beneficial, and indeed Schneyer expressly disclaims that view: "the arbitrary denomination of some social groups as inferior . . . could hardly be socially beneficial. . . ."[47]

The symbolic value of a law can never be evaluated with precision. There will always be people to whom legal affirmation or rejection is more important for what it symbolizes than for what it controls. To paraphrase Gusfield, even if the law is broken it is clear whose law it is. How much such affirmation should count for in the ledger of benefits is a question which the reader must answer for himself. I suggest that a symbolism that is grounded in illusion and productive of social conflict can never be much of a benefit to any society.

The "benefit" side of the ledger adds up to this: apart from their symbolic value, our present laws against marijuana may well deter substantial numbers of individuals from using marijuana experimentally, intermittently, or in moderation—but the benefit to society from preventing such use is probably minimal. Greater benefits might be gained by preventing heavy use—but it seems unlikely that our laws have that effect.

These conclusions rest to some extent on speculation about human behavior and on hypotheses drawn from limited experiments. I will be content if the reader accepts the form of analysis I have suggested, even if he makes different entries on the credit side of the ledger, for against these benefits must be weighed a formidable battery of costs.

COSTS OF THE MARIJUANA LAWS: AN OVERVIEW

The response of the legal system to the use of marijuana stands in sharp contrast to the history of alcohol control. As the Shafer commission has reminded us, "From the very inception of marijuana control legislation, this nation has utilized a policy of a total prohibition. . . ." The distinctive feature of such a policy is that "all marijuana-related behavior is prohibited by law."[48] Violation of the law is punished by the imposition of criminal sanctions;[49] en-

[47] Schneyer, *supra* note 6, at 212–13.
[48] *Signal of Misunderstanding,* 138.
[49] See generally Packer, "The Aims of the Criminal Law Revisited: A Plea for a New Look at 'Substantive Due Process,' " 44 S. *Cal. L. Rev.* 490 (1971).

forcement of the law is accomplished through the full panoply of the criminal process.

As the use of marijuana grew from a trickle to a torrent in the late 1960's and early 1970's, it gradually became apparent to more and more people that society was paying an enormous price as a result of its attempt to deal with marijuana through a total prohibition scheme utilizing the criminal process. Many of the items on the debit side of the ledger are now widely acknowledged, and it will not be necessary to do more than summarize them here and refer the reader to more detailed discussions elsewhere. Other costs, though perhaps mentioned with equal frequency, have not been fully understood, for if they were, the defects of halfway reforms, such as reductions in penalties or the adoption of a partial prohibition approach, would become more apparent.

The most obvious consequence of the marijuana laws is that they have resulted in prison sentences for thousands of persons, most of them young and otherwise law-abiding. It is widely acknowledged today, even by persons strongly opposed to significant liberalization of the marijuana laws, that the penalties prescribed in many (and perhaps most) states are grossly out of proportion to the gravity of the offense.[50] Sentences of twenty, thirty, forty years—even life imprisonment—have been imposed for the possession or sale of marijuana.[51] Kaplan suggests that "as a practical matter" these severe penalties "are very rarely applied." He concedes that "horrible examples do occur every once in a while" but finds that these cases "are so rare as to be more a commentary on the sentencing judge

[50] See, e.g., *N.Y. Times,* Jan. 27, 1971, p. 46, col. 1 (remarks of State Senator Dunne of New York); 58 *A.B.A.J.* 1074–75 (1972) (American Bar Association House of Delegates urges elimination of excessive penalties but votes down a resolution urging repeal of laws against possession and personal use). One year later, the House of Delegates, although continuing to "deplore" the use of marijuana, adopted a resolution urging that "there should be no criminal laws punishing the simple possession of marijuana by users" and that "casual distribution of small amounts not for profit" should be treated as simple possession. See 59 *A.B.A.J.* 1134–35 (1973).

[51] In Houston, Texas, in 1972, a jury sentenced a thirty-four-year-old man to life imprisonment for possession of a pound of marijuana. *N.Y. Times,* Jan. 28, 1972, p. 17, col. 1; see also Gomez v. State, 162 Tex. Crim. 30, 280 S.W.2d 278 (1955) (five to twenty-five years); Garcia v. State, 166 Tex. Crim. 482, 316 S.W.2d 734 (1958) (life); Leal v. State, 332 Tex. Crim. 729 (Tex. Crim. App. 1960) (seventy-five years); Perez v. State, 172 Tex. Crim. 492, 358 S.W.2d 381 (1962) (twenty-five years). Texas has achieved notoriety for severe sentences in marijuana cases, but that state is by no means unique. A panel of Ohio judges sentenced a young couple to twenty to forty years' imprisonment for selling marijuana (*N.Y. Times,* July 18, 1971, p. 48, col. 7). In New Orleans a man was sentenced to fifty years in prison without parole for selling marijuana in a matchbox to undercover agents (*N.Y. Times,* Aug. 10, 1971, p. 21, col. 2).

than upon the defendant." [52] My own survey of marijuana cases that
have reached appellate courts, while far from scientific, indicates
that heavy penalties are by no means as rare as Kaplan believes.[53]

For every person actually sent to prison for a marijuana offense,
scores, perhaps hundreds, more are subjected to the consequences
of arrest. The FBI's Uniform Crime Report showed that 420,700
persons were arrested on marijuana charges during 1973—an increase of more than 100,000 over the figure for 1972.[54] Arrest alone,
quite apart from any subsequent conviction, can have a traumatic
and often long-lasting effect, especially on young persons.[55] Years
after he has forgotten the indignities attendant upon being booked
and spending a night in jail, the individual seeking employment or
admission to the bar may find that his arrest record continues to
haunt him.

These consequences are visited upon persons who, except for
their use of marijuana, are as law-abiding as the average citizen. An
empirical study conducted by the Shafer commission revealed that
"almost all of those arrested are between the ages of 18 and 25,
most have jobs or are in school, and most have had no prior contact
with the criminal justice system." [56] Studies of marijuana arrests in
Houston and California have reported similar findings.[57] Nor is it
only the users who are otherwise law-abiding. The *New York Times*
reported in early 1971 that "most of the *traffickers* in non-addictive
drugs are young, fairly well-educated and from middle- or upper-
middle-class families, and have never been charged with a serious
crime." [58]

Admittedly, only a tiny proportion of marijuana users are ever
arrested, let alone convicted. To focus on the number of arrests
and convictions, however, is to grossly underestimate both the magnitude and the enormity of the problem. The most devastating consequence of the marijuana laws is not the volume of convictions or
arrests, but the fact that they have made criminals out of a large
segment of the population that is otherwise law-abiding.

At first blush it might appear circular to argue that marijuana

---

[52] Kaplan, *supra* note 4, at 33.
[53] See cases cited in *supra* note 51.
[54] *Washington Post*, July 22, 1974, p. A-2, col. 3.
[55] These consequences are described in detail in Kaplan, *supra* note 4, at 31.
[56] *Signal of Misunderstanding*, 144.
[57] Sayer and Rotenberg, "Marijuana in Houston: A Second Report and a
Proposal," 8 *Houston L. Rev.* 209, 238 (1970); Kaplan, *supra* note 4, at 31.
[58] *N.Y. Times*, Feb. 17, 1971, p. 1, col. 5; p. 20, col. 1 [emphasis added].

laws are bad because they make criminals out of marijuana users. After all, extortion laws make criminals out of extortionists and murder laws make criminals out of murderers; the argument seems to depend on an implied premise that the use of marijuana is not harmful—a premise I have explicitly disavowed. This criticism misses the point. The point is that the marijuana laws attach the consequences of criminality to conduct which large numbers of otherwise law-abiding citizens engage in in the belief that what they are doing is unexceptionable.

To the user, laws against marijuana, like the thirteenth stroke of the clock, are not only dubious in themselves; they also cast doubt upon the soundness of the entire mechanism—in this instance, the law. It appears to the user that society is prosecuting him for courting pleasure in his chosen fashion—for seeking nepenthe in a joint instead of a martini. In his eyes a governmental system that labels and punishes individuals as criminals on the basis of conduct that he regards as both harmless and none of the law's business is itself unworthy of trust or respect. The simple fact that a law is widely violated would not be an argument for its repeal. But when a law is widely violated by individuals who believe it to be unjustified and even illegitimate, the result is to foster skepticism about the legitimacy of the entire legal system and thereby to weaken the bonds of shared attitudes that make it possible for a society to function democratically.[59]

For other reasons, too, the marijuana laws tend to foster "a disrespect for all law and the system in general," [60] in the words of the Shafer commission. Because the penalties are so disproportionate, many judges and prosecutors seize every loophole to prevent felony convictions, especially of young middle-class users.[61] Knowledge that the law is being manipulated in this way can breed only cynicism about the whole legal system. Similar attitudes are bred by the disparate sentences handed out for the same crime. Otis Lee Johnson, a militant black leader, was sentenced to thirty years' imprisonment for giving one marijuana cigarette to an undercover police agent.[62] In the same state a Dallas football star received a five-year suspended sentence and was placed on probation for possession of one marijuana cigarette and enough marijuana to fill two

---

[59] *Cf.* Charles Black, *The People and the Court* (New York, 1960), pp. 34–35.
[60] *Signal of Misunderstanding,* 145.
[61] Packer, *Limits of the Criminal Sanction, supra* note 1, at 340.
[62] Johnson v. State, 447 S.W.2d 927 (Tex. Crim. App. 1969); see also Johnson v. Beto, 337 F. Supp. 1371 (S.D. Tex. 1972).

matchboxes.[63] Of course, disparity in sentencing is hardly unique to marijuana crimes, but the disparity tends to be far wider than for other offenses, principally because there is such a lack of consensus about the seriousness of the crime. Statutes permitting an enormously wide range of penalties, especially for sale or distribution, aggravate this tendency.[64]

The effect of marijuana laws on attitudes, however, goes far beyond what people feel about the legal system or the government. Nor is it limited to marijuana smokers or persons who sympathize with their right to go to hell in their own way. By invoking the criminal process to reinforce the designation of the marijuana user as an "enemy deviant," [65] the legislature announces that the user poses a threat to society that may appropriately be countered by the same measures that are deployed against persons who are criminals by anyone's standards.[66] The import of this message is not lost on police officers and others who are responsible for enforcing the criminal laws. Even the judiciary is affected. In the minds of the Nevada Supreme Court judges, for example, a group of people sharing a joint in a motel room were part of the "vast, vague underworld of narcotics," so that the undercover agents who engineered their arrest were not held to "the polite manners practiced in decent society." [67] For the judges of Wisconsin's highest court, the presence of a quantity of marijuana turned an ordinary apartment into a place exactly like a gambling joint or a house of prostitution, and the police could act accordingly.[68] Responses such as these demonstrate that, as Michael Rosenthal puts it, merely labeling users as members of a criminal class tends to make both them and others think of them as criminals and outsiders [69]—persons outside the pale of "decent society," in the words of the Nevada court. Crimi-

[63] *N.Y. Times,* Feb. 22, 1972, p. 47, col. 7.

[64] See Senate Interim Drug Study Committee, *Report: Marijuana in Texas* (Austin, Tex., 1972), 47.

[65] See *supra* p. 24.

[66] It is no answer to suggest that all laws need not be enforced, and all violations of the law need not be investigated, in the same way. This may be true in theory, but in practice once an activity is placed within the purview of the criminal code, tactics used and attitudes acquired in the detection of the more serious crimes tend to be carried over into the detection of all violations. Indeed, for reasons discussed in Part Two, the measures taken to enforce the marijuana laws are often more drastic than those used to detect other crimes.

[67] Crown v. Sheriff, 85 Nev. 522, 458 P.2d 357 (1969), discussed at *infra* pp. 64–65, 70.

[68] State v. Chambers, 55 Wis. 2d 289, 198 N.W.2d 377 (1972), discussed at *infra* pp. 136–37.

[69] Rosenthal, "A Plea for the Amelioration of the Marihuana Laws," 47 *Tex. L. Rev.* 1359, 1370 (1969); see generally Kaplan, *supra* note 4, at 33–37.

nalization thus fosters a pattern of mutual alienation between marijuana smokers and those in the community who are unsympathetic to the use of the drug.

Laws against marijuana do harm to society in more tangible ways as well. The very existence of such laws interferes with drug education programs and makes it far more difficult to convince young people of the consequences of using really dangerous drugs.[70] Efforts to enforce marijuana laws divert scarce law enforcement resources that could be mobilized against crimes which directly threaten the safety of persons and property.[71] Even in communities where the police have given up the attempt to enforce the possession laws, officers may find themselves spending valuable time at the station house and in court following up "inadvertent" discoveries of marijuana. Efforts to investigate distributors will, of course, require considerably more manpower. Nor are the burdens limited to the police; other elements of the law enforcement system, including prosecutors' offices and the courts, suffer also. In the District of Columbia, for example, lawyers in the U.S. attorney's office pointed out late in 1974 that the prosecution of marijuana cases "absorbs a disproportionate amount of our limited resources." As a result, assistant U.S. attorneys fell behind in handling misdemeanor cases involving such crimes as carrying a dangerous weapon and assault. In the same jurisdiction, the chief judge of the superior court warned that a growing misdemeanor caseload—about one-quarter of which consisted of marijuana possession cases—could lead to a backlog in the court's disposition of felony cases.[72]

Even in purely monetary terms, the marijuana laws impose a substantial burden on taxpayers. An exact accounting is obviously impossible, but a study made in 1974 by the California legislature's Select Senate Committee on Control of Marijuana sheds light on the extent of the costs involved. Using a conservative extrapolation from available data, the committee found that in the state of California alone, state and local government agencies were spending more than one hundred million dollars a year in enforcing marijuana laws. This sum would have been enough to fund the state's entire Department of Justice for two years.[73]

[70] See Kaplan, *supra* note 4, at 37–40.

[71] *Ibid.*, 29–31, Senate Interim Drug Study Committee, *supra* note 64, at 37; *cf.* Schneyer, *supra* note 6, at 203–4.

[72] *Washington Post*, Nov. 16, 1974, p. A-1, col. 6; p. A-5, col. 3; Nov. 20, 1974, p. C-13, col. 1; *Newsweek*, Dec. 2, 1974, p. 113.

[73] California Legislature Select Senate Committee on Control of Marijuana, *Marijuana: Beyond Misunderstanding* (Sacramento, 1974), 97–118 and Appendix IV.

In a sense, the point that marijuana laws are bad because they make criminals out of marijuana smokers epitomizes all of the arguments made in this volume. Given the consequences of attaching criminal sanctions to marijuana-related conduct, the rational legislator must decide whether those consequences represent an acceptable price for the benefits to be anticipated from continued criminalization. It is easy to say that "there ought to be a law" to prevent whatever evils are believed to flow from the use of marijuana. It is even easier to do nothing when the law is already on the books and repeal might be thought to carry the seeds of evils yet unknown. What is too easily forgotten, however, is that there is a difference between society's declaring—through the attitudes and behavior of the majority—that an activity is disfavored and the legislature's making it a crime.

Some of the costs of making the use and distribution of marijuana a crime have been explored in the preceding pages. The most devastating and pervasive costs, however, are those which result from the techniques used to enforce the laws. As I shall show in Part Two, laws against marijuana cannot be enforced without requiring the police to resort to tactics that intrude upon the privacy, security, and individual dignity of users and nonusers alike. The conclusion that emerges is that nothing short of total decriminalization will avoid these intrusions. To put this argument into perspective, however, it will be useful to analyze a proposal for less sweeping reform—the report of the National Commission on Marihuana and Drug Abuse.

III

The Shafer Commission
Report

When a problem begins to strain the fabric of our society, the government typically responds by appointing a commission to study the situation. So it was with racism, violence, and crime; [1] so it was with marijuana. In 1971 President Nixon appointed the National Commission on Marihuana and Drug Abuse headed by former Pennsylvania Governor Raymond P. Shafer. In March, 1972, after a year's work, the commission issued its first report.[2] A second report, published in early 1973, surveyed a somewhat broader spectrum of drug use problems but added little to the commission's initial conclusions about marijuana.[3]

THE COMMISSION CLEARS THE AIR

In the pages that follow, I shall have much to say that is critical of the Shafer commission's report. These criticisms should not detract from the important positive contributions which the commission has made to the national debate on marijuana. First, the report effectively rebuts many of the myths whose widespread acceptance

[1] National Advisory Commission on Civil Disorders, *Report* (Washington, D.C., 1968); National Commission on the Causes and Prevention of Violence, *To Establish Justice, to Insure Domestic Tranquility* (Washington, D.C., 1969); President's Commission on Law Enforcement and Administration of Justice, *The Challenge of Crime to a Free Society* (Washington, D.C., 1967) [hereinafter cited as *Challenge of Crime*].

[2] National Commission on Marihuana and Drug Abuse, *Marihuana: A Signal of Misunderstanding* [hereinafter cited as *Signal of Misunderstanding*].

[3] National Commission on Marihuana and Drug Abuse, *Drug Use in America: Problem in Perspective* (Washington, D.C., 1973).

continues to retard intelligent discussion about *Cannabis*. Second, the commission places the marijuana problem in a proper perspective by relating it to other social phenomena and by comparing marijuana with alcohol and tobacco. Third, the commission recognizes that attempting to eliminate the use of marijuana—the goal of society's current legal policy—is neither possible nor desirable.

Rebutting myths about marijuana. The most dismaying aspect of the commission's report is the gap that it reveals between what the public believes about marijuana and what researchers have found to be true. Earlier reports by Kaplan, Grinspoon, Blum, and others have apparently fallen on deaf ears.[4] It is to be hoped that the findings of a federal panel appointed by a Republican president and headed by a former Republican governor will have more of an impact on the public mind.

The report deals at some length with the three most widely held misconceptions about marijuana: the belief that it is addictive, the belief that it is causally linked to crime and other antisocial conduct, and the belief that it is a stepping-stone to the use of more dangerous drugs.

Although most state laws classify marijuana with narcotics such as heroin and opium,[5] marijuana does not share the characteristics of the true narcotics. Most important, marijuana is not addictive. An addict has been defined as "a person who, not requiring the continued use of a drug for the relief of the symptoms of organic disease, has acquired, as a result of repeated administration, an overpowering desire for its continuance, and in whom withdrawal of the drug leads to definite symptoms of mental or physical distress or disorder."[6] This description simply does not fit the marijuana user, as the commission's report makes amply clear. The commission states unequivocally that "cannabis does not lead to physical dependence." The report goes on: "No torturous withdrawal syn-

---

[4] John Kaplan, *Marijuana: The New Prohibition;* Lester Grinspoon, *Marihuana Reconsidered;* Blum, "Mind-Altering Drugs and Dangerous Behavior: Dangerous Drugs," in President's Commission on Law Enforcement and Administration of Justice, *Task Force Report: Narcotics and Drug Abuse* (Washington, D.C., 1967), 21; Mayor's Commission on Marihuana, "The Marihuana Problem in the City of New York," in *The Marihuana Papers,* ed. David Solomon, 277; Erich Goode, *The Marijuana Smokers.*

[5] See Bonnie and Whitebread, "The Forbidden Fruit and the Tree of Knowledge: An Inquiry into the Legal History of American Marijuana Prohibition," 56 *Va. L. Rev.* 971, 1077–79 (1970).

[6] Horace Judson, "The British and Heroin," *New Yorker,* Sept. 24, 1973, p. 93 (quoting Britain's Rolleston commission).

drome follows the sudden cessation of chronic, heavy use of marijuana. Although evidence indicates that heavy, long-term cannabis
users may develop psychological dependence, even then the level
of psychological dependence is no different from the syndrome of
anxiety and restlessness seen when an American stops smoking tobacco cigarettes." [7] This conclusion reaffirms the findings of Kaplan, Grinspoon, and the president's crime commission.[8] Recently
the Illinois Supreme Court has held that classification of marijuana
as a narcotic violates the Equal Protection clause. Other judges
have indicated agreement with this view.[9] In several states legislatures have acted to reclassify marijuana.[10] These decisions, rein-
forcing the commission's conclusions, may finally convince the
public that marijuana is not addictive.

It will be more difficult to scotch the belief that persons who use
marijuana ~~will~~ progress to the use of more dangerous drugs, particularly heroin. In the commission's survey 70 percent of the adult
respondents thought that marijuana makes people want to try
stronger drugs such as heroin.[11] The commission strongly repudiates
this idea: "Whether or not marijuana leads to other drug use depends on the individual, on the social and cultural setting in which
the drug use takes place and on the nature of the drug market. Its
use, however, is neither inevitable nor necessary. The fact should
be emphasized that the overwhelming majority of marijuana users
do not progress to other drugs. . . . When the voluminous testimony given at [1951 congressional] hearings is seriously examined,
no verification is found of a causal relationship between marijuana
use and subsequent heroin use." [12] Once again, the commission's
conclusion is supported by earlier writers—Kaplan, Grinspoon, and
Blum, among others.[13]

Almost as prevalent is the idea that marijuana is causally linked
to crime and other antisocial conduct. As the commission virtually

[7] *Signal of Misunderstanding*, 87.

[8] Kaplan, *supra* note 4, at 164–75; Grinspoon, *supra* note 4, at 256–61;
Challenge of Crime, 13.

[9] People v. McCabe, 49 Ill. 2d 338, 275 N.E.2d 407 (1971); see also Sam v.
State, 500 P.2d 291 (Okla. Crim. 1972); State v. Carus, 118 N.J. Super. 459, 286
A.2d 740 (1972); People v. Sinclair, 387 Mich. 91, 194 N.W.2d 878 (1972)
(opinions of Swainson and Williams, JJ., concurring). For contrary cases, see
supra p. 10, note 29.

[10] *N.Y. Times*, Aug. 8, 1972, p. 39, col. 4.

[11] *Signal of Misunderstanding*, 88.

[12] *Ibid.*, 49, 87–88.

[13] Kaplan, *supra* note 4, at 209–74; Grinspoon, *supra* note 4, at 261–80; Blum,
supra note 4, at 24.

acknowledges, this attitude was created almost entirely by propaganda emanating from the Federal Bureau of Narcotics and was uncritically spread by newspapers and magazines in the 1930's.[14] It would be appropriate if another governmental agency were instrumental in correcting the errors fostered by a predecessor, but the task is a formidable one. The commission's survey indicates that 56 percent of the adult population agrees with the statement that "many crimes are committed by persons who are under the influence of marijuana." [15] The commission's conclusions emphatically repudiate the popular belief:

> [T]he weight of the evidence is that marijuana does not cause violent or aggressive behavior; if anything, marijuana generally serves to inhibit the expression of such behavior. . . .

> No evidence exists that marijuana use will cause or lead to the commission of violent or aggressive behavior by the large majority of psychologically and socially mature individuals in the general population.

> [N]either informed current professional opinion or empirical research, ranging from the 1930's to the present, has produced systematic evidence to support the thesis that marijuana use, by itself, either invariably or generally leads to or causes crime, including acts of violence, juvenile delinquency or aggressive behavior.[16]

Summing up, the commission states, "neither the marijuana user nor the drug itself can be said to constitute a danger to public safety." [17] Here, too, the commission agrees with Grinspoon, Kaplan, and Blum.[18]

Authoritative refutation of these myths may prove to be the commission's most important contribution to the debate about marijuana, but it must be recognized that such myths die hard. Indeed, nearly thirty years ago the Mayor's Commission on Marihuana, appointed by Mayor Fiorello La Guardia of New York, reached exactly the same conclusions,[19] with no apparent effect on public

[14] *Signal of Misunderstanding,* 67–68; *cf.* Grinspoon, *supra* note 4, at 18–33; Kaplan, *supra* note 4, at 91–101.
[15] *Signal of Misunderstanding,* 74–75.
[16] *Ibid.,* 73, 76.
[17] *Ibid.,* 78.
[18] Grinspoon, *supra* note 4, at 337–48; Kaplan, *supra* note 4, at 91–146; Blum, *supra* note 4, at 24–25.
[19] Mayor's Commission on Marihuana, *supra* note 4, at 307 (conclusions 7, 9, 10, 12).

attitudes. Perhaps now that the use of marijuana has spread to "all segments of the U.S. population" [20] it will be possible for the public to accept a more realistic view of the drug.

Perspectives on marijuana. The report makes a second important contribution by placing the marijuana problem in a proper perspective. The Shafer commission tries to show that the increasing use of marijuana is more a symptom than a cause of other social problems and that any threat to public health from marijuana use is dwarfed by the known dangers of alcohol and tobacco. Both points deserve elaboration.

As the commission notes, the use of marijuana is associated in the minds of many people with a series of social phenomena which are perceived as a threat to deeply held values. The older adult especially "perceives youthful marijuana use as part of a much larger pattern of behavior which bodes ill for the future of the nation." (For example, only 9 percent of the over-fifty generation agreed with the statement that "most people who use marijuana lead a normal life.") [21] The use of marijuana, particularly by the young, is thought to lead to idleness, underachievement, political radicalism, and rejection of the work ethic. The commission finds these fears to be largely unfounded, arising to a great extent from a confusion between association and causation.

For example, in discussing the fear that marijuana use leads to idleness and dropping out, the commission points out that "little likelihood exists that the introduction of a single element such as marijuana use would significantly change the basic personality and character structure of the individual to any degree. An individual is more likely to drop out when a number of circumstances have joined at a given point in his lifetime, producing pressures with which he has difficulty in coping." [22]

The commission also reassures parents who fear that marijuana "will undermine or interfere with academic and vocational career development and achievement. . . . No conclusive evidence was found demonstrating that marijuana *by itself* is responsible for academic or vocational failure or 'dropping down,' although it could be one of many contributory reasons." On such matters, of course, conclusive evidence is impossible to obtain; what is more

20 *Signal of Misunderstanding,* 32.
21 *Ibid.,* 93. Nineteen percent of the 34–49 age group and 29 percent of the 26–34 age group were of the same belief.
22 *Ibid.,* 97.

significant is the commission's reminder that adult judgments about youthful achievement (or supposed lack of it) are often made "without concern for what the individual himself feels about his potential, his interests and his goals." [23]

Implicit in this comment is a recognition that the evil of "dropping down" is in the eye of the beholder. Contrary to the implications of some other sections of the report,[24] the commission here appears to accept the legitimacy of values different from those held by the majority. Since most of the social phenomena associated (rightly or wrongly) with marijuana can be judged only in the light of one's own values, this approach, if followed consistently, would significantly weaken the case for restricting the availability of marijuana.

The commission's conclusions on the significance of the "marijuana problem" are worth setting forth in their entirety:

> Viewed against the background of the profound changes of recent years in the fields of economics, politics, religion, family life, housing patterns, civil rights, employment and recreation, the use of marijuana by the nation's youth must be seen as a relatively minor change in social patterns of conduct and as more of a consequence of than a contributor to these major changes.
>
> When the issue of marijuana use is placed in this context of society's larger concerns, marijuana does not emerge as a major issue or threat to the social order. Rather, it is most appropriately viewed as a part of the whole of society's concerns about the growth and development of its young people.
>
> In view of the magnitude and nature of change which our society has experienced during the past 25 years, the thoughtful observer is not likely to attribute any of the major social problems resulting from this change to marijuana use. Similarly, it is unlikely that marijuana will affect the future strength, stability or vitality of our social and political institutions. The fundamental principles and values upon which the society rests are far too enduring to go up in the smoke of a marijuana cigarette.[25]

Developments in the three years since the commission issued its report have only served to emphasize the soundness of these conclusions. Marijuana usage continues to be widespread, yet most of the

23 *Ibid.*, 99.
24 See, e.g., *ibid.*, 128, 134.
25 *Ibid.*, 102.

social phenomena that were commonly associated with drug use in the late 1960's have largely given way to other preoccupations and pursuits.

Throughout its report the Shafer commission compares marijuana with alcohol and tobacco. Three points are particularly noteworthy. First, the commission reminds us that in earlier times both alcohol and tobacco were attacked in language very similar to that used by opponents of marijuana today: "One 18th century pamphleteer advised against the use of any drink 'which is liable to steal away a man's senses and render him foolish, irascible, uncontrollable and dangerous.' Similarly, one 19th century observer attributed delirium tremens, perverted sexuality, impotency, insanity and cancer to the smoking and chewing of tobacco." [26] The point is not that alcohol and tobacco have been proved harmless, but that their perils were so greatly exaggerated. In particular, the nineteenth-century crusaders against alcohol and tobacco, like many present-day opponents of marijuana, refused to accept any distinctions between the consequences of moderate use and the consequences of heavy use. Since a majority of the commission's readers probably use alcohol or tobacco, they are likely to wonder whether propaganda against marijuana may not be as exaggerated as the nineteenth-century pamphlets which the commission quotes.

Second, the commission contrasts the legal history of alcohol with that of marijuana: "The temperance movement was a matter of vigorous public debate; the anti-narcotics movement was not. Temperance legislation was the product of a highly organized nationwide lobby; narcotics legislation was largely ad hoc. Temperance legislation was designed to eradicate known problems resulting from alcohol abuse; narcotics legislation was large anticipatory." [27] This history is significant because it undercuts the argument that because total prohibition laws are now on the books, the burden of proof rests upon those who would change them. This argument might have merit if the laws were the product of informed consideration and vigorous debate; in the light of what actually hap-

[26] Compare these claims with those in an article in the December, 1971, issue of *P.T.A. Magazine:* "(1) The use of marijuana leads acutely, and for several hours to days thereafter, to a disorder of thinking characterized by lack of coherence and an aggravation of pathological thinking processes. (2) The effects of marijuana are cumulative. (3) After a period of prolonged use (say 6 months to a year) changes occur that are similar to those seen in organic brain disease —patches of lucidity amid areas of fogginess."

[27] *Signal of Misunderstanding,* 13.

pened there is less reason to accord much weight to the judgments made by earlier legislators.[28] The blue-ribbon San Francisco Committee on Crime has taken the point one step further:

> Opponents of change in the law argue that if the evidence is uncertain, the status quo should be maintained by leaving the law as it is. But those laws originated when legislators assumed that the dangers of marijuana were far worse than a dispassionate examination of the evidence now available warrants. If that evidence would not warrant enactment, now, of the highly restrictive laws presently on the books, it cannot justify their retention. In a free society there ought always to be a presumption against illegalizing conduct until evidence is produced to warrant criminalization.[29]

Finally, and most important, the Shafer commission points out that the proved dangers of alcohol and tobacco are far more serious than any known or probable dangers of marijuana. For example, alcohol is a factor in half of the 60,000 highway fatalities occurring each year; one-half of all homicides and one-fourth of all suicides are alcohol-related, accounting for a total of 11,700 deaths annually. Cigarette smoking is the major "cause" of lung cancer in men and a significant risk factor contributing to the development of coronary heart disease.[30] The threat to public health arising from the use of alcohol and tobacco is thus far more serious than any peril that can reasonably be attributed to marijuana; yet there are few people today who argue that the sale (let alone the mere possession) of liquor and cigarettes ought to be banned.[31]

The point is not that because we permit the sale of alcohol and tobacco in spite of their deleterious consequences we ought to be equally willing to permit the sale of marijuana. The point, rather, is this: we have made the decision—in the case of alcohol, a very

[28] For a detailed history of marijuana legislation, see Bonnie and Whitebread, *supra* note 5. The authors conclude that the early laws were "essentially kneejerk responses uninformed by scientific study or public debate and colored instead by racial bias and sensationalistic myths" (*ibid.*, 1010). Later, passage of the Uniform Narcotic Drug Act in the states "was attended by little publicity, no scientific study, and even more blatant ethnic aspersions than the earlier laws. In short, the laws went unnoticed by legal commentators, the press, and the public at large, despite the propagandizing efforts of the Bureau of Narcotics" (*ibid.*, 1034).

[29] San Francisco Committee on Crime, *Report* (San Francisco, 1971), quoted in *The Leaflet*, Nov. 1971, p. 3.

[30] *Signal of Misunderstanding*, 15.

[31] Within the last couple of years there has been some talk among public officials of banning the sale of cigarettes. Such a prohibition would be even more unworkable than a ban on marijuana.

conscious decision—not to criminalize the sale of alcohol and tobacco because we recognize that the costs of doing so would exceed
the benefits that would accrue. In other words, we permit the sale
of alcohol and tobacco not because we deny the harm that flows
from their use but because forbidding their sale would result in even
greater harm to society. Once this point is recognized the next step
is to ask whether similar reasoning might be applied to marijuana.
The question does not answer itself, but the magnitude of the risks
that we are willing to accept instead of attempting to prohibit alcohol or tobacco suggests that we ought to be equally cautious in
criminalizing another widely used drug.

Impossibility of eliminating marijuana use. Having found that
most of the dangers associated in the public mind with marijuana
use are grossly exaggerated, the Shafer commission turns to the
question of how society should deal with the drug. The most significant aspect of this discussion is the commission's rejection of
a policy seeking the total elimination of marijuana use, for, as the
report points out, this has been the nation's official policy for the
past two generations.

POLICY CHOICES FOR SOCIETY

In canvassing possible governmental responses to marijuana, the
commission engages in a two-stage analysis. First, the commission
considers four policy options: approval of use, elimination of use,
discouragement of use, and neutrality toward use. Having selected
"discouragement of use, with emphasis on prevention of heavy and
very heavy use" as its generalized aim,[32] the commission then attempts to weigh the advantages and disadvantages of three legal
responses: total prohibition (the present approach), partial prohibition (Kaplan's "vice model") and regulation (Kaplan's "licensing model").[33] Of these, the commission finds partial prohibition to be the most desirable policy at the present time.

The report devotes only three pages to explanation of the commission's reasons for rejecting the policy option of approval of use.
I do not challenge this verdict,[34] but it is worth pointing out that
the question is by no means as clear-cut as the commission's cursory
discussion suggests. The commission states: "Society should not

[32] *Signal of Misunderstanding,* 138.
[33] See Kaplan, *supra* note 4, at 173.
[34] See *supra* pp. 3–6.

approve or encourage the recreational use of any drug, in public or private. Any semblance of encouragement enhances the possibility of abuse and removes, from a psychological standpoint, an effective support of individual restraint." [35] Although the commission concedes that "the use of drugs for pleasure or other nonmedical purposes is not inherently irresponsible," and that "[p]roductivity and recreation both have a place in the American ethical system," [36] the tone of the report suggests an extremely grudging attitude toward the recreational use of drugs. Earlier sections of the report leave the impression that individuals smoke marijuana primarily as a reaction to negative aspects of society. Only occasionally does the report recognize that marijuana smoking might be increasing because many people find it an enjoyable supplement to other pleasures.[37] If the commission were not so skeptical of the possibility that marijuana might take a legitimate place among society's recreations, would the commission be so fearful of the possibility of abuse and so insistent upon the need for society to provide "an effective support of individual restraint"?

The commission's rejection of a policy of approval occasions no surprise. Far more significant is its rejection—in terms no less emphatic—of a policy of eliminating marijuana use. As the commission points out, this has been the "official social policy" of this nation for half a century. The policy of elimination should now be abandoned, the commission recommends, for two reasons: it is "an inappropriate social response," and it is also unattainable. One is reminded of Fred Rodell's celebrated farewell to law reviews: "There are two things wrong with almost all legal writing. One is its style. The other is its content. That, I think, about covers the ground." [38]

The policy is inappropriate, the commission concludes, because "marijuana's relative potential for harm to the vast majority of individual users and its actual impact on society does not justify a social policy designed to seek out and firmly punish those who use it." [39] Earlier sections of this book have indicated some of the ways in which marijuana's potential for harm has been exaggerated over the years, and I shall not develop the point further here except to

[35] *Signal of Misunderstanding,* 129.
[36] *Ibid.,* 128.
[37] Grinspoon, *supra* note 4, at 123–30; Erich Goode, "Turning On for Fun," *N.Y. Times,* Jan. 9, 1971, p. 27, col. 1.
[38] Rodell, "Goodbye to Law Reviews," 23 *Va. L. Rev.* 38 (1936).
[39] *Signal of Misunderstanding,* 130.

ask the obvious question: If marijuana is not so harmful that society should seek to punish those who *use* it, is it nevertheless harmful enough that society should seek to punish those who *supply* it to the users?

Even if an eliminationist policy were thought desirable, the commission suggests, it would be impossible to enforce at this time. It is not clear to what extent the commission is relying on cost-benefit analysis and to what extent on sheer practicality. At one point the commission states that the eliminationist policy, if taken seriously, "would require a great increase in manpower and resources in order to eliminate the use of a drug which simply does not warrant that kind of attention." [40] Here the commission seems to be talking in cost-benefit language. A few paragraphs earlier, however, the commission states that law enforcement personnel recognize that elimination of marijuana use is "unattainable" and "impossible." These words imply that the government could not eliminate the use of marijuana even if greater manpower and resources were available.

As a practical matter, the two rationales come down to pretty much the same thing. In an era of taxpayer revolts and municipal stringency, law enforcement officials know that they will not get the resources that would be necessary to stamp out the use of marijuana. The more interesting question is whether it is worthwhile to use law enforcement resources to deal with marijuana at all.

It appears that the commission had little difficulty in rejecting the policies of approval at one extreme and elimination of use at the other. This left the "unresolved question" of "whether society should try to dissuade its members from using marijuana or should defer entirely to individual judgment in the matter, remaining benignly neutral." The choice between discouragement and neutrality was "a difficult one," but the commission finally opted for discouragement.[41]

The first difficulty in the commission's analysis lies in its framing of the question. Whatever *benign neutrality* might mean in the abstract, the term is quite inappropriate to describe the proposals made by responsible critics of the marijuana laws. John Kaplan, for example, proposes a licensing system that would include strict controls on price and potency, limit the number of outlets at which marijuana could be sold, and prohibit the sale of marijuana to chil-

[40] *Ibid.,* 131.
[41] *Ibid.*

dren.[42] Lester Grinspoon advocates legalization, but he defines it to mean "the freedom for people above a certain age, say 18, to use marijuana (bhang) of a predetermined potency." [43] Thomas Szasz urges that we regard "freedom of self-medication as a fundamental right," but that right would be applicable only to adults and would be subject to "important qualifications." [44]

In short, none of these writers has advocated what Kaplan terms the "sugar candy model." None has suggested that the law should withdraw completely from the marijuana area or that society should allow marijuana to be freely produced, sold, and advertised. On the contrary, most of these writers agree that marijuana should be taxed like a luxury and that restrictions should be imposed on sales and advertising. The choice is not between discouragement and neutrality but between degrees of discouragement.

The report compounds the confusion in terminology by implying that society's policy toward alcohol since Prohibition has been one of neutrality.[45] Can it really be said that society is neutral toward the use of alcohol when virtually every jurisdiction imposes strict restraints on who may buy it, where and when it may be sold, and how it may be advertised; when alcohol is taxed at a far higher rate than nonalcoholic beverages; and when many kinds of alcohol-related behavior in public are subject to criminal punishment? [46]

The distinction which the commission purports to be making between discouragement and neutrality is more accurately regarded as the distinction between Kaplan's vice model (commonly followed today for gambling and prostitution) and his licensing model (exemplified by our controls over alcohol). This difference, in turn, corresponds to the distinction that the commission makes in a later section between partial prohibition and regulation.[47] In other words, the commission uses different language and different labels to make the same distinction in two contexts.[48] This impression is

[42] See *infra* pp. 195–200.
[43] Grinspoon, *supra* note 4, at 411–12.
[44] Thomas Szasz, "The Ethics of Addiction," *Harper's,* April, 1972, p. 77.
[45] See *Signal of Misunderstanding,* 132: "There are many today who feel that if the social impact of alcohol use had then been more fully understood, a policy of discouragement rather than neutrality would have been adopted to minimize the negative aspects of alcohol use."
[46] "In the eyes of the law the liquor business stands on a different footing from other pursuits and is separated or removed from the natural rights, privileges and immunities of the ordinary citizen" (Peppermint Lounge, Inc., v. Wright, 498 S.W.2d 749, 752 [Mo. 1973]).
[47] *Signal of Misunderstanding,* 146–51.
[48] In one context the commission purports to be discussing "the appropriate social control policy" for marijuana (*ibid.,* 129). In the second context the

strengthened by the fact that the arguments and assumptions of fact made in support of the choice of discouragement over neutrality reappear in the commission's defense of partial prohibition as opposed to regulation.

In rejecting a policy of neutrality, the commission is attacking a straw man. This in itself is not as significant as it might be, since most critics of the marijuana laws would probably endorse the commission's recommendation of a "social control policy seeking to discourage marijuana use, while concentrating primarily on the prevention of heavy and very heavy use." [49] The argument arises over how the policy is to be effected and in particular over the role of law. I turn now to the latter question.

Although hybrid approaches may be suggested,[50] the choice for the legal system can be reduced to two alternatives: regulation (the licensing model) or partial prohibition penalizing distributors but not users (the vice model).[51] Having concluded that the costs to society of continuing the total prohibition approach exceed the benefits to be gained, the commission appears to agree that the choice between regulation and continued partial prohibition should also be made on the basis of a cost-benefit analysis.[52] The crucial question is how the cost-benefit calculation changes when partial prohibition is substituted for total prohibition, as opposed to the change that results from the substitution of a policy of regulation.

In answering the crucial question, the commission apparently accepts the reasoning of Professor Schwartz, the reporter for the Model Penal Code: "The argument for maintaining criminal sanctions against professional promoters of 'vice' is essentially that drawing the line there retains some brake on economic exploitation of human weaknesses and some expression of the community's reservations about the activity itself, but minimizes the intolerable side-effects of attempting to make criminals out of millions of users of marijuana. . . . [T]he cost-benefit calculation for law enforcement against sellers is quite different when buyers are also incriminated." [53] I suggest that when marijuana is the "vice" in question

commission purports to be discussing legal techniques for implementing the preferred social policy of discouragement (*ibid.,* 146–48).

[49] *Ibid.,* 134.

[50] See *infra* pp. 191–95, discussing proposals to retain criminal sanctions but reduce penalties.

[51] This is something of an oversimplification, but the distinction mentioned is the crucial one.

[52] This approach is taken more explicitly in a consultants' report prepared for the commission. See *Signal of Misunderstanding, Appendix,* 1146.

[53] Schwartz, book review in 44 *S. Cal. L. Rev.* 528, 531 (1971).

this conclusion does not stand up and that partial prohibition will do little to solve the problems growing out of the increasing use of marijuana. This is so for two reasons. First, the system of partial prohibition proposed by the commission would retain the worst evils of the current system; in other words, the cost side of the ledger would not change significantly. Second, partial prohibition is unlikely to achieve its purpose of discouraging the use of marijuana—especially heavy use. Thus, the gain in benefits would be minimal. Both points will be documented in the following pages.

THE COMMISSION'S PROPOSAL: PARTIAL PROHIBITION

The limited scope of the reforms proposed by the commission should be emphasized. What is recommended is not a simple distinction between possession and distribution, but a complex calculus of regulations under which the sanction to be applied for conduct involving marijuana would depend on several variables. Under the statutory scheme suggested by the commission, state laws would distinguish among four kinds of possession: [54]

(1) Possession in private of marijuana for personal use would no longer be an offense of any kind.

(2) Possession in public of one ounce or less of marijuana would not be an offense—but the marijuana would be contraband subject to summary seizure and forfeiture.

(3) Possession in public of more than one ounce of marijuana would be a criminal offense punishable by a fine of one hundred dollars.

(4) Possession of marijuana with intent to sell (apparently whether in public or in private) would remain a felony.

In addition, public *use* of marijuana would be a criminal offense punishable by a fine of one hundred dollars.[55]

Several points about this scheme deserve note. First, the commission gives no indication of how "possession for personal use" is to be distinguished from "possession with intent to sell." In discussing its recommendations for federal law, the commission points out that in 1965 Congress "placed on the prosecution the burden of

[54] A similar scheme is proposed for federal laws (see *Signal of Misunderstanding*, 151–52), but the commission assumes that the primary responsibility for regulating marijuana will remain with the states (*ibid.*, 159).
[55] *Ibid.*, 153–55.

proof that the possession was for purposes of sale." [56] As the commission must have known, however, courts have not accepted any particular quantity as the dividing line between ordinary possession and possession with intent to sell.[57] It would have been appropriate for the commission to recommend a uniform standard, just as it sets one ounce as the dividing line between public possession that will result in confiscation and public possession that will result in criminal punishment.[58] (This assumes, of course, that a rational line can be drawn between possession for personal use and possession with intent to sell. As will be seen later,[59] this is not the case.)

Second, the commission fails to adequately explain why the mere possession of marijuana for personal use in public should subject the possessor to criminal sanctions or the forfeiture of the drug (depending on the quantity involved). Under the commission's scheme, as commissioners Hughes and Javits point out, "[t]he individual who buys an ounce and a half would be a criminal when he buys on the corner, when he puts it in his pocket, when he gets in his car and drives home, when he is on his doorstep, but not when he crosses the threshold of his home." [60] The prohibition is not only illogical, but it is also, in the ordinary course of events, unenforceable. How can the police discover whether someone walking down the street or driving in his car has in his possession a few ounces of marijuana except by using tactics that violate the spirit, and probably the letter, of the Fourth Amendment? The commission attempts to justify the ban on public possession as a "prophylactic measure for anticipating distribution." [61] In the light of the impossibility of enforcing the ban, it is difficult to see how the stated purpose can be achieved except by giving the police license to stop and search anyone who they suspect is carrying the drug.

[56] *Ibid.*, 156; *cf.* Drug Abuse Control Amendments of 1965, Pub. L. No. 89–74, § 3(b), 79 Stat. 227 (repealed 1970).

[57] Compare, e.g., People v. Jackson, 241 Cal. App. 2d 189, 50 Cal. Rptr. 437 (1966) (defendant convicted of possession with intent to sell on the basis of his possession of 243 grams [8.5 ounces] of marijuana), with Redden v. State, 281 A.2d 490 (Del. 1971) (defendant could not be convicted of possession with intent to sell on the sole basis of his possession of 12 ounces and twenty-nine other small sealed packets of marijuana).

[58] For an example of such a standard, see Bonnie and Whitebread, *supra* note 5, at 1178–79 (possession of more than four ounces would be illegal unless the defendant can show that it was possessed solely for personal use). The authors seek to take the user and small seller out of the criminal process while "ensnaring the mass distributor."

[59] See *infra* pp. 52–53, 180–81.

[60] *Signal of Misunderstanding,* 156n.

[61] *Ibid.,* 160.

Finally, the commission defines *private* very narrowly; apparently
the term is used to refer only to possession or use in the home.[62] If
this definition is taken literally, it would criminalize use in a hotel
room or in a person's front yard. Prosecution in such cases hardly
seems consistent with the "preference for individual privacy" to
which the commission rightly attaches such a high value.[63] The
scope of protected activities will be further narrowed if, as the commission appears to suggest, *the home* is equated with *private dwelling* as the term was used in the National Prohibition Act.[64] In in-
terpreting that act, courts refused to accord immunity from searches
to many places where marijuana could be used without offending
any of the policies cited by the commission as justifying the ban on
public possession.[65]

The contraband feature of the commission's scheme is even more
senseless. The commission states that it "symbolizes the discouragement policy and will exert a major force in keeping use private," [66]
but Commissioners Hughes and Javits point out several flaws in
this approach. First, the contraband provision "serves no useful
law enforcement purpose within the overall partial prohibitory
model." The dissenters continue:

> If marijuana held for personal use within the home is not contra-
> band, why should marijuana held for personal use within one's
> automobile be contraband? The area of operation of the contra-
> band provision is extremely narrow. If one possesses more than
> one ounce of marijuana in public, it may be seized without regard
> to the contraband doctrine since such possession is a criminal
> violation.

> Since the contraband provision does not apply to marijuana pos-
> session and use in private, the only effective area covered by the
> contraband provision is the area of possession in public of less
> than one ounce. The Commission has chosen to remove the stigma
> of the criminal sanction in this kind of case. To impose instead a
> contraband provision, which it is argued is in the nature of a civil
> "in rem" seizure which does not operate against the person, is to

[62] *Ibid.,* 157.
[63] See *ibid.,* 140.
[64] *Ibid.,* n. 1.
[65] See, e.g., Dulek v. United States, 16 F.2d 275 (6th Cir. 1926) (upholding
search of a shack on the defendant's farm); United States v. McGuire, 300 Fed.
98, 100 (N.D. N.Y. 1924) (upholding search of a family residence above a
saloon).
[66] *Signal of Misunderstanding,* 159.

cloud the issue and to weaken the force of the basic decriminalization. A persuasive justification simply has not been made.[67]

Second, the legal implications of the contraband provision "are confusing . . . even among lawyers." Ordinarily an item is classified as contraband either because possession of it is illegal or because it is the fruit or instrumentality of a crime.[68] Under the commission's scheme, possession in public of an ounce or less of marijuana would fall in neither category. The most important questions raised by this anomaly concern the authority of the police to investigate individuals suspected of possession of the contraband. May the policeman justify a warrantless search on the ground that he had probable cause to believe that the suspect was in possession of an ounce or less of marijuana—even though this would not be a crime? [69] Or could the marijuana be regarded as the second- or third-hand fruit of someone else's crime? If not, will the contraband ever be seized except when an individual has been stopped and searched ostensibly for some other purpose?

As a practical matter, the contraband provision of the commission's scheme will probably have little or no effect on police practices. As Paul Chevigny points out, a policeman who finds reasons to stop and search persons whom he suspects of possessing drugs may not be interested in obtaining a conviction; he will be content to get the drug out of circulation.[70] Indeed, if the search uncovers no more than an ounce of marijuana the policeman will be relieved of the bother of taking part in judicial proceedings, while he has the satisfaction of preventing the suspect from making use of the drug. The contraband provision thus serves no purpose except to encourage policemen to continue to look for reasons to search persons who they suspect are marijuana users.[71]

Finally, the dissenters urge that the voice of the commission be

[67] *Ibid.*, 153–54n.
[68] See One 1958 Plymouth Sedan v. Pennsylvania, 380 U.S. 693, 699 (1965).
[69] For a general discussion of the circumstances justifying a warrantless search, see *infra* pp. 90, 112–13.
[70] Paul Chevigny, *Police Power: Police Abuses in New York City* (New York, 1969), 209.
[71] In this regard, the contraband provision is analogous to vaguely worded vagrancy statutes which permit a policeman to arrest "on suspicion" even though the officer has no articulable grounds for thinking that the person has committed a crime. Such statutes have regularly been struck down by the Supreme Court, in part because of the unfettered discretion which they place in the hands of the police. See Papachristou v. City of Jacksonville, 405 U.S. 156, 168–71 (1972).

"loud and clear that the preservation of the right of privacy is of paramount importance and cannot be casually jeopardized in the pursuit of some vague public or law enforcement interest which has not been defined and justified with clarity and precision." [72]

A third anomaly in the commission's scheme is the prohibition of public *use* of marijuana. The commission justifies this ban on three grounds: "No intoxicant should be used in public, both because it may offend others and because the user is risking irresponsible behavior if he should be under its influence in public. Moreover, where marijuana is concerned, continuing societal disapproval requires that the behavior occur only in private if at all." [73] These explanations are not persuasive. The suggestion that no intoxicant should be used in public because it may offend others is unnecessarily broad. There is a difference between prohibiting behavior in circumstances where it causes offense to others and prohibiting that behavior under all circumstances because it may *sometimes* offend others. For example, it may be reasonable to prohibit the drinking of alcoholic beverages in a park frequented by children, but that is hardly an argument for outlawing the tavern or cocktail lounge. Similarly, there will be many public places where the smoking of marijuana will not offend anyone—for example, coffeehouses, "counterculture" restaurants or community centers, and dormitory lounges.[74]

Indeed, it is even questionable whether offense to others is a constitutionally sufficient reason for the exercise of the police power. If communal smoking of marijuana in public is found to be embraced within the right of peaceful assembly, the state could probably not prohibit it simply because it was offensive to some people.[75] Even apart from First Amendment considerations, legislatures may not be able to restrict conduct in public where the only objection is that it may offend the sensibilities of onlookers. For example, miniskirts may offend some people, but a law prohibiting women

---

[72] *Signal of Misunderstanding,* 154n.

[73] *Ibid.,* 160.

[74] Different considerations come into play when the legislature is asked to prohibit cigarette smoking in public places. The legislature must then weigh the health and comfort of nonsmokers against the needs and convenience of cigarette smokers—many of whom are addicted (to tobacco) in a way that the marijuana user is not. Of course, if smoking generally is prohibited in a particular class of public places, it would be appropriate to ban marijuana smoking as well.

[75] For a recent application of the underlying doctrine, see Hess v. Indiana, 414 U.S. 105 (1973).

from wearing miniskirts in public would be of dubious constitutionality, to say the least.[76] Even nudity in public may be protected under some circumstances.[77] Justice Harlan's comment about four-letter expletives may be applied to many kinds of public behavior: "[I]t is . . . often true that one man's vulgarity is another's lyric. Indeed, we think it is largely because governmental officials cannot make principled distinctions in this area that the Constitution leaves matters of taste and style so largely to the individual." [78]

As for the risk of irresponsible behavior in public by persons under the influence of marijuana, it is sufficient to prohibit "disorderly conduct associated with public use of or intoxication by marijuana," [79] as the commission recommends be done. Finally, the ban on public use is likely to have a symbolic effect contrary to the commission's expectations, for it will tend to encourage the mystique which many young people are said to associate with marijuana and which the commission is so anxious to dispel.

The commission's recommendations on distribution and sale are even more confusing—so confusing, in fact, that two members who dissent in part from the recommendations appear to misunderstand them. The report proposes the following scheme:

(1) The distribution (a) in *private* (b) of small amounts (c) for no remuneration or "insignificant remuneration not involving a profit" would no longer be an offense.

(2) The distribution (a) in *public* (b) of small amounts (c) for no remuneration or "insignificant remuneration not involving a profit" would be a criminal offense punishable by a fine of one hundred dollars.

(3) Sale or distribution for profit would be a felony.[80]

Penalties for distribution, then, appear to depend on three factors: whether the transaction takes place in public or in private, the quantity of marijuana involved, and whether or not the transaction is for profit. Unfortunately, the commission discusses only a few of the possible combinations of these variables.

Commissioners Hughes and Javits, who dissent in part from the

[76] *Cf.* People v. O'Gorman, 274 N.Y. 284, 8 N.E.2d 862 (1937); see generally Herbert Packer, *The Limits of the Criminal Sanction*, 264–66.
[77] *Cf.* State v. Rocker, 52 Hawaii 336, 475 P.2d 684 (1970); State v. Miller, 501 P.2d 363, 368 (Hawaii 1972) (dissenting opinion); In re Smith, 7 Cal. 3d 362, 497 P.2d 807, 102 Cal. Rptr. 335 (1972).
[78] Cohen v. California, 403 U.S. 15, 25 (1971).
[79] *Signal of Misunderstanding*, 154.
[80] See *ibid.*, 151–67.

majority's recommendations, understand the commission to recommend that the "totally donative transfer" would not be subject to criminal penalty "regardless of where it takes place." [81] The report itself, however, recommends that the states should prohibit "all transfers outside the home, whether or not for remuneration." [82] This conclusion is justified on the same basis as the recommended ban on use in public, and is vulnerable for the same reasons.[83] Further, as the dissenters point out, "casual not-for-profit transfers," even when they take place in public, are "necessarily incident to private possession and use," [84] which the commission recommends be permitted. The inconsistency is aggravated by the commission's narrow understanding of what is private.

The commission's classification of marijuana transfers rests on the assumption that workable distinctions can be made—if not by the legislature, then by the courts [85]—between commercial sales and casual distributions. Whatever relevance this distinction might have for heroin, it bears little relation to the realities of marijuana distribution.

As a prototype of the casual not-for-profit transfer the commission cites the situation in which "a college student makes a quasi-donative transfer of one or two marijuana cigarettes and receives fifty cents or a dollar in exchange to cover the cost of the marijuana." [86] This kind of transaction is virtually nonexistent today. Almost no one purchases individual joints; most low-level exchanges involve at least an ounce of marijuana, enough to make fifty to seventy joints.[87] Even the "nickel bag"—the five-dollar purchase of one-quarter or one-third of an ounce—has become largely obsolete. When someone does transfer one or two joints he would not expect remuneration, certainly not in cash. A more accurate picture of these one- or two-joint transactions is suggested by the remark of a Skidmore coed: "Where a man used to bring candy and flowers, he now brings grass." [88]

The fundamental difficulty with the commission's approach is that it is impossible to identify the casual transfer and the com-

[81] *Ibid.*, 155n.
[82] *Ibid.*, 160.
[83] See *supra* pp. 50–51.
[84] *Signal of Misunderstanding*, 155–56n.
[85] See *ibid.*, 158n.
[86] *Ibid.*
[87] Goode, *Marijuana Smokers, supra* note 4, at 248; *N.Y. Times*, Nov. 20, 1972, p. 47, col. 1.
[88] *N.Y. Times*, Nov. 20, 1972, p. 47, col. 3.

mercial transfer as distinct kinds of transactions. If the word is used in its ordinary sense, virtually all marijuana transactions are "casual"—that is, "occurring without regularity; occasional. . . ." [89] If the commission's dichotomy has meaning at all, it is only to suggest two ends of a continuum.

This conclusion rests on three independent studies of the marijuana market published over the past four years—one by sociologist Erich Goode, a second by *New York Times* reporter Wayne King, and a third by *Times* reporter Robert D. McFadden.[90] A person who buys an ounce of marijuana will probably get it from a friend or acquaintance who has himself purchased no more than a pound or perhaps a kilo (2.2 pounds). It would be unrealistic, however, to term the latter a *dealer*—one who is regularly in the business of buying the drug at "wholesale" and selling it at "retail." His own purchase of the larger quantity may have been fortuitous, prompted by the happenstance of its being available; the next time he may buy no more than an ounce or two. Having bought the pound or kilo, he will typically keep some for his own use, give some to friends or guests, perhaps use some to cancel debts, and sell the remainder. The price at which he sells will be highly variable. To close friends the price would be the dealer's cost. Less intimate friends would pay more, but less than the retail price. Strangers or casual acquaintances would pay the full retail price.

The person who sells a large quantity of marijuana—several pounds or more—may not be a regular dealer either; he may have been offered a chance to buy the drug at a low price and is selling the bulk of it so that he can smoke free himself. At the top of the distribution funnel even the person who smuggles marijuana into this country from Mexico (the most common source) may not necessarily be a commercial seller in the sense that the commission suggests. He, too, may be an amateur or one-time smuggler whose purpose is to bring in and sell enough marijuana so that what he smokes costs him nothing.

Some transactions, of course, will be commercial by any standard. Here the problem is not one of identification but rather one of enforcement. For reasons which will be developed later in this volume,[91] the government has been notoriously unsuccessful in ap-

[89] *Webster's 7th New Collegiate Dictionary*, s.v. "casual."
[90] Goode, *Marijuana Smokers, supra* note 4; *N.Y. Times*, Feb. 17, 1971, p. 1, col. 5; p. 20, col. 1; Nov. 20, 1972, p. 1, col. 5; p. 47, col. 1.
[91] See *infra* pp. 181–84.

prehending the commercial trafficker and is not likely to do better in the future.

The most confusing aspect of the commission's scheme involves the variable of quantity. Not-for-profit transfers of *small* amounts would be legal as long as the transaction takes place in private, but what about not-for-profit transfers of *large* amounts? Commissioners Hughes and Javits understand the commission to recommend that the transfer of large amounts for "significant" remuneration not involving a profit be subject to criminal penalty,[92] but this is not stated in the report. Actually, if prohibiting sales made any sense at all, it would be more practical to draw the line at transfers of large quantities, regardless of their characterization, rather than to attempt to distinguish between sales for profit and not-for-profit transfers. The commission's reasons for prohibiting transfers generally, however, do not withstand analysis, as will be seen later.[93]

In short, the distinctions which the commission advocates cannot help but produce confusion among law-enforcement officials and bitterness among users, whose freedom may depend on arbitrary characterizations divorced from reality. The commission's scheme might nevertheless be defensible if its enactment could be expected to mitigate the most serious negative effects of present laws—those resulting from the techniques used to enforce them. Unfortunately, the substitution of partial prohibition for total prohibition is likely to have little effect on police practices, as I shall show in Part Two.

[92] *Signal of Misunderstanding,* 156n.
[93] See especially *infra* pp. 165–66, 174–75, 180–84.

PART TWO

Introduction

The most serious costs of the marijuana laws are those that result from the way in which the laws are enforced. In the following chapters I shall show that these costs are necessary consequences of any attempt to deal with marijuana through the criminal process.[1] The partial prohibition recommended by the Shafer commission would thus perpetuate the most serious negative effects of the present system. In summary:

(1) The partial prohibition scheme advocated by the commission would require for its enforcement, almost as much as does the present system, the use of police practices that approach the limits of constitutional guarantees and that conflict most strongly with the values of privacy, spontaneity, and individual dignity.

(2) The laws retained under the commission's scheme would continue to furnish excuses for the police to harass "people they don't like for other reasons."[2] Selective enforcement and the operation of chance would still be the crucial factors in many, if not most, marijuana arrests.

(3) As long as the Exclusionary Rule is retained by the courts, the police, in order to support arrests or searches under the commission's scheme, will continue to shade their testimony and even to perjure themselves in suppression hearings.

[1] The narratives in these chapters are drawn principally from the appellate opinions cited. I have interwoven direct quotations, paraphrasing, and comment; in the interest of readability I have not always indicated which phrases and sentences are quoted directly. The interested reader may consult the reported case. See the note on citations, p. xi.

[2] National Commission on Marihuana and Drug Abuse, *Marihuana: A Signal of Misunderstanding,* 146.

These conclusions will be documented in detail in the following pages. Preliminarily, however, it may be useful to examine briefly the shortcomings of the commission's approach to these problems.

As one of its reasons for rejecting "the total prohibition approach and its variations" the commission cites the techniques required to enforce laws against possession for personal use. "Possession of marihuana is generally a private behavior; in order to find it, the police many times must operate on the edge of constitutional limitations. Arrests without probable cause, illegal searches and selective enforcement occur often enough to arouse concern about the integrity of the criminal process." [3] Conversely, the commission lists as one of the benefits of the partial prohibition scheme the prospect of "[r]elieving the law enforcement community of the responsibility of enforcing a law of questionable utility, and one which they cannot fully enforce, thereby allowing concentration on drug trafficking and crimes against persons and property. . . ." [4]

Unfortunately, the commission never addresses itself to the question of whether the police practices that the commission finds so objectionable in the detection of possession might not be equally ubiquitous in, and even necessary to, the detection of drug trafficking and other activities which the commission would continue to prohibit. Brief reflection and a study of appellate cases will show that enforcement of a partial prohibition will require the same dubious practices that law enforcement officials have found necessary to enforce the present scheme of total prohibition.

When the legislature decides to deal with a particular kind of conduct through the criminal process, implementation of that decision is placed in the hands of law enforcement officials—policemen, prosecutors, and judges. The police have essentially two roles: preventing or interrupting the commission of crimes, and identifying and apprehending the persons who commit them. The commission recognizes that when the crime is possession of marijuana the police must often operate "on the edge of constitutional limitations" in order to carry out either function. The reasons for this are obvious, but they are worth reiterating.

Police difficulties in apprehending possessors of marijuana stem essentially from two facts: marijuana is used in private, and in the

[3] *Ibid.*, 146, 145.
[4] *Ibid.*, 150. It is not clear whether the commission refers to crimes against persons and property committed by drug users or whether the commission is talking generally about the kind of activity which everyone agrees is properly the target of the criminal law.

ordinary course of events no one who knows that a "crime" has been committed will report it to the police. It is the combination of these circumstances that renders normal police techniques impotent. As a consequence the police are compelled to use tactics that infringe most strongly upon the values of privacy, spontaneity, and individual dignity.[5] What is worse, these tactics are used not only to obtain evidence against a person suspected of committing a crime that has previously been witnessed or reported, but also to discover whether any crime has been committed.[6] As Herbert Packer has noted in a widely quoted paragraph:

> Quite without regard to the niceties of the constitutional law of search and seizure, there is the greatest difference between, on the one hand, breaking into a man's house to arrest him when you have probable cause to believe that he has already committed a crime (like robbery or burglary) and your interest is in arresting him, and, on the other, doing so when you have probable cause to believe that he is in the process of committing a crime there (like possession of narcotics) and your interest is in securing evidence that a crime is being committed. The second is much more of a bootstrap operation than the first. It is also much likelier to occur than the first, and the chances of making a mistake are far greater.[7]

Allowing the police to use intrusive tactics in the second situation has other undesirable consequences. Police officers may themselves participate in criminal transactions. Resort to unsavory investigative tactics is likely to diminish their self-respect. Citizens who desire to aid the police may be encouraged to spy on their neighbors.

The commission acknowledges the validity of this analysis for the crime of possession but fails to explain why it does not apply with equal force to crimes of sale or transfer. Such transactions are no less private and no less consensual. In the absence of a fortuitous disclosure, law enforcement officials will not be able to detect these crimes or apprehend their perpetrators without the use of the same tactics used to enforce laws against possession.[8]

[5] *Cf.* Harlan, J., dissenting in United States v. White, 401 U.S. 745, 787–88 (1971); Herbert Packer, *The Limits of the Criminal Sanction,* 284.

[6] Jerome Skolnick, *Justice without Trial* (New York, 1966), 115.

[7] Packer, *supra* note 5, at 285.

[8] The commission may have concluded that the use of such tactics is less reprehensible when the buyer is not the target (*cf.* Schwartz, book review in 44 *S. Cal. L. Rev.* 528, 531 [1971]), but this conclusion is inconsistent with what is known about the distribution of marijuana. See *infra* pp. 180–81.

IV

Deception, Betrayal, and Police Participation

In the ordinary course of events, the persons who know from experience or observation where and by whom marijuana is being used will not voluntarily share their knowledge with law enforcement officials. To obtain that information, the police must either disguise their identity or rely on an intermediary who, unsuspected by the users, will act as a police spy.[1] It is hardly surprising, therefore, that the most valuable tools in the enforcement of marijuana laws are undercover agents and informers and the deceptive practices that are an essential part of their activities.[2] Indeed, the detection of marijuana law violations, as of other consensual crimes, "would be all but impossible without the use of traps, decoys and deception."[3]

INFILTRATION BY UNDERCOVER AGENTS

The best-known and most spectacular tactic for apprehending violators of the marijuana laws is the use of undercover agents who in-

[1] Of course the police may also detect violations of the marijuana laws through searches of individuals, their homes, and their effects, but with some exceptions the police will not be able to make a lawful search until they have obtained information from an undercover agent or an informer. The statement in the text also excludes the detection of marijuana law violations as a by-product of other investigations. See chapters 5 and 6.

[2] See William McDonald, *The Enforcement of Narcotic and Dangerous Drug Laws in the District of Columbia* (Georgetown University Law Center Institute of Criminal Law and Procedure, 1973), 64.

[3] Note, "Judicial Control of Secret Agents," 76 *Yale L. J.* 994 (1967).

filtrate the marijuana subculture.[4] Undercover agents may aid in securing arrests in several ways. Often the agent will attempt to purchase marijuana from a suspect, thus providing evidence of a sale.[5] Sometimes the agent's information may be used as the basis for obtaining a search warrant.[6] In other cases the undercover agent will accompany other police officers to a house or apartment where, as a purported friend of the householder, he has seen marijuana. The resident will usually have no hesitation about admitting the agent, and through this subterfuge the other officers also obtain entrance—without need for a warrant.[7] In Vermont an undercover agent—bearded and casually dressed—adopted the technique of giving rides to hitchhikers in the hope of obtaining information about drug activity.[8]

The case of John Sinclair, the radical poet, provides a classic example of the work of undercover agents.[9] The Narcotics Bureau of the Detroit Police Department assigned two agents, a patrolman and a policewoman, to infiltrate an establishment called the Artists' Workshop. The workshop was a meeting place for "heads" in the Wayne State University area.[10] Sinclair, who had achieved notoriety

[4] It is not entirely accurate to speak of the "marijuana subculture" since, as the national commission has reported, use has now spread to "all socioeconomic groups and occupations" (National Commission on Marihuana and Drug Abuse, *Marihuana: A Signal of Misunderstanding*, 32). However, the police seldom direct their enforcement efforts against the middle-class suburban user. *Cf.* Kaplan, "Forward, Marijuana Laws: An Empirical Study of Enforcement and Administration in Los Angeles County," 15 *U.C.L.A. L. Rev.* 1499, 1505 (1968). Thus, a police undercover agent will seek to infiltrate groups conventionally associated with the use of marijuana—the young, the students, and those who are unconventional in their dress or life-style.

[5] See, e.g., McKelva v. State, 453 S.W.2d 298 (Tex. Crim. App. 1970); State v. Boccelli, 105 Ariz. 495, 467 P.2d 740 (1970), discussed at *infra* pp. 81–82; McKay v. State, 489 P.2d 145 (Alaska 1971); Bennett v. State, 477 S.W.2d 497 (Ark. 1972); People *ex rel.* Dunbar v. District Court, 494 P.2d 841 (Colo. 1972).

[6] See, e.g., State v. Monteith, 477 P.2d 224 (Ore. App. 1970).

[7] See, e.g., State v. Darroch, 492 P.2d 308 (Ore. App. 1971) (an undercover agent, after buying hashish from the defendant, purposely left the front door slightly ajar for other agents' entry); State v. Cazes, 262 La. 202, 263 So. 2d 8 (1972) (an agent, after seeing marijuana in a matchbox, summoned police); State v. Alexander, 495 P.2d 51 (Ore. App. 1972) (similar).

[8] See State v. White, 129 Vt. 220, 274 A.2d 690 (1971). The ruse served its purpose in at least the one instance. We do not know how many other hitchhikers may have taken the driver into their confidence, not knowing that he was a policeman.

[9] People v. Sinclair, 387 Mich. 91, 194 N.W.2d 878 (1972).

[10] "According to testimony, a 'head' means 'a user of marijuana'" (McKelva v. State, 453 S.W.2d at 299 n. 1 [Tex. Crim. App. 1970]). Compare with *The Barnhart Dictionary of New English since 1963* (New York, 1973), which defines *head* as "1. a drug addict. 2. a devotee; fan."

as a leader of the Ann Arbor hippie community and as a political activist, lived in an apartment above the store. Patrolman Kapagian grew a beard and let his hair grow long. For three months in late 1966 and early 1967 he and the patrolwoman, both using aliases, took part in the activities of the workshop. As Justice Swainson of the Michigan Supreme Court described it:

> The officers assisted in doing typing and other odd chores at the Artists' Workshop, including sweeping floors and collating literature. They sat in at communal dinners and provided the food for one of these dinners. They joined a group called LEMAR, which advocated that marijuana be legalized. They listened to poetry and helped in the preparation of certain literature. Patrolman Kapagian visited the shop and saw defendant approximately two or three times a week until the defendant's arrest. As part of the assignment, Patrol[man] Kapagian took a job at the Candle Shop. Patrolman Kapagian was equipped with a Portatalk radio transmitter which allowed him to keep in contact with other police officers stationed outside and nearby.[11]

The officers' masquerade, so matter-of-factly narrated by Justice Swainson, would be farcical if presented on a stage, but in real life it was no laughing matter. For three months John Sinclair and his friends talked and worked with "Louis Cory" and "Pat Green," not knowing that the newcomers had joined their activities only to secure evidence against them. Nor did they know that the man they called Louis Cory was carrying a device that enabled him to report their activities to fellow policemen. It is fair to assume that Sinclair and his friends will be less trusting with the next stranger who offers to sweep the floor or share the cost of dinner.[12]

A similar subterfuge led to a thirty-year sentence, later upset by a federal district court, for Lee Otis Johnson, a militant black leader in Houston, Texas. The authorities apparently assigned a black police recruit to infiltrate the commune-style house where Johnson lived. The rookie began chauffeuring Johnson around town and bought food and supplies for the house. One evening Johnson asked his new acquaintance to drive him to a friend's house to obtain

[11] 387 Mich. at 100, 194 N.W.2d at 880.
[12] A similar masquerade was used in State v. Monteith, 477 P.2d 224 (Ore. App. 1970). See also State v. Steward, 496 P.2d 40 (Ore. App. 1972).

some marijuana. When Johnson returned from the house to the car he gave one joint to the agent. The agent then arrested him.[13]

Perhaps the most frightening example of police undercover work is the subterfuge which led to the conviction of Leslie Fiedler, the novelist and critic, for "maintain[ing] a place where [a] narcotic drug [was] unlawfully used."[14] In February, 1967, the Buffalo Narcotics Squad decided to launch an investigation of Fiedler, who had aroused controversy by his advocacy of the legalization of marijuana and other unpopular causes. A member of the squad went to a Buffalo hospital to talk with a seventeen-year-old girl named Marsha, who was then a patient in the psychiatric ward. He asked her if she could gain entrance to the Fiedler home. The girl replied that she knew Fiedler's daughter and could gain access through her. The officer said that the police "wanted to get certain information from the Fiedlers" and asked Marsha to act as an undercover agent in their home. She agreed.

How the narcotics squad happened to get in touch with Marsha is not clear. The girl later gave several conflicting stories, and it may be that she volunteered her services. What *is* clear is that the police sent a spy into the Fiedler household and that the spy was a young girl who was at best mentally unbalanced and at worst psychotic.[15]

For several weeks the girl came and went in the Fiedlers' house. The Fiedlers realized that there was something odd about her, for "[s]he had the habit of disappearing and reappearing with a set of unconvincing and contradictory stories about what exactly had happened to her. . . . It would have been tempting to believe her a spy, except that she looked not so much like someone with a mission as someone at a loss. . . ."[16] What Fiedler did not know is that when the girl visited his home she carried an electronic eavesdrop-

[13] See Johnson v. State, 447 S.W.2d 927 (Tex. Crim. App. 1969); Johnson v. Beto, 337 F. Supp. 1371 (S.D. Tex. 1972). Some of the facts in this paragraph are taken from *The Leaflet*, July–Aug., 1972, p. 1.

[14] N.Y. Penal Law of 1909 § 1533, as amended L. 1960, c. 526; L. 1965, c. 741 (now N.Y. Penal Law of 1967 § 240.45). The facts in this account are taken from the dissenting opinion of Goldman, J., in People v. [Kurt] Fiedler, 30 A.D.2d 476, 477, 294 N.Y.S.2d 368, 370 (1968), affirming the conviction of Dr. Fiedler's son for possession of marijuana, and from Fiedler's book about the arrest and the events leading up to it, *Being Busted* (New York, 1969).

[15] See Fiedler, *supra* note 14, at 200–206. The girl may have decided on her own to attempt to "plant" marijuana in the Fiedlers' house. See *ibid.*, 208.

[16] *Ibid.*, 136, 198.

ping device about the size of a cigarette pack that picked up all conversations within its range. Anything said in the house by members of the family or by visitors was carried to the "uninvited ear" of the police officer listening and making notes at the other end.[17] A more complete invasion of "the last refuge of the individual" [18] could hardly be imagined.[19]

During the period of Marsha's visits the Fiedler home was watched "on and off" by the police. Then for ten days the house was placed under twenty-four-hour surveillance.[20] On the basis of the surveillance and the information provided by Marsha the police obtained a search warrant. On April 28, 1967, six police officers entered Fiedler's home and arrested members of his family and several visitors on various drug charges. More than five years later Fiedler's conviction was reversed by the New York State Court of Appeals on the ground that "no crime was charged or proved." [21] In the interim Fiedler lost a lecturing appointment at the University of Amsterdam, had his home insurance cancelled, and was denied a fellowship.[22]

These cases may suggest that the use of undercover agents is reserved for political activists and other unpopular figures. The truth is otherwise, as Robert Yance and Jack Crown learned to their sorrow in 1969. The two men were staying at a motel in Reno, Nevada. Yance met a girl named Sheila Summers and a man named Ben Jiminez. Apparently he felt that a quick rapport had developed, for he invited them to his room. "There is some implication," the Nevada court states, "that Sheila used her sexual wiles to get to the room with the men." Crown was already in the room when the three arrived. "From a closet Yance produced a quantity of marijuana, rolled a cigarette, and offered it to [Ben and Sheila] after lighting it. The 'joint' . . . was passed around from Yance to Jim, to Sheila, to Crown, back to Sheila from Crown, and then

17 United States v. Katz, 389 U.S. 347, 359 (1967).

18 Ramsey Clark, *Crime in America* (New York, 1970), 287, quoted in United States v. White, 401 U.S. 745, 764 (1971) (dissenting opinion).

19 At this point it is probably unnecessary to add that the police did not have a warrant for the surveillance they undertook.

20 See *infra* p. 92.

21 People v. Fiedler, 31 N.Y.2d 176, 286 N.E.2d 878, 335 N.Y.S.2d 377 (1972). The court stated: "It was never contemplated that criminal taint would attach to a family home should members of the family on one occasion smoke marijuana or hashish there" (31 N.Y.2d at 180, 286 N.E.2d at 879, 335 N.Y.S.2d at 379).

22 *N.Y. Times,* July 7, 1972, p. 1, col. 4; p. 7, col. 1.

to Yance." What Crown and Yance did not know was that Sheila and Ben were undercover agents working for the Reno police department. After sharing the joint with their new acquaintances, Sheila and Ben left—only to return later with other police officers. They then helped the police to force their way into the motel room —all without benefit of search warrant.[23]

If Sheila Summers did use her "sexual wiles" to get into the motel room with the men, as the Nevada court suggests, she would not be the only Delilah to be found in the reports. In Saint Augustine, Florida, an undercover agent named Mrs. Thompson "hung out" at a bar near the beach, drinking beer and meeting people who she hoped would tell her about the drug trade. Tom Spencer, a young man who had an apartment a block away, saw Mrs. Thompson at a table, bought her a beer, and invited her to his apartment. Once they were there, the talk turned to the subject of marijuana—not, one suspects, by chance. A friend of Spencer's had left some marijuana in a closet, but there was nothing in the apartment with which to smoke it. Mrs. Thompson helpfully volunteered to buy cigarette papers. Spencer's roommate drove her to a store, where she bought the papers with money supplied by the state. When they returned to the apartment they rolled two marijuana cigarettes and smoked one of them; Mrs. Thompson took the other one with her, probably to have its contents analyzed. Spencer was later arrested and found guilty of possessing the marijuana, but the appeals court threw out his conviction, saying that "[i]t would be naive . . . not to recognize the implied promise in return for which the appellant must commit a crime. . . . It is beneath the dignity of the state of Florida to allow female agents to appear to be of questionable virtue in order to lure men into committing the crime of smoking marijuana." [24]

At a rock festival in Florida four men were standing around their van when another man, apparently a photographer, approached them and started taking pictures. The four invited the photographer inside, and he shot some film there as well. The men asked, "Is there anything else you'd care to see?" "Well," the photographer replied, "the only thing I don't have is somebody sitting on the canal bank smoking marijuana." The four men obligingly produced hand-rolled marijuana cigarettes and smoked them for the benefit of the photographer's camera. The photographer "simulated" smok-

23 Crown v. Sheriff, 85 Nev. 522, 458 P.2d 357 (1969).
24 Spencer v. State, 263 So. 2d 282 (Fla. App. 1972).

ing with them,[25] then left. His destination was a sheriff's car, from which he called two deputy sheriffs. There was some delay because the deputies' car became stuck in the mud (an occupational hazard at rock festivals), but after a few minutes the photographer—himself a deputy sheriff—pointed out the van to his fellow law enforcement officers. The result was the arrest of the four men. They and their van were searched; marijuana and LSD were seized.[26]

The threat that such activities pose to individual liberties can hardly be overestimated. To begin with, the extent to which undercover agents actually infiltrate groups like the Artists' Workshop or Leslie Fiedler's family is almost irrelevant. A few such instances, widely publicized (as they always are when the agent's cover is broken), must inevitably breed an attitude of mistrust and fear among members of groups who think themselves potential targets of such investigations. Justice Harlan's comment on the practice of third-party bugging is even more applicable here: "The impact . . . must . . . be . . . to undermine that confidence and sense of security in dealing with one another that is characteristic of individual relationships between citizens in a free society." [27]

Unfortunately, not all judges share Justice Harlan's perceptions. In an Oregon case, for example, the court upheld a warrantless seizure of marijuana in the defendant's home on the ground that the drug was "in plain view" to an undercover agent who was visiting the defendant as his guest.[28] To the argument that two United States Supreme Court decisions invalidated the seizure,[29] the Oregon court replied that the cases did not govern because "[t]here was no intrusion upon defendant's privacy" during the time that the undercover agent saw the marijuana. "As far as defendant knew," the court states, "these were not officers but his friends and he treated them and admitted them to his home as such. It was while they were in his house in this status, in the room to which they had

[25] The word *simulated* is the court's. One might conclude that the photographer took the joint when his turn came, but that—apparently unlike the Nevada agents —he only pretended to smoke. Or did he smoke but not inhale? *Cf.* State v. Uresko, 16 Ariz. App. 369, 370, 493 P.2d 536, 537 (1972) ("The agents pretended to be smoking in order not to arouse suspicion"); Ochoa v. State, 444 S.W.2d 763, 764 (Tex. Crim. App. 1969) ("Officer Griffin related he pretended to smoke and did not inhale").

[26] State v. Rouse, 239 So. 2d 79 (Fla. App. 1970).

[27] United States v. White, 401 U.S. at 787 (dissenting opinion).

[28] State v. Alexander, 495 P.2d 51 (Ore. App. 1972). The "plain view" doctrine is discussed at *infra* pp. 113–15.

[29] Chimel v. California, 395 U.S. 752 (1969); Coolidge v. New Hampshire, 403 U.S. 443 (1971).

been invited, that Officer Kock observed what he said he recognized as a baggie of marijuana." Because he was "still in [his] 'drug culture' manner of dress," he was "in a place where he [had] a right to be," and anything he observed was fair game.

The court sees nothing anomalous in holding that the use of an arrest warrant or a search warrant is "an intrusion upon privacy," while there is no intrusion when a narcotics agent in the guise of a friend visits a home under false pretenses and scrutinizes the room looking for evidence with which to incriminate his host. Surely, if the average citizen were asked whether an orderly search by a policeman who has announced his purpose or a covert visit by an undercover agent would be more likely to undermine his "sense of security in dealing with [other people]" and smother the "spontaneity that liberates daily life," [30] he would find the court's choice to be bizarre and even perverse. As one writer puts it:

> . . . The actual inconvenience of a police search, conducted politely at a reasonable hour, is relatively slight. The assault on the personality lies mainly in the fact that the police have chosen the individual for testing and investigation, and that the individual must consider himself subject to such scrutiny at the whim of the police. But this is precisely the same sort of intrusion as that represented by undercover investigation and solicitation. The use of secret agents, indeed, has the additional odious characteristic that the target does not even know that he is ringed by the state, his reactions probed and his words marked.[31]

It must be conceded, of course, that several United States Supreme Court decisions have rejected Fourth Amendment claims based on the activities of undercover agents.[32] These decisions rest on the premise that the amendment affords no protection to a *wrongdoer's* misplaced confidence that his companions will not report his conversations and acts to the police.[33] The flaw in this approach—to quote Justice Harlan—is that "[by] casting its 'risk analysis' solely in terms of the expectations and risks that 'wrongdoers' or 'one contemplating illegal activities' ought to bear," the Court "does not simply mandate that criminals must daily run the

[30] United States v. White, 401 U.S. at 787 (Harlan, J., dissenting).
[31] Note, *supra* note 3, at 1010–11.
[32] Hoffa v. United States, 385 U.S. 293 (1966); Lewis v. United States, 385 U.S. 206 (1966).
[33] Hoffa v. United States, 385 U.S. at 302; United States v. White, 401 U.S. at 749.

risk of [government agents] prying on their private affairs; it subjects each and every law-abiding member of society to that risk." [34]
The Fiedler and Sinclair subterfuges demonstrate how real that
risk is: every visitor to the Fiedler home ran the risk that his words
would be transmitted to a police monitoring station; every member
of the Detroit commune conducted his life for two months under
the watchful eye of a pair of police officers. Whatever one might
say about the Court's decisions as a matter of constitutional interpretation, it is hard to avoid the conclusion that infiltration by
undercover agents threatens the values underlying the Fourth
Amendment at least as much as do the practices that traditionally
have been thought to be within its scope.

Unfortunately, even Justice Harlan stopped short of the conclusion to which his analysis should have led him; although he condemned warrantless third-party bugging, he saw no constitutional
objection to the uncontrolled launching of undercover agents. As
Nathan Lewin has written, however:

> . . . The fears which Justice Harlan [expresses] in [his] dissent
> are not really products of the electronic eavesdrop; the spontaneity,
> frivolity, impetuosity and defiance of our conversation would all
> be "smothered" if we thought that the person in whom we are con-
> fiding has been assigned by the authorities to surveil us and report
> our every deed and word. A far greater danger to our free society
> is presented by the prospect that friends and associates may be em-
> ployed as government spies than by the possibility that an informer
> with whom we speak may be instantaneously transmitting our con-
> versation to a nearby receiver. . . .
> . . . By approving of the uncontrolled launching of the informer
> but balking at his use of a radio transmitter, Justices Douglas,
> Harlan, Brennan and Marshall have swallowed the pig and choked
> on its tail.[35]

Despite his belief that surveillance by government spies threatens
"the preservation of privacy and free discourse," Lewin would not
outlaw the practice; rather, he would require that the recruitment
and use of undercover agents be subjected to judicial control. Under his approach, whenever law enforcement officials make the
decision to use an agent "on a mission which includes seemingly

---

[34] United States v. White, 401 U.S. at 789 (Harlan, J., dissenting).
[35] Nathan Lewin, "Privacy and the 'Third Party Bug,'" *New Republic*, April 17,
1971, p. 15.

confidential conversations and private transactions with [a] suspect," they would have to obtain a warrant from a magistrate; this
means that they would have to have probable cause to believe that
the law is being violated.[36] Such a rule could eliminate the worst
excesses of overzealous law enforcement, but recent developments
suggest that it might not do even that. A warrant requirement in
the federal no-knock law did not prevent a series of violent raids by
narcotics agents on the homes of innocent families in the early
1970's.[37] And quite apart from particular abuses, prior judicial
authorization for search and seizure warrants has proved to be, in
the words of the former district attorney of Philadelphia, "more a
matter of form than of substance in guaranteeing the existence of
probable cause to substantiate the need for a search." [38] Many
studies have shown that judges and other magistrates often issue
warrants after no more than a perfunctory review of the police
affidavits made in support of them.[39] In the one instance in which
Congress, concerned about intrusions on privacy, did attempt to
require extraordinary safeguards for the issuance of court orders
permitting surveillance, the government flouted the legislative mandate.[40]

    I do not suggest that infiltration by undercover agents can never
be justified. With genuine judicial supervision it may be an appropriate and even necessary tactic in investigating organized
crime or municipal corruption. The difficulty is that once the use
of undercover agents is accepted as a legitimate tool of law enforcement, distinctions among crimes tend to be forgotten. The
police will not easily be persuaded that although society deems
marijuana to be so harmful that its use and distribution should be

---

[36] For a proposed system of judicial control of undercover agents, see Note,
supra note 3, at 1014–19.

[37] See *N.Y. Times,* June 25, 1973, p. 1, col. 5. The statute is 21 U.S.C. § 879
(b) (enacted Oct. 27, 1970). Largely because of the outcry over these raids, the
no-knock authority was repealed by Pub. L. No. 93–481 (1974).

[38] Quoted in Ira Glasser and Herman Schwartz, "Your Phone Is a Party Line,"
Harper's, Oct., 1972, p. 114.

[39] See, e.g., LaFave and Remington, "Controlling the Police: The Judge's Role
in Making and Reviewing Law Enforcement Decisions," 63 *Mich. L. Rev.* 987
(1965); Miller and Tiffany, "Prosecutor Dominance of the Warrant Decision: A
Study of Current Practices," 1964 *Wash. U. L. Q.* 1. Although, as LaFave and
Remington put it, "there is greater judicial concern over the issuance of search
warrants than over the issuance of arrest warrants" (*supra* this note, at 993), even
search warrant requests often do not receive careful scrutiny. See LaFave, "Administrative Searches and the Fourth Amendment," 1967 *Sup. Ct. Rev.* 1, 27.

[40] See United States v. Giordano, 416 U.S. 505 (1974).

stamped out through the criminal process, the police should nevertheless refrain from using tactics which have proved effective in
combatting other consensual crimes. Such restraint is even less likely
when the courts, far from drawing distinctions among crimes, tend
to assimilate marijuana offenses with conduct for which criminal
sanctions are more generally regarded as proper. The Nevada case
discussed earlier demonstrates the point well. In affirming the conviction of the two individuals who had shared a joint with the undercover agents, the Nevada Supreme Court said, "This court has
already approved the use of police informers in the prosecution of
the narcotics traffic [citation omitted]. . . . Policemen dealing in
the vast, vague underworld of narcotics are not held to the polite
manners practiced in decent society." [41]

That the court can equate a group of people passing around a
joint of marijuana in a motel room with "the vast, vague underworld of narcotics" evidences a dismaying ignorance of the realities
of marijuana smoking. Even more alarming is the court's assumption that people who smoke marijuana have thereby relinquished
the protections accorded members of "decent society." Unfortunately, as long as marijuana laws remain on the books there will be
prosecutors and courts who will take this view. The effect on attitudes has been described in an earlier chapter. More tangible consequences—the loss of privacy and security—will be felt by unknown numbers of persons, many of whom have committed no
crime except having acquaintance with someone whom the police
have chosen, without judicial check, to investigate.

The fact that undercover agents have been used so extensively
in the investigation of marijuana crimes is of particular significance
in evaluating the Shafer commission's partial prohibition scheme.
The use of undercover agents is costly. The Detroit Police Department lost the services of two officers for three months while they
swept floors and ate communal dinners at the Artists' Workshop in
an attempt to apprehend narcotics violators.[42] The Buffalo Police
Department expended considerable manpower in maintaining a

[41] Crown v. Sheriff, 85 Nev. at 524, 458 P.2d at 358.
[42] It was widely believed that Sinclair alone was the target of the investigation.
Sinclair had been active in organizing the "hip people" in the community and,
according to the magazine *Rolling Stone,* this work "prompted Police Lt. Warner
Stringfellow to threaten: 'I know what you are; we'll get you this time and drown
you, you worthless prick.'" Sinclair responded to the threat with a poem dedicated
to the officer. The two agents began their work within two weeks of this exchange.
Rolling Stone, Feb. 17, 1972, p. 6, col. 4.

twenty-four-hour surveillance on the Fiedler house for ten days. Police departments will seldom go to this trouble and expense merely to apprehend possessors or users.[43] As a result, officials seeking to enforce the laws which the commission proposes to retain would have no less incentive to use undercover agents.

AID FROM INFORMERS

Closely related to the use of undercover agents is the use of informers. Informers fall into three categories: the police informer, who works on a regular basis for law enforcement officials; the arrestee informer; and the citizen informer. Often a person arrested for a relatively minor offense will agree to cooperate with the police by implicating other violators in return for more lenient treatment for himself. In other cases the police receive unsolicited information from citizens—frequently friends or relatives of the person incriminated. The police informer, the arrestee informer, and the casual citizen informer aid the police for different reasons, but the motivation will not make much difference to the person who has been betrayed by someone he trusted.

The methods of the police informer are illustrated by a recent Illinois case.[44] The facts were in dispute, but even the version most favorable to the prosecution raises questions about the propriety of tactics used by the police.[45] The informer, Yates, had known David Ramirez for about six months (or possibly six weeks—the informer gave conflicting testimony). The two of them went to a restaurant with Ramirez's girlfriend Leona Mamach. Yates asked Ramirez about the marijuana he was to purchase; apparently Yates and Ramirez had discussed the transaction previously. Ramirez said he had the drug. Yates then called the police department to make arrangements to meet some detectives. Two officers came to the

[43] It may be suggested that in both of the cited instances the police were less interested in uncovering marijuana-related behavior than in sending a political activist to jail. In both cases, however, the defendants were accused—and convicted—of more serious charges than simple possession. Moreover, as the preceding pages have shown, similar tactics are used against the obscure as well as the notorious.

[44] People v. Ramirez, 124 Ill. App. 2d 407, 260 N.E.2d 435 (1970).

[45] If one accepted the defendant's version of the events, one would have to conclude that he was framed. This would hardly place the police in a better light. For a similar case in which a police informer did apparently attempt to frame the defendant, see Smith v. State, 485 P.2d 771 (Okla. Crim. 1971). See also State v. Anselmo, 260 La. 306, 256 So. 2d 98 (1972) (informer falsely told police that he had been at a "pot party" and had obtained marijuana there).

restaurant. Yates excused himself, went outside, and told one of the officers that he could make a purchase of marijuana from Ramirez. He added that he had made similar purchases from others for other policemen.

The officer searched Yates, going through his pockets and the linings of his suit, and had him take off his shoes. He then gave Yates a prerecorded five-dollar bill. Ramirez and Mamach came out of the restaurant and rejoined Yates. The three walked together for several blocks. What Ramirez and the girl did not know was that the police officers were following them in a squad car. During the walk (according to Yates's testimony) the girl took from her brassiere an envelope containing marijuana and gave it to Ramirez, who transferred it to Yates. Yates gave the five-dollar bill to Ramirez, who gave the money to Mamach.

When the transaction was over, Yates entered a building while Ramirez and Mamach waited outside. Yates phoned police headquarters to state that the deal had been completed. This information was relayed to the officers in the squad car. One of the officers entered the building and received the envelope containing the marijuana from Yates, who told the officer that the girl had the money. The officer placed Ramirez under arrest and, upon finding the prerecorded five-dollar bill in a cigarette package in the possession of Mamach, arrested her also. The girl pleaded guilty to a charge of possession (though she testified at Ramirez's trial that she was innocent); Ramirez was convicted of selling the marijuana.

Two points stand out from this narrative. One is the extent to which the informer and the detectives participated in the crime. Although their conduct probably did not constitute entrapment in a legal sense (since Ramirez was a willing seller),[46] they did supply the money and the buyer for the transaction. A second interesting aspect of the case is the complete trust which Ramirez and his girlfriend apparently had in their false friend Yates. In hindsight, Yates's conduct must have appeared somewhat strange (he disappeared twice during the afternoon without much of an explanation), but at the time neither Ramirez nor Mamach felt any suspicions. The significance of their lack of concern will be discussed in chapter 7.

In cases like *Ramirez* the informer functions as a "decoy," to use Packer's term.[47] More often the informer simply "puts the finger"

[46] See *infra* pp. 79–80.
[47] Herbert Packer, *The Limits of the Criminal Sanction*, 284–86. The decoy stratagem was also used in State v. Chudy, 108 Ariz. 23, 492 P.2d 402 (1972).

on a suspect. At Troy State University in Alabama, for example, two student informers provided police officers with the names of other students whose rooms were to be searched for the presence of marijuana.[48] Often the informer's account is quite detailed, providing evidence of his success in achieving intimacy with those whom he expects to betray.[49]

Kaplan suggests that the typical marijuana user is "much less likely [than the typical heroin addict] to violate the strong ethic against 'turning in' his source—especially since the source so often is a close friend." [50] This consideration, of course, does not apply to the professional informer, who will not be turning in a true friend. The appellate reports include numerous marijuana cases involving informers who work regularly for the police.[51] Nor is the arrestee informant as uncommon as Kaplan believes. Ordinarily, the courts have no occasion to explore the informer's motives, but sometimes one can read between the lines and surmise that he cooperated in exchange for more lenient treatment.[52] In other cases this conclusion is virtually inescapable. A California woman, charged with possession of marijuana, worked with police officers in securing the arrest of several friends (including her former fiancé!) for various drug offenses. The woman testified that she had done so out of a desire to perform a public service, but the court found her account "inherently incredible" and concluded that she had betrayed her friends in the hope of obtaining leniency for herself.[53] In Houston, students who have been turned in to the police by their parents often agree to cooperate in return for the dropping of charges.[54] Similar deals are made in other jurisdictions.[55]

A sheriff's deputy gave a marked bill to a high school student so that she could purchase a lid of marijuana from an acquaintance. The girl purchased a second lid with her own money, but got rid of it after "apparently having [had] a change of heart." See also State v. Thacker, 496 P.2d 729 (Ore. App. 1972); Burns v. State, 473 S.W.2d 19 (Tex. Crim. App. 1971) (college student was given marked money to purchase drugs from off-duty soldiers).

[48] Piazzola v. Watkins, 442 F.2d 284, 286 (5th Cir. 1971).

[49] See, e.g., Muggley v. State, 473 S.W.2d 470 (Tex. Crim. App. 1971); State v. Wood, 262 La. 259, 263 So. 2d 28 (1972).

[50] John Kaplan, *Marijuana: The New Prohibition,* 340.

[51] See, e.g., People v. Pacheco, 27 Cal. App. 3d 70, 103 Cal. Rptr. 583 (1972) (the informant was responsible for at least fifty arrests); State v. Wood, 262 La. 259, 263 So. 2d 28 (1972) (the informant was responsible for seven or eight convictions).

[52] See, e.g., Earman v. State, 265 So. 2d 695 (Fla. 1972).

[53] People v. Uhlemann, 8 Cal. 3d 393, 503 P.2d 277, 105 Cal. Rptr. 21 (1972).

[54] Sayer and Rotenberg, "Marijuana in Houston: A Second Report and a Proposal," 8 *Houston L. Rev.* 209, 216–17 (1970).

[55] See, e.g., Wood v. Commonwealth; 213 Va. 363, 192 S.E.2d 762 (1972) (arrested for a second offense of possession, a man suggested to a detective that

The casual citizen informer is quite a different breed. At the risk of introducing an unnecessarily personal note, I must express surprise at the number of cases in which people have reported not only strangers but also friends, friends of friends, and even relatives for possession of marijuana—often of very small quantities.[56] The motives, if they can be discerned or surmised, are as varied as the circumstances.

Sometimes the informer is a neighbor. Two persons were arrested in a Tucson apartment after the man next door notified the police that he smelled what he believed to be the odor of burning marijuana coming from beneath the door of the adjoining apartment.[57] The manager of a duplex in New York called the police when two of his tenants told him they had spent their rent money to buy drugs but that they would sell the drugs and use the proceeds to pay the rent.[58] In Oregon two boys found a marijuana plant growing in a fenced area on a nearby ranch owned by a couple named Stanton. They cut the plant and gave it to their father, who in turn gave it to the police. A search and arrest followed.[59] Another Oregonian went on a neighbor's property to retrieve a football. "Acting on his own initiative," he picked part of a plant growing on a garden plot which the neighbor had been cultivating since his arrival a month or two earlier. The trespasser turned the plant over to the police, who identified it as marijuana, obtained a search warrant, and arrested the householder.[60]

One can only speculate about the motives of the informers in these cases. The Arizona apartment dweller may have been bothered by the sweet smell of burning marijuana. The apartment manager in New York appears to have been annoyed because he could not collect the rent on time. In the two Oregon cases the discovery of the marijuana may not have been entirely accidental. In *Stanton,*

he could "set up a buy"); Smith v. State, 485 P.2d 771 (Okla. Crim. 1971) (an AWOL soldier was promised return to prior rank for effective informer work); LeDent v. Wolff, 334 F. Supp. 64 (D. Nebr. 1971). See also Frank Donner, "The Confessions of an FBI Informer," *Harper's,* Dec., 1972, p. 55 (a Vietnam veteran rescued by the FBI from a pending marijuana charge became an informer against an antiwar group).

56 Reporter J. Anthony Lukas, covering the Chicago conspiracy trial, was astonished and depressed to find "how easily ordinary Americans could be persuaded to spy on each other." Anthony Lukas, *The Barnyard Epithet and Other Obscenities* (New York, Perennial Library ed., 1970), 62. But see *infra* pp. 147–49.

57 State v. McGuire, 13 Ariz. App. 539, 479 P.2d 187 (1971).

58 People v. E., 38 A.D.2d 394, 330 N.Y.S.2d 3 (1972).

59 State v. Stanton, 490 P.2d 1275 (Ore. App. 1971).

60 State v. Rutherford, 477 P.2d 911 (Ore. App. 1970).

the defendant's premises were known as the "Green Parrot Goat Ranch"; one may surmise that the couple who lived there appeared unconventional to their neighbors. Reading between the lines in the football case, one might guess that the defendant had failed to satisfy his neighbors' curiosity about what he was growing in his little garden.[61]

In other cases the informers' motives are even more obscure. A sixteen-year-old boy found marijuana and narcotics paraphernalia in a home in which he was baby-sitting. He brought the items to the police, who obtained a search warrant and searched the premises. The only elucidating fact is the comment that the baby-sitter had "previously contacted the police." [62] In Los Angeles a refrigerator repairman phoned the police to tell them that while repairing a refrigerator he had found two bags containing a substance which appeared to be marijuana. He then took part in a ruse which permitted the police to enter without arousing the householder's suspicion.[63] In several cases the police have been tipped off about the presence of marijuana by maids in motels.[64]

A school superintendent in Rialto, California, told the police about a marijuana party which he believed would be taking place at a house where several teachers in his district lived. The police snooped around and then raided the party.[65] In Springfield, Oregon, a woman told a police officer that she had found marijuana in the pocket of a pair of trousers worn by a man who had stayed overnight in her house as a guest. She signed a "little note" consenting to the search of her house, led the officer to the guest bedroom, and pointed to a pair of pants lying on the floor. According to the officer, a plastic bag containing marijuana was visible, half in and half out of the pocket.[66]

[61] See 477 P.2d at 912: "The defendant moved into a house in Klamath Falls. A few days after he moved in, he began to tend a small plot of ground, as if he were planting a garden. This plot of ground was located about 60 feet from his house in a small cleared area variously described as either in defendant's yard or in a lot adjoining his yard. Three of defendant's neighbors observed defendant tending, digging, watering and raking the plot on several occasions."
[62] People v. Legard, 12 Cal. App. 3d 1006, 91 Cal. Rptr. 257 (1970).
[63] People v. Mesaris, 14 Cal. App. 3d 71, 91 Cal. Rptr. 837 (1970). See further discussion at *infra* p. 107.
[64] See, e.g., People v. Benson, 490 P.2d 1287 (Colo. 1971); State v. Treadway, 28 Utah 2d 160, 499 P.2d 846 (1972); Krauss v. Superior Court, 9 Cal. App. 3d 793, 88 Cal. Rptr. 612 (1970); Purvis v. Wiseman, 298 F. Supp. 761 (D. Ore. 1969).
[65] Mann v. Superior Court, 3 Cal. 3d 1, 472 P.2d 468, 88 Cal. Rptr. 380 (1970). Other aspects of this case are discussed at *infra* p. 97.
[66] State v. Cate, 491 P.2d 627 (Ore. App. 1971).

In New Jersey, a sixteen-year-old baby-sitter opened a package that was delivered to the home where she was working. She discovered that the package contained marijuana (which she recognized from her high school health education classes). The sitter immediately telephoned a girlfriend and told her about the package. The girlfriend in turn told her mother, who notified the police. Two officers were sent to the home where the sitter was working. She admitted them and gave them the package. The man who had hired her and the woman who had delivered the package were both arrested.[67]

In Mississippi, Wayne Barker stopped at the home of a friend's parents to ask for his friend's address. The friend's mother gave Barker the information he wanted, and Barker gave her three cigarettes, telling her they were marijuana and asking her to try them. (He added that they were better than drinking because you would not get a hangover.) The mother told her husband about the conversation and gave him the cigarettes. The husband went to the police, who obtained a search warrant for Barker's residence.[68]

The train of events that led to the arrest of Delvin Young began when a girlfriend, seventeen, and her thirteen-year-old sister Peggy visited his home. The older girl asked, "Where is the grass?" Young brought out some marijuana, rolled three cigarettes, and passed them around to the older girl and another man. The four then went for an automobile ride, during which the three older persons smoked more marijuana. Apparently Peggy did not participate —or so she told the police when she gave them the information on the basis of which the warrant was issued.[69]

Probably the most unfortunate victim of a citizen informer was Robert Sorenson of Killeen, Texas. Sorenson left home at the age of sixteen to go to work. He returned three years later and agreed with his parents that as soon as he became employed he would pay them ten dollars a week rental for his room. About two weeks

[67] State v. Frank, 112 N.J. Super. 592, 272 A.2d 309 (1971). For a similar case, see *N.Y. Times*, Jan. 25, 1971, p. 17, col. 6 (a ten-year-old boy turned in his baby-sitter and three other teenagers for marijuana violations; he said he learned to recognize the smell of the drug at a state police exhibit and learned what marijuana looked like by watching public service TV programs).

[68] Barker v. State, 241 So. 2d 355 (Miss. 1970).

[69] People v. Young, 12 Cal. App. 3d 878, 90 Cal. Rptr. 924 (1970). Cases like this one inevitably prompt speculation about the motives and relationships of the individuals involved. Was young Peggy piqued at being left out of the marijuana smoking? What prompted the woman in Oregon to turn in a man who had stayed overnight in her home as her guest?

after his return his mother went into his room to put two clean shirts in his closet. While hanging the shirts up she noticed an unusual odor, which she believed to be that of marijuana. (She had had occasion to smell marijuana before; under what circumstances we do not know.) She said later, "I took it upon myself to look and see if I could find it, to see if it was there, and I did find it myself there."

Over the weekend Mrs. Sorenson left the marijuana where she had found it, assuming that her son would tell her about it or dispose of it. Apparently he did not, for sometime thereafter she decided to talk to the family minister. She took some of the green substance with her in order to be certain it was marijuana. What the minister told her we do not know, but Mrs. Sorenson then went to the Killeen police department, thinking "under the circumstances that existed this would be my only alternative." She and her husband signed a "consent to search" form for the entire residence. Police officers made a cursory search of the rest of the home and then went to Robert's room. As Robert watched, the officers opened his closet and found a brown jacket. In the inside pocket were a plastic bag and two bottles containing marijuana and four hypodermic needles. Robert was arrested. Earlier that day he had started working on his new job. His mother was still holding the paycheck he had received from his employer for his first day's work.[70]

This case is not unique. Sayer and Rotenberg found a "surprising number of parents who will turn in their children to the police." Forty juveniles were reported to the Houston police department by one or both of their parents for marijuana offenses in 1969.[71] During a twelve-month period in San Mateo County, California, 7 of the 133 defendants in marijuana cases first came to the attention of the police when they were referred by their families.[72] In New York the parents of two college students asked the police to arrest their sons for possession of marijuana. (After serving as complainants against their children, the parents hired a lawyer for them.)[73] The mayor of an Ohio town turned his nineteen-year-old son over to the police for dispensing marijuana to a minor—a crime that carried a maximum penalty of thirty years to life. The minor who

[70] Sorenson v. State, 478 S.W.2d 532 (Tex. Crim. App. 1972).
[71] Sayer and Rotenberg, *supra* note 54, at 239 and n. 196.
[72] Comment, "Possession of Marijuana in San Mateo County: Some Social Costs of Criminalization," 22 *Stan. L. Rev.* 101, 127 (Table 4) (1969).
[73] *N.Y. Times,* Feb. 27, 1967, p. 33, col. 1.

had received the marijuana was the brother of the arrested youth.[74]

Informers pose much the same threat to privacy and security as do undercover agents, but the use of informers is in some ways even more repugnant to the ideals of a free and open society. The police informer, often trading his own security for that of his friends and acquaintances, will sometimes fabricate evidence in order to win the favor of the law enforcement officials on whose good will he is dependent.[75] Still more distasteful is the spectacle of parents who turn in their children to the police—or children who turn in their parents. However admirable the motivation might be in a particular case,[76] repeated instances of informing by friends or members of the family suggest an alarming resemblance to Russia of the Stalinist purges or Oceania of Orwell's *1984*. As with the use of undercover agents, the actual extent to which the police make use of informers is less important than the extent to which the practice is believed to exist.

Some people may think that the refrigerator repairman, the babysitter, and even Mrs. Sorenson were only doing their duty as citizens. Unfortunately, the line between good citizenship and vigilantism is a thin one. It is not only the guilty who are subjected to police snooping or interrogation as a result of citizens' reports. In Hartford, Connecticut, for example, a "bust the pusher" campaign, asking for anonymous calls to a special telephone number, drew 828 tips in a seven-month period. Ten arrests were attributed to the project; 37 others arrested were mentioned in tips but were already under investigation. Presumably the remaining tips—more than 700 of them—lacked sufficient foundation to justify an arrest, let alone a conviction.[77] One wonders how many innocent persons were placed under surveillance or otherwise investigated as a result of these anonymous calls.

It may be suggested that society would hardly benefit if citizens did not report strangers prowling around a neighbor's property or the screams of a girl in the street below. There are important differences, however, between crimes such as burglary and rape on the one hand and marijuana offenses on the other. Even if one believes that the use of marijuana is harmful to society, the harm is hardly

[74] *N.Y. Times,* Mar. 3, 1973, p. 14, col. 6.

[75] See, e.g., Smith v. State, 485 P.2d 771 (Okla. Crim. 1971); State v. Anselmo, 260 La. 306, 256 So. 2d 98 (1972).

[76] The Ohio mayor, for example, refused to pay his son's bail, saying, "This is for his benefit."

[77] *N.Y. Times,* Aug. 2, 1972, p. 45, col. 5.

as immediate and specific as the injury by a burglar or rapist. Further, the chances that the informer will be in error are much greater when he is reporting someone's possession of or dealing in marijuana instead of a crime against persons or property. The opportunities to inform on someone for personal motives are also greater. Finally, even if many citizens' reports prove to be reliable, the interest in law enforcement must be balanced against the danger of creating a society in which no one is ever quite sure that the man who repairs his refrigerator, the girl who baby-sits with his children, or the neighbors who ask him about his gardening activities will not turn him in to the police on the basis of real or imagined evidence that marijuana is to be found in his possession.

As long as marijuana laws remain on the books, however, there will be citizens who will feel obliged—out of whatever motives—to report persons who they suspect are violating those laws. In this respect, adoption of the partial prohibition scheme recommended by the Shafer commission would hardly change the situation at all. The commission would retain so many laws against the possession and distribution of marijuana that the "good" citizen would still have many opportunities to report activities which he believes to be unlawful. Society must decide whether the benefits of criminal laws against marijuana are great enough to justify the loss of trust and security resulting from this kind of informing.

Nor would adoption of the commission's recommendations significantly affect the practice of using arrestee informants. Although law enforcement officials would in many cases not have the threat of a simple possession charge to use as a lever, the commission would retain a sufficient battery of minor marijuana offenses [78] so that a person desiring to avoid a criminal record might still agree to cooperate by informing against "dealers" [79] in return for more lenient treatment for himself.

ENTRAPMENT AND POLICE PARTICIPATION IN CRIME

Undercover agents and informers do not limit themselves to observing and reporting what others have done; often they are active participants in transactions which they hope will lead to an arrest.

[78] National Commission on Marihuana and Drug Abuse, *Marijuana: Signal of Misunderstanding,* 153–54.

[79] This term is misleading if it implies that dealers can be meaningfully distinguished from users. See *infra* pp. 180–81.

Commonly they make inquiries to find someone who will sell them marijuana. When through luck or persuasion they succeed, they will buy the drug, often with money provided by the police.[80] Sometimes they resort to practices which the courts label entrapment. However, in most jurisdictions, including the federal courts, entrapment can be used as a defense only in narrow circumstances. Government agents may solicit or encourage an individual to commit a crime; they may importune, deceive, and even supply materials without which the crime could not be committed. The prosecution will be barred only if the jury concludes that the police agents have induced the defendant to engage in illegal conduct when he was not otherwise predisposed to do so.[81] What this means is that quite apart from any improper activities by overzealous agents, law enforcement officials seeking to apprehend marijuana law violators are free not only to use deception but also to engage in many forms of illegal conduct.

The classic case, once again, is that of John Sinclair.[82] I have already described how two police officers infiltrated the Artists' Workshop, where Sinclair spent much of his time, and won his confidence.[83] On several occasions the two agents asked Sinclair to obtain marijuana for them. Early in the evening of December 22, 1966, Sinclair appeared at the workshop and asked Louis Cory (Patrolman Kapagian) and Pat Green (Policewoman Lovelace) whether they had received any marijuana the previous night. The officers said they had, adding that they were looking for more. About two hours later Kapagian told Sinclair that he and "Pat" had to leave. Sinclair asked them to go upstairs with him to his apartment. Once inside the apartment, Sinclair rolled a joint for Kapagian, who put it in a partially filled cigarette pack. Sinclair then rolled a second cigarette, lit it, and handed it to Kapagian. Kapagian said he did not want to smoke it then because he had to drive and the cigarette would make him dizzy. Sinclair stubbed out the cigarette, and Kapagian gave it to Lovelace, who put it in the cigarette pack with the other joint. The two officers left. Two days later Sinclair was arrested and charged with the unlawful sale and

---

[80] See, e.g., State v. Kasai, 27 Utah 2d 326, 495 P.2d 1265 (1972); State v. Reichenberger, 209 Kan. 210, 495 P.2d 919 (1972); and cases cited in *supra* notes 5 and 47.

[81] The Supreme Court recently reaffirmed this doctrine in United States v. Russell, 411 U.S. 423 (1973).

[82] People v. Sinclair, 387 Mich. 91, 194 N.W.2d 878.

[83] See *supra* pp. 61–62.

possession of two marijuana cigarettes. The trial judge dismissed the count for unlawful sale on the ground that Sinclair had been entrapped by the two officers, but Sinclair was convicted of unlawful possession and sentenced to nine and one-half to ten years' imprisonment. Nearly three years after his conviction, and five and one-half years after the alleged unlawful sale, Sinclair was freed by a decision of the Michigan Supreme Court.[84]

In some cases law enforcement officials have virtually manufactured the crime for which the defendant was charged. One victim of such a stratagem was Frederick Boccelli of Arizona. Shortly after he arrived home from work one day, a casual acquaintance named Gaylord Junkins knocked on the door and was invited into the living room. Unknown to Boccelli, Junkins was an informer for the state narcotics bureau. Junkins asked Boccelli if he wanted to buy a "lid" (approximately one ounce) of marijuana. Boccelli replied, "No, I don't have the money." Junkins then asked if it was all right to leave the marijuana at Boccelli's house, because Junkins wanted to look for another buyer and did not want to carry the drug with him. Boccelli agreed, and Junkins left after placing the marijuana on a table in the living room.

Junkins then went to a meeting with two state narcotics agents. One, Gary Richardson, went with Junkins to Boccelli's home. Junkins introduced Richardson to Boccelli and then left the room in accordance with the plan previously arranged by the two agents. Richardson asked Boccelli if he had the "grass." Boccelli replied, "Yes, it's on the table." Richardson picked up the marijuana and asked Boccelli how much he wanted for it. Boccelli initially asked for $10.00 but settled for $9.25 because that was the amount Richardson had in change. Richardson gave the money to Boccelli. He and Junkins left Boccelli's home shortly thereafter. Although the marijuana belonged to Junkins, Boccelli did not give him the $9.25.

The defense of entrapment was accepted by the state supreme court, which reversed Boccelli's conviction, saying: "The sum of the uncontradicted testimony is that the State's agents supplied all the ingredients of the offense: the plan, the marijuana, the buyer, the money for the purchase. Finally, even the intent to sell was implanted by Richardson's inquiry of appellant as to how much he

---

[84] For a similar case in which the defendant was an obscure individual who, as far as the record showed, had never possessed or sold marijuana before, see Peters v. State, 450 S.W.2d 276 (Ark. 1970).

wanted for the 'grass.' The criminal conduct is clearly the product of the creative activity of the law enforcement officers." [85]

The police may manufacture marijuana crimes in more subtle ways as well. In the state of Washington, two paid informers masquerading as brother and sister were introduced to a young man named Morgan. Morgan had given up marijuana smoking a month or so earlier, but he had two cigarettes left over; they were at his girlfriend's house. Within a week, the agents had asked him on four separate occasions how they could buy marijuana. Morgan steadily insisted that he had no idea where to get any. The girl, who had previously offered "to become his bed partner," as the court delicately puts it, now offered to trade tranquilizer tablets for some marijuana. Since Morgan had been troubled by headaches and insomnia, he accepted the tranquilizers, then went to his girlfriend's house with the two agents and gave them the leftover cigarettes. He was charged with unlawful delivery of a controlled substance and found guilty. The appeals court ordered a new trial, saying that the jury, if properly instructed on the defense of entrapment, could find from the evidence that Morgan "was induced or lured into delivering [the drug] through the concerted efforts of the police informants." [86]

Justice Frankfurter has explained the distaste which courts—and probably most citizens—feel for the practice of entrapment:

> The courts refuse to convict an entrapped defendant . . . because, even if his guilt be admitted, the methods employed on behalf of the Government to bring about conviction cannot be countenanced. As Mr. Justice Holmes said . . . , "It is desirable that criminals should be detected, and to that end that all available evidence should be used. It also is desirable that the Government should not itself foster and pay for other crimes, when they are the means by which the evidence is to be obtained. . . . [F]or my part I think it a less evil that some criminals should escape than that the Government should play an ignoble part." Insofar as they are used as instrumentalities in the administration of criminal justice, the . . . courts have an obligation to set their face against enforcement of the law by lawless means or means that violate

[85] State v. Boccelli, 105 Ariz. at 497, 467 P.2d at 742. For another case in which the court found the police "guilty of unconscionable conduct by entrapping a defendant into acting as a conduit for the sale of marijuana," see Rogers v. State, 277 So. 2d 838, 839 (Fla. App. 1973).

[86] State v. Morgan, 9 Wash. App. 757, 515 P.2d 829 (1973).

rationally vindicated standards of justice, and to refuse to sustain such methods by effectuating them. . . . Public confidence in the fair and honorable administration of justice, upon which ultimately depends the rule of law, is the transcending value at stake.[87]

When police agents participate in the illegal conduct or even encourage it without furnishing *all* the ingredients of the offense, courts seldom accept the defense of entrapment, although many of the evils associated with the practice are present. For example, in the Florida case in which the deputy sheriff posed as a photographer and told the defendants he needed a picture of people smoking marijuana, the court left it to the jury to decide whether the defense of entrapment had been proved.[88] Nor is this an extreme example. Often an undercover agent will repeatedly ask an individual to sell marijuana to him, returning again and again to renew the request after being turned down. Sometimes the individual finally buys a quantity of marijuana from someone and immediately resells it to the agent at the same price; the obvious explanation is that he has done so in the hope of putting an end to the persistent solicitation. Convictions obtained through such tactics are routinely upheld.[89]

A few examples will demonstrate the pattern. In Ohio a man named Lehman, having been found in possession of one marijuana cigarette, agreed to cooperate with the police by attempting to purchase marijuana from a man named McDonald, whom he had met while in the service. Lehman called McDonald three or four times and was refused each time; as Lehman put it, McDonald "seemed reluctant." Finally, McDonald agreed to make a sale. The court found no entrapment.[90] In Maine a college student "looking to a future career in crime detection" volunteered to be an undercover drug agent on campus. He took to his role with gusto; as the court describes it: "[T]o gain the trust of the people involved with drugs at the college, Oberstein engaged in frequent extensive dis-

[87] Sherman v. United States, 356 U.S. 369, 380 (1958) (concurring opinion).
[88] State v. Rouse, 239 So. 2d 79 (Fla. App. 1970), *supra* pp. 65–66.
[89] See, in addition to the cases discussed below, Alston v. State, 258 So. 2d 436 (Miss. 1972) (defendant refused several requests by an undercover agent).
[90] State v. McDonald, 32 Ohio App. 2d 231, 289 N.E.2d 583 (1972). One would like to know more about the informer Lehman. The court tells us that the police, armed with a search warrant, searched his residence and found the one joint in the pocket of his sports coat. Surely that was not what the police expected to find when they went to the trouble of obtaining a warrant. Did they have additional evidence against Lehman that prompted him to help them in incriminating McDonald?

cussions of drugs . . . and, generally speaking, conveyed an attitude that he himself advocated the use of marijuana and did at times encourage people to do so. In fact, Oberstein once actually participated in the smoking of some hashish with the appellant and certain other students." For reasons that are not explained, Oberstein apparently focused his attentions on a fellow student named Allen. Starting in September, he asked on the average of once a week if Allen would get him a nickel bag. For two months his requests were unavailing. Finally, on November 6 Allen handed Oberstein an envelope containing the drug, and Oberstein gave him five dollars. The court, acknowledging that "[n]owhere in the evidence is there any suggestion that Allen was making a profit on the transaction," nevertheless upheld his conviction for unlawful sale.[91]

The police played an even more equivocal role in a Georgia case. Two members of the narcotics squad made the acquaintance of several girls who, as the court tells us, "were used as entrees for making contacts with sellers of drugs." The officers said they wanted to buy a pound of marijuana, and the girls took them to the apartment of Timothy Brooks and his wife. Brooks, however, did not have any marijuana. That might have been the end of the matter, but the girls, pleading that someone was badly in need of the drug, urged him to call people in an effort to locate some. Reluctantly, Brooks did so. The officers supplied $175 for a purchase. Brooks "demurred somewhat," in the words of the court, but finally he and his wife went with their visitors to meet someone who produced about a pound of marijuana wrapped in a newspaper. The undercover policemen pressed Brooks to haggle the price down on their behalf; as one of them later testified, "$175 was a little bit high to what we had been paying for it." The price was set at $165, and $10 was returned to the officers. When the marijuana was inspected, it proved "trashy"; the price was again reduced by $10, and another $10 was refunded to the officers. Brooks and his wife kept none of the money, but were prosecuted for selling the marijuana. She was acquitted; he was convicted. To three of the court of appeals judges the facts showed not only that the entire transaction took place "at the suggestion and instigation" of the police officers, but also that Brooks had not sold the marijuana at all;

---

[91] State v. Allen, 292 A.2d 167 (Me. 1972). Of course it is pure speculation to say that the agent focused his attentions on Allen. For all we know, he may have similarly importuned dozens of other students who he thought (or hoped) would agree to sell marijuana to him.

rather, he had acted as agent for the police in *buying* it. The majority of the court, however, allowed the conviction to stand.[92]

The doctrine that police officers may engage in illegal conduct in order to apprehend others who violate the law was carried to its bizarre but logical conclusion in a series of decisions in Ohio and Texas. The Ohio court first held that "in order to give the appearance of validity to his conduct," an undercover agent may smoke marijuana. Having gone that far, the court did not shrink from the next step: it ruled that an agent seeking "to ferret out the illegal drug trade" may sell and deliver drugs to others.[93] The effect, as one lawyer remarked after the decision was announced, was to "reduce the entire law enforcement picture to a matter of big crooks chasing little ones." [94] Since the court offered no explanation and cited no authorities in support of its conclusion, we do not know how the judges might have refuted this analysis. In any event, it remained for the Texas Court of Criminal Appeals to give the doctrine its final *reductio ad absurdum*. The two cases in which it did so deserve examination, for even if the holdings are unusual, the police practices and the judicial attitudes that produced them are not.

In Amarillo an undercover agent named Griffin, dressed as a "hippie," went to the Hong Kong Lounge one evening and sat down at a table with a group of five people who were already there. He was acquainted with four of the five—Willie John Via and his wife and Ray and Fred Salazar—but he did not know the fifth, a man named Ochoa. Griffin announced that he had arranged to purchase some marijuana that night. Shortly thereafter a woman appeared, and Griffin bought a lid from her. (A lid, this court informs us, is the amount it would take to fill a Prince Albert can.) The woman had brought one and one-half matchboxes more marijuana than Griffin had ordered. Via and Fred Salazar bought the surplus, and the entire purchase was placed in a plastic bag. The group then

[92] Brooks v. State, 125 Ga. App. 867, 189 S.E.2d 448 (1972). The report of the case gives no clue whether the officers arrested the individual who sold the marijuana to Brooks.

[93] Both decisions are reported in State v. Rowan, 32 Ohio App. 2d 142, 288 N.E.2d 829 (1972). The holdings were cited with apparent approval in State v. Hsie, 36 Ohio App. 2d 99, 105, 303 N.E.2d 89, 94 (1973). The undercover agent involved in Rowan's case was investigated by a grand jury but not indicted. Witnesses at Rowan's trial testified that the agent had both bought and sold drugs for profit. By the time the decision was handed down, the agent was no longer with the sheriff's office; it was reported he had left law enforcement altogether. See *Akron Beacon Journal,* Nov. 2, 1972, p. 1.

[94] *Akron Beacon Journal,* Nov. 2, 1972, p. 1.

went to the Vias' house, where Griffin measured out one and one-half matchboxes of marijuana, from which Via and Salazar rolled eleven cigarettes. Via lit the largest of the cigarettes and took it into the living room, where it was passed from hand to hand and smoked by Via, the two Salazars, Ochoa, and Griffin. (Griffin testified that he "pretended to smoke and did not inhale.") A short while later, Ochoa was arrested and charged with possession of marijuana—the "possession" having taken place during the time he shared the joint with his three friends and the undercover agent. He was convicted and sentenced to five years' imprisonment. On appeal the judgment was affirmed. The court conceded that "Griffin was responsible for marijuana being available on the night in question," but held that this did not vitiate the conviction, for Griffin had not himself handed the joint to Ochoa and therefore Griffin "was . . . not the person who caused [Ochoa] to participate" in the offense.[95]

However dubious this distinction might be, one would think that the court, having made it, would reverse a conviction obtained after an undercover agent *had* himself handed marijuana to a defendant charged with possession. The issue was starkly raised a few years later by a case originating in Llano County, not far from Austin. An informer named Horton went to the home of a man named Berryhill and bought ten dollars' worth of marijuana (one lid) with money furnished by the sheriff. Berryhill had several other visitors at the time, including a man named Brewer. Although some members of the group had apparently been smoking marijuana before Horton arrived, there was no evidence that Brewer was among them. Horton handed Brewer some of the marijuana he had just bought, asking him if he wanted to roll a couple of joints and smoke them before Horton left. Brewer thought he had cigarette papers with him, but he did not, so he immediately handed the marijuana back to Horton. Brewer was then arrested. The trial court found that he had unlawfully possessed marijuana, and his parole was revoked. Again the court of appeals affirmed, rejecting Brewer's argument that Horton was an accomplice witness whose testimony required corroboration: "An undercover agent who purchases marijuana is not an accomplice witness so long as he does

---

[95] Ochoa v. State, 444 S.W.2d 763 (Tex. Crim. App. 1969). Ochoa argued that the evidence did not show that he had had possession of the marijuana. The court noted that he had participated in the smoking of the one cigarette, then stated: "A narcotic drug may be jointly possessed by two or more persons." One hopes that no pun was intended.

not bring about the crime, but merely obtains evidence to be used against those engaged in the traffic. . . ." [96]

What the Texas court seems to have forgotten is that Horton's evidence was not being used against anyone "engaged in the traffic." Brewer was not charged with selling marijuana, nor was there even a suggestion that he had been involved in drug trafficking. The same was true in Ochoa's case; indeed, the undercover agent had never heard of Ochoa until the night he met him at the Hong Kong Lounge. The two decisions thus stand the Ohio court's rationale on its head: they permit the police to engage in trafficking in order to obtain convictions for possession. To put the matter more baldly, what the court has held is that it is legitimate for the police to buy marijuana, hand it to someone, and then arrest him for possessing it!

Police participation in marijuana crimes has undesirable consequences whether or not the officer's conduct can be characterized as entrapment. As Herbert Packer has pointed out, putting oneself in the position of a shopper for illegal drugs is bound to have a degrading effect on law enforcement officers. One wonders if Patrolman Kapagian and Policewoman Lovelace had quite the same respect for law—or for themselves—when they returned to ordinary police work after entrapping John Sinclair. Nor will it be easy for the police to maintain their moral authority if as a matter of routine they not only violate the laws they are attempting to enforce but also urge and induce others to do so. To quote Packer again, "there is a substantial difference between occasionally using this technique, as in the detection of espionage and bribery, and making it a way of life, as in the case of drug and sex offenses." [97]

Packer's warning about what happens when illegal activities become "a way of life" for law enforcement personnel was grimly borne out in 1973 by an epidemic of violent raids by federal narcotics agents on the homes of innocent families. People could not easily understand how federal officers could have smashed through doors, destroyed furniture, and shouted obscenities at unresisting women and children. One agent's explanation summed up the transformation of attitudes that made the raids possible: "If you spend weeks undercover, living in a hole and dealing with drug people,

[96] Brewer v. State, 500 S.W.2d 504 (Tex Crim. App. 1973). The Ochoa decision was cited both for the proposition quoted in the text and for the holding that Brewer had not established the defense of entrapment. The court did not explain why the distinction emphasized in *Ochoa* was suddenly irrelevant.
[97] Packer, *supra* note 47, at 286.

your whole life-style changes and perhaps your morals too. Some-times there's a thin line between the hunted and the hunter." [98] The tactics described in this chapter suggest that in the enforcement of the marijuana laws the line all too often disappears entirely.

Police use of entrapment and related practices would probably remain unchanged under the scheme proposed by the Shafer com-mission. Although there are occasional exceptions, like the two Texas cases discussed in this section, such tactics are typically used against persons the police believe to be dealers. Since most kinds of distribution would remain criminal under partial prohibition, the police would have no less incentive to enforce the law through the use of decoys, and society would continue to pay the costs described by Justice Frankfurter and Professor Packer.

[98] *N.Y. Times,* June 25, 1973, p. 22, col. 7.

V

Surveillance and Snooping

The slogan "Big Brother Is Watching You" has come to symbolize the spectre of a totalitarian government watching every move its citizens make.[1] Happily, for most persons in the United States Big Brother remains only a fictional creation. For persons whom the police believe to be connected in any way with marijuana activities, however, Big Brother is often very much a reality. Two kinds of investigatory tactics contribute significantly to this result: surveillance and what I have termed *snooping*. Before turning to these practices, however, it may be useful to give a brief sketch of the law relating to searches and seizures.

We may begin with the text of the Fourth Amendment: "The right of the people to be secure in their persons, houses, papers, and effects, against unreasonable searches and seizures, shall not be violated, and no Warrants shall issue, but upon probable cause, supported by Oath or affirmation, and particularly describing the place to be searched, and the persons or things to be seized." Even more than other important clauses of the Constitution, this language teems with problems of interpretation. Is every intrusion upon an individual's person, house, papers, or effects to be considered a search? By what criteria is a court (or a police officer) to determine whether a search or seizure is reasonable? What is the relationship between the warrant requirement (the second clause of the amendment) and the prohibition against "unreasonable" searches and seizures (the first clause)? Over the years, the Supreme Court has struggled to fashion a coherent body of law that would provide

[1] The phrase comes, of course, from George Orwell's novel *1984* (London, 1949).

answers to these questions. The Court's decisions, as the justices themselves have conceded, point in different directions and embrace inconsistent approaches.[2] Nevertheless, one basic rule has emerged: "searches conducted outside the judicial process, without prior approval by judge or magistrate, are *per se* unreasonable under the Fourth Amendment—subject only to a few specifically established and well-delineated exceptions."[3]

This ringing declaration tells something less than the whole story. It is disingenuous, at best, to say that the exceptions to the warrant requirement are "well delineated"; the fact is that few constitutional issues have given rise to such sharp disagreements, both within the Supreme Court and among lower courts, as the scope and application of the various exceptions.[4] Some of these exceptions have, at times, been interpreted so broadly that they have threatened to swallow up the rule.[5] At the enforcement level, as I have already noted, warrant applications are often approved so perfunctorily that the protections of the requirement are largely lost.[6]

In spite of these difficulties, the warrant procedure remains the ideal, and for good reason. The "right to be let alone," as Justice Brandeis observed in a famous opinion, is "the most comprehensive of rights and the right most valued by civilized men."[7] The Supreme Court has attempted to assure that the determination of when that right must reasonably yield to the right of search will be made by a "neutral and detached magistrate," not by "the officer engaged in the often competitive enterprise of ferreting out crime."[8] Or, as the

[2] See, e.g., Coolidge v. New Hampshire, 403 U.S. 443, 483 (1971); Cady v. Dombrowski, 413 U.S. 433, 440 (1973).

[3] Katz v. United States, 389 U.S. 347, 357 (1967). Justice Harlan attempted to sum up the Court's decisions by stating that "official investigatory action that impinges on privacy must typically, in order to be constitutionally permissible, be subjected to the warrant requirement" (United States v. White, 401 U.S. 745, 781 [1971] [dissenting opinion]).

[4] See, e.g., Schneckloth v. Bustamente, 412 U.S. 218 (1973) (search pursuant to consent); Chimel v. California, 395 U.S. 752 (1969) (search incident to a lawful arrest); Coolidge v. New Hampshire, 403 U.S. 443 (1971) (seizure of evidence "in plain view"); Cady v. Dombrowski, 413 U.S. 433 (1973) (automobile searches); Adams v. Williams, 407 U.S. 143 (1972) (search for weapons after investigatory stop).

[5] See, e.g., United States v. Robinson, 94 S. Ct. 467 (1973) (search incident to arrest for traffic violation); United States v. Rabinowitz, 339 U.S. 56 (1950), overruled in Chimel v. California, 395 U.S. 752 (1969) (search of premises incident to lawful arrest).

[6] See *supra* p. 69.

[7] Olmstead v. United States, 277 U.S. 438, 478 (1928) (dissenting opinion).

[8] Johnson v. United States, 333 U.S. 10, 13–14 (1948).

Court put it in a later case, the Constitution requires "that the deliberate, impartial judgment of a judicial officer . . . be interposed between the citizen and the police." [9]

SURVEILLANCE

Electronic surveillance has been the subject of much discussion and litigation in recent years,[10] but little attention has been paid to the much more common police practice of visual surveillance. Admittedly, having one's home watched is a lesser intrusion on privacy than having one's conversations overheard or recorded. But the intrusion cannot be denied, especially when the watchers take note of who comes and goes and of what people do whenever their activities happen to be visible from the police vantage point.

A few examples taken from appellate cases will give the reader an idea of the kinds of surveillance police have engaged in. Near Kansas City, Missouri, the sheriff and his deputies kept a house under surveillance because "they were attracted to the premises by the number of people entering and leaving. . . ." The house had been rented three days earlier by three students from a local college.[11] Acting on the basis of an informant's tip, two Saint Louis police officers kept watch on the doorway of an apartment through two sets of seven-power binoculars. They maintained the surveillance for parts of several nights.[12] A police officer in Brockton, Massachusetts, observed an apartment building "every night on patrol," to a certain extent, "[b]ecause of certain people that inhabit[ed] the premises." [13]

In New Brunswick, New Jersey, a narcotics detective received information that "there was possibly a pot party going on" at 1 Nielson Street. Six months earlier he had had the premises under surveillance. On the night in question he and another officer returned to the area to observe the house again. The state argued later that the officers were there to investigate a noise complaint, but as the court remarked, it was clear that "the focus of attention was not at

[9] Wong Sun v. United States, 371 U.S. 471, 481–82 (1963).

[10] See, e.g., United States v. White, 401 U.S. 745 (1971) (especially the dissenting opinions of Justice Douglas, at 756, and Justice Harlan, at 768); United States v. District Court, 407 U.S. 297 (1972); American Bar Association Project on Standards for Criminal Justice, *Standards Relating to Electronic Surveillance* (approved draft, 1971).

[11] State v. McGee, 473 S.W.2d 686 (Mo. 1971).

[12] State v. Speed, 458 S.W.2d 301 (Mo. 1970).

[13] Commonwealth v. Cohen, 268 N.E.2d 357, 358 (Mass. 1971).

all upon noise, but the possibility of uncovering narcotics activity."
The two officers "set up" about fifteen feet from the house and
watched for twenty to thirty minutes. During that time they saw
several people arrive, stay a short while, and leave. One of the detectives recognized a person whom he had once arrested in a narcotics raid. The officers entered the house, found marijuana and
hashish, and arrested five men who were inside. In reversing one of
the resulting convictions, the court stated, "We have here a classic
example of search grounded on mere suspicion. . . . Noise coupled with visitors is an extremely shaky foundation for a warrantless search." [14]

Surveillance was also one of the techniques used by the Buffalo
police in their investigation of Leslie Fiedler.[15] Fiedler writes of
his experience, "What is remarkable is to live under 'surveillance,'
a situation in which privacy ceases to exist. . . . Slowly I had become aware of the fact that my phone kept fading in and out because it was probably being tapped; that those cars turning around
in nearby driveways or parked strategically so that their occupants
could peer in my windows, though unmarked, belonged to the
police; that the 'bread van' haunting our neighborhood contained
cops; and that at least one 'friend' of my children was a spy." [16]

The indiscriminate intrusions on individual liberty which can
result from police surveillance are pointed up by a Colorado case.
Police in a Denver suburb kept a house under surveillance for
more than a week. During that time the occupant was not at home.
One evening the police were advised that a large quantity of marijuana would be delivered to the premises. As the police were watching, a man drove up the long driveway, proceeded toward the
house, and then (apparently discovering that no one was at home)
attempted to drive back out. The police officers quickly surrounded
the vehicle, the driver stopped the car, and he and his passenger got
out, offering no resistance. The police realized that neither of the
men in the car was the occupant of the residence and that neither
was known to be a subject of the investigation. Indeed, they had no
reasonable grounds to believe that the men had committed a criminal offense of any kind. Nevertheless, the police spread-eagled
both men against the car and searched them. A police officer patted
down their outer clothing and frisked their inner clothing. During

14 State v. Allen, 113 N.J. Super. 245, 250, 273 A.2d 587, 590 (1970).
15 See *supra* pp. 63–64.
16 Leslie Fiedler, *Being Busted*, 136.

this pat-down and frisk the policeman felt a lump in the driver's shirt pocket. Further search disclosed that the lump was a plastic bag containing marijuana seeds. A telephone address book also was taken, for reasons that are not explained. By means of a similar procedure the officer took a quantity of cigarette papers from the passenger. Charges (the nature of which is not stated) were filed against both men.[17]

In this case the police search uncovered incriminating evidence; because the search was held to be exploratory and without probable cause, the evidence was suppressed and the prosecution presumably abandoned. Some people might therefore regard the outcome of the episode as a draw, but this is to miss the point. Navran and his passenger Niezguski could just as easily have been innocent of any crime. The police had no reason to think otherwise; all they knew was that the two men were visiting the home of a person who had been implicated in marijuana trafficking by a confidential informant. This fact was enough to subject the two men to the humiliation of being searched while spread-eagled against their car.[18] If the search had uncovered nothing incriminating, they would have been sent on their way, perhaps with an apology, perhaps not. The matter would never have reached the attention of a court—unless, of course, Navran and Niezguski were quixotic enough to seek damages for violation of their civil rights.[19] Presumably a similar fate awaits anyone else in Arapahoe County who is unlucky enough to visit a person whose home is placed under surveillance after a tip from an informant.

Surveillance is not limited to individual homes. In Saint Louis two police officers parked in an unmarked automobile "watching the narcotic traffic (*persons and automobiles in general*) in that area." [20] Plainclothes detectives in Harlingen, Texas, having been told by a police informer that someone would be "pass[ing] marijuana to his friends and us[ing] it," began surveillance of a park.[21] In West Palm Beach, Florida, four narcotic agents conducted a surveillance of the area around a theatre. They saw what they be-

[17] People v. Navran, 483 P.2d 228 (Colo. 1971).

[18] *Cf.* Terry v. Ohio, 392 U.S. 1, 16–17 (1968): "A careful exploration of the outer surfaces of a person's clothing all over his or her body in an attempt to find weapons . . . is a serious intrusion upon the sanctity of the person, which may inflict great indignity and arouse strong resentment, and is not to be undertaken lightly." See also *ibid.*, 24–25.

[19] See Monroe v. Pape, 365 U.S. 167 (1961).

[20] State v. Boykins, 434 S.W.2d 484, 485 (Mo. 1968) [emphasis added].

[21] Muggley v. State, 473 S.W.2d 470 (Tex. Crim. App. 1971).

lieved to be a "narcotics transaction," and in unmarked cars they
followed the automobiles of two of the participants. When one of
the agents saw a person in one of the cars smoking what appeared
to be a marijuana cigarette, he stopped the car and arrested all of
the passengers.[22]

While no statistics are available, it is likely that the incidents of
surveillance which come to the attention of courts represent no
more than a tiny proportion of the total. Indeed, when the surveillance provides no basis for further police action, the subjects themselves may not even realize that their comings and goings have been
subjected to police scrutiny. Surveillance is in this sense like wiretapping and other forms of electronic eavesdropping, but with an
important difference: visual surveillance by itself is unlikely to
violate the Fourth Amendment, however much of an intrusion on
privacy it might be.[23] One consequence is that the police need not
obtain judicial authorization before setting up watch around someone's home or place of business as they must do before engaging
in most forms of electronic surveillance.[24] Moreover, unwonted surveillance is not subject even to the limited restraints resulting from
police awareness of the Exclusionary Rule.

What is perhaps most alarming is the casualness with which the
police set up watch around someone's house. It is justification
enough that there is a lot of coming and going or that persons
suspected of using drugs have visited there or that an anonymous
informant has reported a "pot party." [25] Given the absence of legal
restraints and the lack of any need to justify surveillance to anyone
outside the police hierarchy, this casualness will surprise no one.
More unsettling is the unconcerned acceptance of the practice by
the courts. While courts are probably powerless to do anything
about it,[26] it would be reassuring to see judicial recognition of the
dangers of widespread surveillance.

22 State v. Profera, 239 So. 2d 867 (Fla. App. 1970).

23 Cf. Laird v. Tatum, 408 U.S. 1 (1972); Giancana v. Johnson, No. 63 C 1145
(N.D. Ill. 1963), reversed on other grounds, 335 F.2d 366 (7th Cir. 1964). See
generally Livingston Hall, Yale Kamisar, Wayne LaFave, and Jerrold Israel,
Modern Criminal Procedure (3d ed., St. Paul, 1969), 228–29.

24 See United States v. District Court, 407 U.S. 297 (1972); but cf. United
States v. White, 401 U.S. 745 (1971).

25 See, in addition to the cases cited in the preceding notes, Berger v. Commonwealth, 213 Va. 54, 189 S.E.2d 360 (1972) (a house was observed by police for
two months; the affidavit in support of the warrant request did not explain why).

26 In this respect the Exclusionary Rule, see *infra* p. 104, is probably a strong
barrier to reform. In the light of recent Fourth Amendment developments, see

There is little reason to expect any significant change in police surveillance practices if the Shafer commission's partial prohibition scheme is adopted. As long as many marijuana transactions remain illegal, the police will find a need to watch the homes of people whom they suspect to be dealers or distributors. The result is that many innocent people—not only suspects but also their visitors, friends, and neighbors—will conduct their activities under the skeptical eyes of law enforcement personnel. As with other such practices, the effects are felt not only by those who are actually watched (they may not even be aware of it), but also by those who will never be quite sure that they are *not* being watched.[27]

SNOOPING

Some readers may feel that police surveillance of someone's house from a distance of ten or fifteen feet (as in the New Jersey case) does not present a significant threat to the privacy of the persons who live there.[28] Very often, however, the police do not confine themselves to watching from a distance but go much closer—peering through windows, poking around back yards and garages, even picking through the householder's trash. I have labeled such practices *snooping*. This is an inelegant and perhaps inexact term, but it is an appropriate characterization of police investigatory tactics that fall between surveillance on the one hand and more conventional searches on the other.

Snooping differs from surveillance in that it *is* subject to the restraints of the Fourth Amendment, or at least those restraints that result from the operation of the Exclusionary Rule. The courts appear to have recognized that the problem also differs from the mine-run of search-and-seizure cases, for rather than using the ordinary tools of Fourth Amendment analysis (asking whether the search comes within one of the exceptions to the general rule requiring a warrant), the leading cases have focused on the issue of reasonable

infra pp. 95–96, it might be argued that some kinds of visual surveillance constitute an "unreasonable intrusion" on a "reasonable expectation of privacy" and are therefore unconstitutional. Few courts are likely to accept this argument, however, as long as the consequence of holding such practices unconstitutional is the suppression at trial of all evidence secured as a fruit of the surveillance.

[27] *Cf.* Orwell, *supra* note 1, at 7: "There was, of course, no way of knowing whether you were being watched at any given moment. . . . You had to live— did live, from habit that became instinct—in the assumption that every sound you made was overheard and, except in darkness, every movement scrutinized."

[28] State v. Allen, 113 N.J. Super. 245, 273 A.2d 587 (1970), *supra* pp. 91–92.

expectations of privacy. If the snooping was an "unreasonable governmental intrusion" on a "reasonable expectation of privacy," [29] evidence discovered as a result of that snooping will be excluded at the defendant's trial. The usual result is that the charges will have to be dismissed.

Many of the snooping cases follow a common pattern. The police receive a tip from an informant that "narcotic activities" are taking place in a dwelling. An officer will poke around the premises— often trespassing—to seek evidence confirming the tip. He will not have a warrant. If he finds incriminating evidence he will usually return with a warrant, conduct a new search, and arrest the owner or occupant. Sometimes the police will proceed with the search and arrest without bothering to obtain a warrant, but if they do they run the risk that the evidence will be suppressed on Fourth Amendment grounds. (Even if a warrant is obtained, moreover, the evidence may still be suppressed under the "fruit of the poisonous tree" doctrine.) [30]

As with surveillance, if the initial snooping proves fruitless the police will ordinarily proceed no further in their investigation. Even if someone is arrested and charged, the defendant may be freed at some stage of the proceedings because the Fourth Amendment is successfully invoked to invalidate the search or arrest. Whatever the outcome, however, the real harm has already been accomplished —the invasion of privacy.

Although the phrase "reasonable expectation of privacy" does not appear in any United States Supreme Court decision, the test is a justifiable extrapolation from the opinions in *Katz* v. *United States,* the 1967 wiretapping case.[31] Unlike some of the earlier Fourth Amendment tests,[32] this approach permits courts to address themselves directly to the conflicting values involved when the

[29] People v. Krivda, 5 Cal. 3d 357, 364, 486 P.2d 1262, 1267, 96 Cal. Rptr. 62 (1971). See Brief for Respondent at 1c, California v. Krivda, 409 U.S. 33 (1972).

[30] Under this doctrine, any evidence directly or indirectly obtained as the result of an illegal search may not be admitted against a defendant. See, e.g., Wong Sun v. United States, 371 U.S. at 484–87; Peterson v. United States, 411 F.2d 1074, 1078 (8th Cir. 1969). The classic statement is by Justice Holmes: "The essence of a provision forbidding the acquisition of evidence in a certain way is that not merely evidence so acquired shall not be used before the court but that it shall not be used at all" (Silverthorne Lumber Co. v. United States, 251 U.S. 385, 392 [1920]). But see United States v. Calandra, 94 S. Ct. 613 (1974).

[31] 389 U.S. 347. For a critique of *Katz* and its progeny, see Amsterdam, "Perspectives on the Fourth Amendment," 58 *Minn. L. Rev.* 349, 382–85 (1974).

[32] Gouled v. United States, 255 U.S. 298 (1921) ("mere evidence" rule); Hester v. United States, 265 U.S. 57 (1924) (curtilage); Olmstead v. United States, 277 U.S. 438 (1928) (trespass).

police seek evidence of crimes for which there are no witnesses and no complainants. For the purposes of this study, however, the decisions are less important for their ultimate holdings than for what they reveal about methods used by police to investigate persons suspected of possessing or dealing in marijuana.

A California case illustrates the pattern I have described. The police had been told that there might be a marijuana party at a house where several high school teachers lived. The house was on an acre of ground, enclosed by walls on two sides. The police—admittedly trespassing without a warrant—walked across the yard through a grove of orange trees to the front of the house, where three windows opened into the dining room. Bushes were growing along the house in front of the windows, so close that their branches brushed against the panes. To get a clear view of what was going on inside, the officers had to stand between the bushes and the house. The testimony was in conflict about how far the shades were drawn on the windows, but even if they were drawn to within two or three feet from the sill, as one of the officers stated, it would probably have been necessary to crouch in order to see inside. The view was further obstructed by thin curtains that covered the windows. The officers watched the activities in the dining room for about fifteen minutes from their position between the bushes and the house. When they saw people smoking what they believed to be marijuana, they entered the house and arrested everyone present.[33]

A similar intrusion resulted in the arrest of Edward and Eleanor Vidaurri of La Mesa, Californa. Their home was hidden by hedges, trees, bushes, shrubbery, foliage, plants, and flowers in the front yard. The back yard was enclosed by block walls and wooden and wire fences four to six feet high and by more foliage. As the court put it, "These features and the elevation of the house and lot made it impossible to see from the front street into the area along the left side of the house, let alone into the back yard." Nevertheless, police officers opened the gate to the back yard, went in, and searched for growing marijuana plants in the garden and flower beds. When they found them, they pulled them up and kept them as evidence. The Vidaurris were subjected to this investigation as the result of a tip from an agricultural inspector who had himself trespassed on their back yard in search of an insect pest.[34]

[33] Mann v. Superior Court, 3 Cal. 3d 1, 472 P.2d 468, 88 Cal. Rptr. 380 (1970). For other aspects of this case, see *supra* p. 75.
[34] Vidaurri v. Superior Court, 13 Cal. App. 3d 550, 91 Cal. Rptr. 704 (1970). See also People v. Bradley, 1 Cal. 3d 80, 460 P.2d 129, 81 Cal. Rptr. 457 (1969).

An East Palo Alto man told police that he had observed what appeared to be marijuana plants growing in his neighbor's back yard. A police officer came over and discovered that the plants could be seen only by peeking through a half-inch opening between the planks of a wooden fence that separated the two properties. The portion of the yard in which the plants were growing was also covered with a large sheet of plastic. Nevertheless, on the basis of his observations the officer was able to obtain a warrant authorizing him to search not only the yard but also the entire house. Both the magistrate and the appellate court accepted the officer's explanation that articles used in the processing of marijuana were located inside the house. They did so even though the officer had not seen the inside of the house and his statements about what was there were no more than surmise.[35]

Snooping is not limited to California. In Florida a police officer watched what was going on in an apartment from a position on an outside fire escape.[36] In New York the manager of a two-family dwelling told the police that the tenants in the upper apartment were selling drugs. Two officers arrived and were admitted to the locked vestibule by the manager. The officers climbed a flight of stairs which gave access only to the apartment and looked inside through the open door.[37]

An investigatory tactic that has come to the attention of courts recently is that of rummaging through trash cans to find evidence of marijuana use. In the leading case, *People* v. *Krivda*,[38] the police

---

Bradley lived in an apartment attached to a garage behind a house. The garage building stood at the end of a driveway that ran alongside the house. Behind the house and to the west of the garage building was a large fenced-in yard. Told by an informer of unknown reliability that Bradley was growing marijuana near a fig tree at the rear of his residence, a narcotics officer trespassed on the yard to inspect the area near the fig tree. He found a marijuana plant growing in a keg. It was necessary for him to come within almost a foot of the tree—twenty feet from Bradley's door and the path to his house—before he could identify the plant as marijuana. Moreover, the officer testified that the plant was covered by foliage. As Justice Tobriner stated in dissent, Bradley could reasonably expect that strangers calling at his residence would stay in the approximate vicinity of the door and pathway; thus, they would not be able to see the marijuana plant clearly enough to identify it. The majority, however, held that the search did not violate Bradley's reasonable expectations of privacy.

[35] Hart v. Superior Court, 21 Cal. App. 3d 496, 98 Cal. Rptr. 565 (1971).

[36] State v. Clarke, 242 So. 2d 791 (Fla. App. 1970).

[37] People v. E., 38 A.D.2d 394, 330 N.Y.S.2d 3 (1972). Other aspects of this case are discussed at *supra* p. 74.

[38] 5 Cal. 3d 357, 486 P.2d 1262, 96 Cal. Rptr. 62 (1961), *vacated and remanded*, 409 U.S. 33 (1972), *on remand*, 8 Cal. 3d 572, 504 P.2d 457, 105 Cal.

investigation was triggered by a telephone call from an anonymous informant who said that "Roger," "Judy," and "Frankie," residing at 1901 Nolden, Los Angeles, were engaging in sex and narcotic activities and were injecting Judy's two children with methedrine. Two officers located the premises, a single-family dwelling, observed two young girls in front, and ran a utility check which showed that Judy Krivda paid the utilities there. They also learned —presumably from police files—that Edward Krivda, whose wife was named Judy, had previously been arrested for narcotics activity.[39]

Three weeks after the anonymous call the officers returned to the address and saw several trash barrels in front of the house on the parkway adjacent to the sidewalk. Apparently the trash collectors were just about to arrive at the Krivda residence. The police stopped them about half a block away and asked them to empty the well of their truck and pick up the trash in the cans in front of 1901 Nolden. The trash collectors did as they were asked and then stopped the truck a block from the house, where the officers examined the contents of the well. They found five paper sacks containing miscellaneous marijuana debris and marijuana seeds. One sack also contained several partially burned marijuana cigarettes and some papers with the residents' names. The officers then returned to the vicinity of the Krivda house and kept it under surveillance. They saw a man named Roger Minor come out, pick up the trash barrels, and carry them to the front porch. The police then entered the house, found additional marijuana and paraphernalia, and arrested Minor and Judy Krivda.

In an earlier California case a Riverside County man told the police that he had seen on his neighbor's back porch a large plastic bag containing packages, one of which was torn and contained a dark green vegetable substance that looked like alfalfa but didn't smell like alfalfa and had a "small funny type seed." (Presumably the informer suspected that it was marijuana, or he would not have told the police about it.) Two officers walked down the railroad tracks behind the residence where the marijuana had been observed

Rptr. 521 (1973), *cert. denied,* 412 U.S. 919 (1973). The case was taken for review by the United States Supreme Court but remanded to the California court because it was not clear whether the California decision rested on the federal or the state constitution. When the California court responded that the decision rested on both constitutions, the United States Supreme Court declined to review it.

[39] The court does not indicate the disposition of the charges or whether Judy had been implicated in the earlier investigation.

by the neighbor. They entered the back yard of the house and saw three trash cans two or three feet from the door of the back porch. The officers rummaged through the trash. In one of the cans they found a bag containing marijuana—"possibly enough to roll a couple of cigarettes or more." One of the detectives took the marijuana back to his office to examine it more carefully. A group of policemen then returned to the area of the suspects' house, where they conducted a stakeout from 12:30 A.M. until 4:30 A.M. When the householder returned he was arrested.[40]

The lengths to which police will go in order to apprehend users of marijuana are illustrated by the case of Robert Croker of Laramie, Wyoming. According to an officer's affidavit, Croker was "known to officers of the Laramie Police Department as a user and possessor of marijuana prior to Oct. 30, 1968." How the officers acquired this knowledge is not stated. It was not through an arrest, for Croker was not arrested until October 30, when he was found in possession of 179 grams of marijuana. Even then he was apparently not convicted. Nevertheless, the police pursued their investigation of his activities, and on February 16, 1969, they decided to place his garbage cans under surveillance.

The garbage cans were kept inside a wooden picket fence enclosing the back yard of Croker's house. The yard bordered an alley, and the garbage cans—covered by lids—were placed near a small gate that opened into the alley. At regular intervals the city garbage collectors entered the premises through the gate and emptied the contents of the cans into a large green plastic barrel. The contents of the barrel were then deposited in a truck, which transported them to the city dump.

The police asked the garbage collectors not to dump the contents of Croker's barrel into the truck but to turn them over to the officers. This was done on four separate occasions between February 19 and March 1. The first search of the trash barrel uncovered plant stems and seeds of marijuana. The second search uncovered nothing (except, presumably, Croker's ordinary garbage). During the third search the police found one hand-rolled cigarette butt containing marijuana. On March 1 another cigarette butt containing marijuana and four marijuana seeds were discovered. The police then obtained a search warrant, searched Croker's home, and arrested him for possession of marijuana.[41]

<hr />

[40] People v. Edwards, 71 Cal. 2d 1096, 458 P.2d 713, 80 Cal. Rptr. 633 (1969).
[41] Croker v. State, 477 P.2d 122 (Wyo. 1970).

In at least one Kansas town, inspection of garbage for evidence of marijuana use has become a routine part of the sheriff's work. After every teen-age party, the sheriff told *Newsweek,* "[w]e go through the incinerators the next morning to see if it was a beer party or not." If it was a beer party, the investigation ends; if it was not, the householder can presumably expect a visit from a sheriff's deputy.[42]

Reports of police officers solemnly searching through someone's garbage conjure up such ludicrous images that it may be difficult to take the tactic seriously. More than one satirist has found the subject irresistible, and a few years ago columnist Jack Anderson caused something of a stir by rummaging through the trash of J. Edgar Hoover and publishing an inventory of what he found. Nevertheless, the practice is no joke. Justice Louis Burke of the California Supreme Court put the matter this way: "We can readily ascribe many reasons why residents would not want their castaway clothing, letters, medicine bottles or other telltale refuse and trash to be examined by neighbors or others, at least not until the trash has lost its identity and meaning by becoming part of a large conglomeration of trash elsewhere. Half truths leading to rumor and gossip may readily flow from an attempt to 'read' the contents of another's trash." [43] A person's garbage is a reflection, indeed, an extension, of his life. Sifting through that garbage violates his security in a less acute but no less real way than breaking into his home.[44]

Several points stand out in the snooping cases generally. One is the way in which questionable procedures are pyramided on one another. An informer's tip leads to a trespass, which in turn leads to a no-knock entry.[45] A neighbor's tip brings an officer to peek through a fence, resulting in a search of the house, which he has not seen, as well as the yard, which he has.[46] Suspicion and an earlier arrest persuade officers to poke through a man's garbage, and on the basis of their snooping they obtain a warrant to search the house.[47]

[42] *Newsweek,* Sept. 11, 1972, p. 24.

[43] People v. Krivda, 5 Cal. 3d at 366, 486 P.2d at 1268, 96 Cal. Rptr. at 68.

[44] In this regard, it is worth emphasizing that the intrusions described in this chapter would be lawful and proper if the police had a valid warrant issued on the basis of affidavits showing that they had probable cause to believe that specific items connected with criminal activity would be found in the particular place to be searched. In virtually all of the cases, however, the information available to the police at the time of the intrusion did not rise to the level of probable cause.

[45] Mann v. Superior Court, 3 Cal. 3d 1, 472 P.2d 468, 88 Cal. Rptr. 380 (1970), *supra* pp. 75 and 97.

[46] Hart v. Superior Court, 21 Cal. App. 3d 496, 98 Cal. Rptr. 565 (1971), *supra* p. 98.

[47] Croker v. State, 477 P.2d 122 (Wyo. 1970), *supra* p. 100.

A second point is the willingness of police to trespass on private property without attempting to obtain a warrant. Third—and perhaps most dismaying—is the mechanical, crabbed approach of many courts to intrusions such as the ones I have described.[48] Some courts seem to be looking for ways to validate the actions of the police, however intrusive they might be. Conversely, there seems to be little appreciation of the privacy interests involved.

Two other points, mentioned earlier in different contexts, are relevant here as well. First, it cannot be emphasized too often that it is not only the guilty whose parties will be spied upon and whose garbage will be scrutinized as the result of a neighbor's tip; the innocent as well will find their privacy invaded. Second, snooping, like decoy work, is bound to have a "degrading effect . . . on law enforcement officers." [49] Little harm will be done, perhaps, if the police occasionally rummage through garbage or crouch in the bushes watching a party in order to detect espionage or bribery, but when the police take seriously the job of enforcing criminal laws against marijuana, such tactics become a "way of life." [50] The result must be to tarnish the image of the policeman held not only by the public but also by the policeman himself.

The extremely limited decriminalization proposed by the Shafer commission would probably have little effect on the use of snooping practices by the police. Like surveillance and infiltration by undercover agents, most forms of snooping require so much manpower that the police are not likely to resort to them unless they expect to find more than a small amount of marijuana for personal use. (This may not be true when the police are seeking to incriminate a person for reasons other than his use of marijuana,[51] but such practices are hardly to be encouraged.) Partial prohibition would thus do nothing to halt the intrusions on privacy and the damage to police self-respect which result from the continued use of snooping tactics.

[48] See especially *ibid.;* Hart v. Superior Court, 21 Cal. App. 3d 496, 98 Cal. Rptr. 565 (1971), *supra* p. 98; and State v. Clarke, 242 So. 2d 791 (Fla. App. 1970), *supra* p. 98.
[49] Herbert Packer, *The Limits of the Criminal Sanction,* 286.
[50] *Ibid.*
[51] See People v. Sinclair, 387 Mich. 91, 194 N.W.2d 878 (1972), discussed *supra* pp. 61–62 and 80–81; State v. Johnson, 447 S.W.2d 927 (Tex. Crim. App. 1969), discussed *supra* pp. 62–63.

VI

Unlawful or Questionable Searches and Seizures

Surveillance, snooping, infiltration by undercover agents and informers, practices bordering on (or constituting) entrapment: these are the techniques used by the police in directed, concerted efforts to apprehend marijuana law violators. The vast majority of marijuana arrests, however, can be traced to spontaneous encounters, on the street or elsewhere, with one or more policemen.[1] Unfortunately, a large proportion of those arrests result from police conduct that violates the spirit if not the letter of the Fourth Amendment's prohibition against unreasonable searches and seizures. Cases of this sort are so numerous that I can do no more than sketch the most common patterns.

Preliminarily, it is necessary to point out that the problem is even worse than the reported court decisions suggest. First, the appellate cases represent only a tiny fraction of the unlawful or questionable searches and arrests, and they may not necessarily be the most flagrant examples. If no marijuana is found, the lawfulness of the police conduct will not come under judicial scrutiny. (Exceptions to this may occur when the policeman files a "cover charge" against the suspect in order to justify the arrest and search.) [2] If marijuana is discovered, but through a clear and unarguable violation of the Fourth Amendment, the case may never come before a court anyway because the prosecuting attorney will probably agree to a dismissal. When the violation is somewhat less flagrant, so that the

[1] *Spontaneous* is often the wrong term; see *infra* pp. 140, 146–47.
[2] Paul Chevigny, *Police Power: Police Abuses in New York City,* 232.

charges may or may not stand up in court, the prosecutor will probably bargain with the defendant's attorney for a plea of guilty to a lesser offense.[3]

Second, whether the arrest or search in a particular case is ultimately held by a court to be lawful is almost beside the point. The court has said only that in the light of all the facts the search was not unreasonable; the invasion of privacy is no less real and no less jarring to the victim no matter how persuasive the court finds the justification. What is worse, decisions like that of the Wyoming Supreme Court in the *Croker* case tend to have a self-expanding effect: every time a warrantless search is validated despite the questionable circumstances, the police will have that much less incentive to seek a warrant on the next occasion, even if the circumstances are less exigent and the justification less weighty.[4] As Justice Robert H. Jackson once put it, "the extent of any privilege of search and seizure without warrant which we sustain, the officers interpret and apply themselves and will push to the limit." [5] The courts, in turn, may feel pressure to approve the still-more-dubious search, not necessarily because the police have relied on the earlier decisions, but because the Exclusionary Rule means that a guilty person will go free if the search is found invalid.

At the other extreme, one should not fall into the trap of assuming that tactics which receive judicial disapproval will thereafter be renounced by the police. The fact is that constitutional decisions by courts have far less effect on police practices than is often realized.[6] As a practical matter, the only sanction for violation of the Fourth Amendment is the exclusion at trial of the illegally obtained evidence; if the police are not primarily interested in securing a conviction, this sanction will be no deterrent at all. A recent empirical study pointed up some of the not-so-subtle motiva-

[3] The reason the prosecutor agrees to the dismissal or the plea to a lesser offense is that under the Exclusionary Rule evidence obtained through an unconstitutional search or seizure cannot be used in a criminal prosecution. For a concise description of the Exclusionary Rule and its ramifications, see Jerrold Israel and Wayne LaFave, *Criminal Procedure in a Nutshell* (St. Paul, 1971), 28–32.

[4] Croker v. State, 477 P.2d 122 (Wyo. 1970), discussed *supra* p. 100.

[5] Brinegar v. United States, 338 U.S. 160, 182 (1948) (dissenting opinion); *cf.* Jerome Skolnick, *Justice without Trial,* 224.

[6] Even the Supreme Court's well-publicized (and harshly criticized) decision in Miranda v. Arizona, 384 U.S. 436 (1966), was widely ignored by the police. For a concise summary of empirical studies on the impact (or lack of it) of the Miranda opinion on police interrogation practices, see Livingston Hall, Yale Kamisar, Wayne LaFave, and Jerrold Israel, *Modern Criminal Procedure,* 552–55.

tions that may prompt an officer to make a marijuana arrest even though he knows or suspects that the crucial evidence will be thrown out by a court:

> A policeman who is unwilling to lie about probable cause or to conceal a prior illegal search may still be inclined to make an arrest for possession of marijuana, even if he is aware that it will not stand up under judicial scrutiny. At a minimum he will have confiscated a supply of an illegal drug. The defendant will be jailed and have to post bail, and in many cases will have to hire a lawyer; these alone serve as forms of punishment. Finally, there is always the possibility that the defendant will plead guilty to a lesser offense rather than risk a felony conviction.[7]

When the case does go to court, there is substantial evidence to suggest that police often lie in order to bring their conduct within the limits of the practices sanctioned by judicial decisions.[8]

Finally it must be noted also that police-citizen encounters which result in marijuana arrests may not be as spontaneous as they appear on the surface. Policemen often focus their attention on persons whose hairstyle, dress, or other characteristics are associated in the policeman's mind with drug usage.[9] The result is that arrests which appear to be the by-product of the investigation of other offenses may actually be part of an effort to apprehend marijuana law violators.

Searches that result in the discovery of marijuana are seldom made on the basis of warrants (except when the police are acting on the basis of a tip from an informant). Instead, the police assert that the search came within one of the exceptions to the Fourth Amendment's warrant requirement—for example, that the marijuana was "in plain view" or that it was found in a search incident to a lawful arrest or that the search was a "frisk" within the scope of the Supreme Court's 1968 stop-and-frisk decisions.[10] The question is whether these exceptions are being properly invoked or whether, on the contrary, the letter and spirit of the constitutional guarantee are being flouted. In seeking the answer it is appropriate to divide the cases into three categories, depending on whether the

[7] Comment, "Possession of Marijuana in San Mateo County: Some Social Costs of Criminalization," 22 *Stan. L. Rev.* 101, 115 (1969); see also Skolnick, *supra* note 5, at 219–24.

[8] See *infra,* chapter 9.

[9] See *infra,* chapter 7.

[10] See *infra* pp. 113–15, 124–26.

marijuana is found in a person's home, as the consequence of an arrest for a traffic violation, or in the course of an encounter on the street.

ARRESTS, SEARCHES, AND SEIZURES IN THE HOME

When a pedestrian or a person in a motor vehicle is arrested for violation of the marijuana laws, the arrest is usually claimed to be the by-product of police investigation of other offenses. This is seldom the case with persons arrested in their (or someone else's) home, but occasionally it happens. Most commonly the police are dispatched in response to a complaint about a noisy party. Upon arriving, the police smell the odor of marijuana or see marijuana cigarettes "in plain view." Those present are then arrested for possession.[11] Sometimes the circumstances suggest that the noise investigation is a pretext, with marijuana law violations the real target of the police visit.[12]

These cases are exceptions. Most residential arrests for marijuana offenses result from an informer's tip alleging "narcotics activities" or "a pot party" or simply the presence of marijuana. Occasionally the police obtain a search warrant,[13] but more often they do not, and indeed under present law many of the tips would not justify the issuance of a warrant.[14] What the police usually do is visit the premises in question. Sometimes they will set up a surveillance or snoop around the property, as described in the preceding chapter. If their suspicions are not dispelled, they will seek to gain entry into the residence. Questionable procedures are often used in two phases of the investigation: getting inside, and, once inside, in looking for evidence or other suspects.

To gain entry into a residence without a search warrant the

[11] See, e.g., People v. Struckle, 480 P.2d 845 (Colo. 1971) (odor); State v. Easterling, 185 S.E.2d 366 (S.C. 1971) (rejecting the state's argument that drugs were "in plain view"); State v. Howard, 16 Ariz. App. 231, 493 P.2d 133 (1972).

[12] See, e.g., State v. Allen, 113 N.J. Super. 245, 273 A.2d 587 (1970), *supra* pp. 91–92. In State v. Johnson, 162 Conn. 215, 292 A.2d 903 (1972), police officers with a warrant authorizing them to search for dynamite looked in the refrigerator and found marijuana.

[13] See, e.g., Torres v. State, 253 So. 2d 450 (Fla. 1971); Comm. v. Tirpak, 216 Pa. Super. 310, 263 A.2d 917 (1970); State v. McGee, 473 S.W.2d 686 (Mo. 1971); Poole v. State, 247 So. 2d 443 (Fla. 1971).

[14] See, e.g., Mann v. Superior Court, 3 Cal. 3d 1, 6–7, 472 P.2d 468, 471, 88 Cal. Rptr. 380, 383 (1970); People v. Mesaris, 14 Cal. App. 3d 71, 76 n. 4, 91 Cal. Rptr. 837, 840 (1970).

police often use trickery.[15] In South Carolina Clarence Easterling heard a knock at the door during a party at his house. "Who is it?" he asked. "Clarence," the person outside replied. Easterling opened the door and was confronted by four police officers, who entered and found hashish in a tinfoil plate on the floor.[16] A New York policeman, having been told by an informant that a pot party was in progress at a Long Island address, obtained entry by falsely telling the man who came to the door, "I just hit a car."[17] The lead singer of a rock music group was arrested in a Minnesota motel after he opened the door of his room to a policeman disguised as a "hippie," who falsely said that he was supposed to meet a friend of the singer's there. (The singer left the door open; the officer, standing in the doorway, saw, from a distance of six or seven feet, a cigarette box from which six hand-rolled cigarettes protruded.)[18]

In California a repairman found marijuana in a refrigerator and phoned the police. Three officers in civilian clothes proceeded to the house where the repairman was working, knocked on the door, and asked for the repairman. The woman who answered the door said, "He is in the kitchen," and pointed in the appropriate direction. The officers went to the kitchen, identified themselves to the repairman, took the marijuana, and arrested those in the house. They then searched the rest of the house and found more marijuana. When another resident arrived, he, too, was arrested and searched. The police had no warrants for any of their investigations. The court found the arrests and searches to be invalid, saying, "An entry which is obtained by the police through an opened door for an ostensible purpose different from their real purpose is not a consensual entry because of the trickery involved in obtaining the consent."[19] (In the Minnesota and New York cases, however, the courts found the ruses to be permissible.)

A more elaborate subterfuge was used against Daymond Monteith, age nineteen, of Klamath Falls, Oregon. Monteith had become acquainted with a man he knew as John Henderson. Under his long hair and beard, Henderson was really Paul Wood, an undercover agent for the city police department. Wood visited Monteith at various times and attended parties at his house. On the

[15] See also the cases involving undercover agents in *supra,* chapter 4.
[16] State v. Easterling, 185 S.E.2d 366 (S.C. 1971). The evidence was excluded because it was not "in plain view" until the officers had entered.
[17] People v. Troy, 70 Misc. 2d 799, 334 N.Y.S.2d 953 (Sp. Term 1972).
[18] State v. Buchwald, 293 Minn. 74, 196 N.W.2d 445 (1972).
[19] People v. Mesaris, 14 Cal. App. 3d at 75, 91 Cal. Rptr. at 840 (1970).

basis of what he learned during these visits he obtained a search warrant. Several officers went with him to serve it. While the other officers waited nearby, Wood knocked on the door. Someone inside asked, "Who's there?" Wood replied, "John." A person whose voice he did not recognize said, "Come in." Wood entered and saw Monteith seated alone at a table in the kitchen, with marijuana in front of him. Wood asked if he could purchase some of the marijuana, but Monteith said he did not have enough to sell. At this point the other officers entered, searched the premises, and arrested Montieth and five other people who were in the house. The purpose of the delay between Wood's entry and the entrance of the other officers was to prevent the destruction of the marijuana. The court found the stratagem permissible.[20]

Sometimes subterfuge is not necessary. In California a narcotics officer named Narron, acting on the basis of an informant's tip, trespassed on a householder's property and found a marijuana plant growing in the yard.[21] The officer tried to obtain a search warrant but was unsuccessful because no judge was available. He nevertheless returned to the suspect's residence accompanied by four other officers—at 3:15 A.M. The door to the apartment was open, probably for ventilation (the search took place in July). From outside the apartment Narron, by the light of a flashlight, saw a man who appeared to be asleep on a bed. Without knocking, asking permission, or speaking, four of the officers entered the room. The man on the bed got up. Narron showed his identification, again with the aid of a flashlight, and identified himself. The officers told the man on the bed that he was under arrest for possession of marijuana and informed him of his "constitutional rights" (the quotation marks are the court's). They also asked whether he minded if a search was made of the house. The man replied, "No, go ahead." The ensuing search disclosed more marijuana.

Although the evidence obtained in the search was held inadmissible, the California court rested its decision on a narrow statutory ground: "[W]e are satisfied in view of the purposes of section 844 . . . that the demand and explanation requirements of that section . . . apply where, as here, officers walk into a dwelling through an open door at nighttime when the occupant apparently is asleep."[22]

[20] State v. Monteith, 477 P.2d 224 (Ore. App. 1970).
[21] This aspect of the case is discussed *supra* p. 97, note 34.
[22] People v. Bradley, 1 Cal. 3d 80, 87, 460 P.2d 129, 133, 81 Cal. Rptr. 457, 461 (1969).

Section 844, like similar statutes in other states, permits a police officer to break into a house in order to make an arrest "after having demanded admittance and explained the purpose for which admittance is desired." [23] A narrow ruling, avoiding constitutional issues and confining itself to the facts of the case, is not necessarily to be condemned. What is dismaying is the court's lack of concern for the threat to privacy posed by the officers' tactics. The majority decision, as the dissenters point out, leaves open the possibility that the officers' entry would have been lawful if it had been made during the day or if the man on the bed had been awake.[24] The entry would clearly have been lawful if the officers had complied with the statute by demanding admittance and explaining their purpose. Clearly, too, if the door had been closed and the person inside had refused to open it after the officers made their "demand and explanation," the officers could have broken open the door and gained entry anyway. What this means is that as long as the officers make the required "demand and explanation" they are privileged to enter a person's home at any time of day or night in order to arrest him for possession of a few marijuana plants—or, presumably, any other amount of marijuana sufficient to support a felony conviction. (Under the Shafer commission's scheme, this amount would apparently include any amount greater than what is deemed appropriate "for personal use.") The officers need not even have a warrant as long as they have "reasonable cause to believe that the person to be arrested has committed a felony, whether or not a felony has in fact been committed." [25] Upon entering, they may make a lawful search incident to the arrest—including any areas within the "immediate control" of the suspect.[26] Moreover, the of-

[23] The statute provides, in relevant part, that "[t]o make an arrest, . . . a peace officer, may break open the door or window of the house in which the person to be arrested is, or in which [the officer has] reasonable grounds for believing him to be, after having demanded admittance and explained the purpose for which admittance is desired" (Calif. Penal Code § 844). The statute codifies a common law rule dating back to an English decision of 1603, Semayne's Case, 77 Eng. Rep. 194.

[24] The court states that in order to avoid any possible illegality it would be "advisable" for officers before entering a house through an open door to make an arrest "to always demand admittance and explain the purpose for which they desire admittance unless the case comes within an established exception to section 844" (1 Cal. 3d at 88 n. 1, 460 P.2d at 133, 81 Cal. Rptr. at 461).

[25] Calif. Penal Code § 836.

[26] Chimel v. California, 395 U.S. 752, 763 (1969). *Cf. 1973 Supplement* to Hall, Kamisar, LaFave and Israel, *supra* note 6, at 83: "Many of the cases which have applied the Chimel 'immediate control' test seem to assume that

ficers need not even comply with the "demand and explanation" requirement if they have reason to believe that contraband will be destroyed if they announce their purpose before entering.[27]

Legislatures in some jurisdictions have recently sought to codify and perhaps expand the various exceptions to the "demand and explanation" requirement.[28] Controversy has raged over the wisdom as well as the constitutionality of these no-knock statutes,[29] but the broad issues thus raised need not be canvassed here. The question, rather, is this: Does the use of marijuana pose a sufficiently serious threat to society to justify authorizing police officers to enter homes unannounced or break down doors or awaken sleeping house-holders—without judicial sanction, often on the basis of neighbor's tip—in order to apprehend users or dealers? There is no middle ground; as long as any marijuana transactions are classified as felonies, these techniques will be used to enforce the prohibition.[30]

It is conceivable that because of the strong possibility of error or harassment, the legislature might enact strict controls on search-and-seizure practices in the enforcement of laws against possession or of sumptuary laws generally. This approach would probably mitigate the most deleterious consequences of those laws; indeed, it might be tantamount to making their enforcement impossible. The effect would be to legislate the phenomenon of patterned evasion described by Robin Williams and Joseph Gusfield.[31] Whether or not this kind of legislative schizophrenia would be desirable, it is highly unlikely; the trend in search-and-seizure statutes has been in the direction of expanding the authority of the police.

Once the police have gained entry into a residence, they often

defendants maintain control over a considerable area even after they have been arrested."

[27] See Ker v. California, 374 U.S. 23 (1963).

[28] The best-known example is the District of Columbia Court Reform and Criminal Procedure Act of 1970, adding § 23–591(c) to the District of Columbia Code. This section was repealed on Oct. 26, 1974 (Pub. L. No. 93–481).

[29] See, e.g., Note, "Police Practices and the Threatened Destruction of Tangible Evidence," 84 *Harv. L. Rev.* 1465 (1971); Note, "Announcement in Police Entries," 80 *Yale L. J.* 139 (1970).

[30] This is not to say that forcible or unannounced entries are never proper. No one would insist that an officer knock and announce his authority or purpose before attempting to apprehend armed suspects who have already shot other police-men. The difficulty is that once forced entries become accepted as a legitimate tactic in "exigent" circumstances, the notion of "exigency" is easily watered down, just as distinctions among crimes tend to be forgotten. Nor can it be assumed, in the light of recent experience (see *supra* p. 69), that a warrant requirement will effectively prevent abuses.

[31] See *supra* pp. 22–24.

use improper or questionable techniques in looking for further evidence or other suspects.[32] A common procedure is to search for additional persons in other parts of the house even though there is no evidence that other persons are present, let alone that they are engaged in criminal activity. The California court appears to have held that when police officers, upon entering a house, find evidence that a pot party is in progress, they may search anywhere in the house for other suspects.[33] This decision is difficult to defend. First, it is inconsistent with the spirit, and probably with the letter, of the United States Supreme Court's ruling in *Chimel* v. *California.* There the Supreme Court stated: "There is no . . . justification for routinely searching rooms other than that in which an arrest occurs. . . ."[34] Second, the California court seems to assume that when some people in a house are smoking marijuana, everyone else in the house is probably "turning on" also. The state court does not consider the possibility that the nonusers at the gathering deliberately separated themselves from the marijuana smokers (or vice versa).[35] One result is that anyone who happens to be in a house where some people are smoking marijuana may find himself subjected to arrest and search. The ruling also means that an innocent host may find that his entire house is subjected to a police search because some of his guests have been discourteous enough to smoke marijuana.

Another common practice is to search or frisk persons who happen to visit a residence while an arrest or search is in progress, whether or not there are reasonable grounds to suspect the visitor of any crime. Sometimes the officer claims to be searching for weapons.[36] In a Wisconsin case the court stated: "The defendant . . . was not . . . entering a purely private home. Exactly as if gambling equipment or prostitutes plying their trade had been found on the premises, the apartment, once the quantity of illegal drugs were found stored in it, became something more than someone's private residence. The fact that a premises is a gambling joint, house of prostitution or narcotics den may not be known to the one who walks in, but it is known to the police officers and it is a

---

[32] See, in addition to the cases cited in this section, the discussion of the plain view doctrine and its abuse, *infra* pp. 155–56.

[33] People v. Block, 6 Cal. 3d 239, 491 P.2d 9, 98 Cal. Rptr. 657 (1971).

[34] Chimel v. California, 395 U.S. at 763.

[35] See *infra* pp. 173–74.

[36] See, e.g., State v. Chambers, 55 Wis. 2d 289, 198 N.W.2d 377 (1972); People v. Roach, 15 Cal. App. 3d 628, 93 Cal. Rptr. 354 (1971).

factor they can consider in reasonably concluding that one who walks into the premises might be armed." [37] The court was referring to an apartment where an earlier search had uncovered a quantity of marijuana but no other drugs and no weapons. In other words, the presence of a drug that has been used by twenty-four million people in this country is sufficient to turn a private residence into premises that are "exactly" like a gambling joint or a house of prostitution. When courts take this attitude, it is easy for a policeman to think that he can get away with anything in dealing with marijuana users.

Even more dangerous is the message that decisions like this one convey to the intelligent but often alienated individuals who make up a large proportion of regular marijuana users. The student who invites a few friends over for an evening of pot and wine is told that he is no better than the proprietor of a gambling den or a brothel. It is hardly to be wondered that his skepticism about the dominant culture often turns into cynicism and a rejection of society's values.[38] This cynicism is likely to be magnified when the student reads that prominent members of the establishment have been given injections of amphetamine by a wealthy doctor,[39] or when he hears repeated television advertisement for mood-altering drugs.[40]

VEHICULAR ARRESTS

A high proportion—probably between one-third and one-half—of all marijuana arrests take place after a police officer has stopped an automobile, supposedly to investigate a violation of traffic or vehicle laws.[41] Sometimes the marijuana is found in the car and sometimes on the person of the driver or a passenger. All too often

[37] State v. Chambers, 55 Wis. 2d at 297–98, 198 N.W.2d at 380–81.

[38] See Comment, *supra* note 7, at 118–21.

[39] *N.Y. Times*, Dec. 12, 1972, p. 1, col. 1.

[40] See *N.Y. Times*, Nov. 15, 1972, p. 94, col. 4 (FCC Commissioner called for legislation to regulate TV drug advertising).

[41] In the Shafer commission's study of state arrests, 69 percent of all marijuana arrests arose from "spontaneous or accidental situations," and "well over half" of those occurred when police stopped an automobile and saw or smelled marijuana. National Commission on Marihuana and Drug Abuse, *Marihuana: A Signal of Misunderstanding*, 110. In the Stanford study, 56 of the 133 defendants first came to the attention of the police in a situation involving an automobile. Comment, *supra* note 7, at 127. In Washington, D.C., a police study found that 17 percent of the marijuana arrests resulted from traffic arrests, while another 42 percent occurred "spontaneously" when uniformed officers "happen[ed] to see marijuana being smoked or sold on the street as they [made] their rounds" (*Washington Post*, Aug. 20, 1973, p. C–1, col. 6).

the contraband is discovered in a search which violates the Fourth Amendment.

When marijuana is found after an automobile has been stopped for a traffic violation, the police, invoking the most common exception to the warrant requirement, usually seek to show that the drug was discovered in a search incident to a lawful arrest. The argument comes up against two obstacles.[42] For most traffic violations the police do not make a full custody arrest but simply issue a citation and allow the offender to proceed on his way.[43] Second, whether or not the police take the offender into custody, the rationale of the arrest exception does not, in the circumstances of the typical traffic stop, support the kind of search that would turn up a cache of marijuana either on the driver's person or in the vehicle. The authority to search incident to arrest is grounded in part on the need to find and preserve evidence or "fruits" of the crime for which the arrest is made and in part on the need to remove any concealed weapons that might threaten the safety of the arresting officer.[44] Obviously, except in the rarest of instances, there can be no evidence or fruits of a traffic violation, and thus a search cannot be validated on that basis.[45] The matter of weapons is more complex. For the moment suffice it to say that a genuine concern for the officer's safety would not justify a search beyond "the area from within which [the suspect] might gain possession of a weapon," [46] nor, ordinarily, would it give the officer reason to open a cigarette pack or wallet or other small package found on the person of the arrestee. Because most courts have recognized the force of these considerations, the police, rather than resting on the broad exception to the warrant requirement, attempt to show that their search was justified by special circumstances. Five kinds of special circumstances are repeatedly claimed.

Marijuana in plain view. Strictly speaking, the "plain view" doctrine is not an exception to the warrant requirement, since the

---

[42] Sometimes it may be possible to argue that the arrest was improper, but it will be a poor police officer who would not be able to justify a vehicular arrest. As a Missouri judge has commented, "Few drivers . . . can drive any considerable distance without violating some traffic law or ordinance" (State v. Robinson, 447 S.W.2d 71, 74 [Mo. 1969] [concurring opinion]); but see Gustafson v. Florida, 94 S. Ct. 488, 492 (1973) (Stewart, J., concurring).

[43] See People v. Superior Court (Simon), 7 Cal. 3d 186, 199, 496 P.2d 1205, 1215, 101 Cal. Rptr. 837, 847 (1972).

[44] United States v. Robinson, 94 S. Ct. 467, 476–77 (1973).

[45] People v. Marsh, 20 N.Y. 2d 98, 101, 228 N.E.2d 783, 785, 281 N.Y.S.2d 789, 792 (1967).

[46] Chimel v. California, 395 U.S. at 763.

theory is that no search takes place when an object can be readily seen from a lawful vantage point.[47] The practical problem is that it is often difficult to believe police officers' assertions that the marijuana which they seized was really in plain view. A study of marijuana arrests in one California county in a twelve-month period turned up five cases in which officers claimed "that from outside a car at night they were able to observe marijuana seeds, marijuana debris, or a single 'roach' inside the car on the floor." As the author points out, "the interior of an automobile is lit dimly (if at all), . . . the floor is generally covered with dark carpeting or rubber mats, . . . dirt and other debris are usually present, . . . and seeds and particles of marijuana rarely exceed one-sixteenth of an inch in any dimension." [48]

In spite of these obstacles, police officers continue to report finding marijuana in plain view. For example, a Denver officer testified that after writing a ticket for double parking he looked inside the car to see if the registration was attached to the steering post. He then saw a clear plastic bag, containing a green plantlike substance, partially concealed by a blanket on the front seat. This observation was held to justify an arrest, which in turn justified a search of the rest of the car.[49] Similar cases can be found in other jurisdictions.[50]

The "plain view" doctrine lends itself to a second kind of abuse: often the object which the officer claims to have seen is not a clear plastic bag containing a green plantlike substance (which is perhaps more likely to be marijuana than anything else), but some other item which would suggest the presence of marijuana only to a person who already expected to find it. In Stockton, California, for example, an officer seized a "handrolled cigarette in white paper," which he claimed to have seen "in plain view" on the back seat of a

[47] See LaFave, "Search and Seizure: 'The Course of True Law . . . Has Not . . . Run Smooth,'" 1966 *U. Ill. L. F.* 255, 333–43. A few years ago the Supreme Court expressed the rule as follows: "[O]bjects falling in plain view of an officer who has a right to be in the position to have that view are subject to seizure and may be introduced in evidence" (Harris v. United States, 390 U.S. 234, 236 [1968] [*per curiam*]). More recently, a plurality of the Court has stated that the plain view exception applies only where the discovery is "inadvertent" (Coolidge v. New Hampshire, 403 U.S. 443, 469 [1971]). The issue arose in the context of a search incident to the arrest of a man in his home, and it is not clear to what extent the "inadvertent discovery" requirement applies in other situations.

[48] Comment, *supra* note 7, at 116.

[49] People v. Marquez, 168 Colo. 219, 450 P.2d 349 (1969).

[50] E.g., Hughes v. State, 86 Nev. 584, 471 P.2d 245 (1970); State v. Devine, 496 P.2d 51 (Ore. App. 1972).

station wagon. (The arrest took place at night, and the only illumination came from the vehicle's dome light.) The officer did not tell how he could distinguish between a hand-rolled tobacco cigarette and a hand-rolled marijuana cigarette.[51]

In other cases officers have sought to justify seizures or arrests by resort to a logical fallacy: because in their experience marijuana is usually or commonly carried in a certain kind of container, they claim that *any* such container is likely to contain marijuana.[52] Thus, in Maryland an arresting officer testified that he looked into the car and "observed on the front seat two brown envelopes, and, from my past experience, knowing that these envelopes are used for narcotic drugs, I examined the envelopes." [53] A California officer who had stopped a panel truck for having a defective brake light searched the truck after observing in the open glove compartment and in the bed of the truck two closed penny matchboxes and two paper matchbooks with the top halves of their covers missing. He testified that matchbook covers are often used as holders for the ends of marijuana cigarettes and that penny matchboxes are frequently used as containers for five-dollar purchases of marijuana.[54] In neither case, apparently, did it occur to the officers that brown envelopes, matchbooks, and matchboxes may be used for purposes not associated with marijuana (or that they might simply be left in a car for no purpose at all). [55]

[51] The court commented: "It is a matter of common knowledge that hand-rolled tobacco cigarettes have found a new popularity reflecting current individualistic attitudes, changing styles, and availability of new 'do-it-yourself' supplies, and increases in the price of factory-mades. Hand-rolled cigarettes 'in white paper' are not unusual, and it would be unjust to automatically subject possessors of them to arrest on marijuana charges or their cars to search" (Thomas v. Superior Court, 22 Cal. App. 3d 972, 977, 99 Cal. Rptr. 647, 650 [1972]). See also State v. Buchwald, 293 Minn. at 83, 196 N.W.2d at 450–51 (1972) (Otis, J., dissenting).

[52] These cases are not limited to searches following traffic arrests. In California, for example, a man was arrested as he emerged from his apartment carrying a brown paper bag. The officer claimed that marijuana "is usually carried in bulk in [that] kind of a sack." The court pointed out that "a great variety of items, such . . . as children's lunches are also carried in such bags." The only reason for the officers' suspicion was an unverified tip from a man the officers had met for the first time an hour earlier. People v. Goodo, 147 Cal. App. 2d 7, 304 P.2d 776 (1956). In New York, officers seized four envelopes "of a small size and common variety" after one teenager was observed giving them to another teenager. People v. Corrado, 22 N.Y. 2d 308, 239 N.E.2d 526, 292 N.Y.S.2d 648 (1968).

[53] Taylor v. State, 9 Md. App. 402, 264 A.2d 870 (1970).

[54] People v. Hana, 7 Cal. App. 3d 402, 86 Cal. Rptr. 721 (1970).

[55] The same may be said of packages wrapped in aluminum foil. See People v. Ware, 484 P.2d 103 (Colo. 1972); Remers v. Superior Court, 2 Cal. 3d 659, 407 P.2d 11, 87 Cal. Rptr. 202 (1970).

Furtive gesture. In many cases, probable cause to search a vehicle that has been stopped for a traffic offense has been predicated on "furtive gestures" or "furtive movements" of an occupant of the vehicle. The theory, in the words of the California Supreme Court, is that "although the officer does not actually *see* any contraband from outside the vehicle, he may reasonably *infer* from the timing and direction of the occupant's movement that the latter is in fact in possession of contraband which he is endeavoring to hide." [56] The difficulty with the theory, as the court noted, is that "from the viewpoint of the *observer,* an innocent gesture can often be mistaken for a guilty movement." [57] After a comprehensive review of the California cases, the court concluded: "The near-insufficiency of the evidence of probable cause upheld in certain of the cited Court of Appeal decisions suggests that police reliance on so called 'furtive movements' has on occasion been little short of a subterfuge, and that in order to conduct a search on the basis of mere suspicion or intuition, guilty significance has been claimed for gestures or surrounding circumstances that were equally or more likely to be wholly innocent." [58] As further evidence that the "furtive gesture" exception has been used as a "subterfuge" by the police (with the cooperation of the courts),[59] Justice Mosk cited the *U.C.L.A. Law Review* study of marijuana law enforcement in Los Angeles County.[60] A similar study by the editors of the *Stanford Law Review,* referred to earlier, also supports the court's conclusion.[61] Cases in other jurisdictions indicate that the problem is not confined to California.[62]

Odor. Often a police officer, having stopped a vehicle, will smell, or claim to have smelled, the odor of marijuana inside the car. For some courts that odor is enough to justify searching the persons in the car and arresting them if marijuana is found.[63] As

---

[56] People v. Superior Court (Kiefer), 3 Cal. 3d 807, 817, 478 P.2d 449, 454, 91 Cal. Rptr. 729, 734 (1970).

[57] 3 Cal. 3d at 818, 478 P.2d at 455, 91 Cal. Rptr. at 735.

[58] 3 Cal. 3d at 827, 478 P.2d at 462, 91 Cal. Rptr. at 742.

[59] This point seems to be implicit in Justice Mosk's opinion.

[60] Note, "Marijuana Laws: An Empirical Study of Enforcement and Administration in Los Angeles County," 15 *U.C.L.A. L. Rev.* 1501 (1968).

[61] Comment, *supra* note 7, at 118–21.

[62] E.g., Cowdin v. People, 491 P.2d 569 (Colo. 1971); *cf.* Pace v. State, 461 S.W.2d 409 (Tex. Crim. App. 1970).

[63] See, e.g., People v. Erb, 128 Ill. App. 2d 126, 261 N.E.2d 431 (1970); People v. Jackson, 241 Cal. App. 2d 189, 50 Cal. Rptr. 437 (1966). In early 1974, *Time* magazine reported that Los Angeles had recently had a rash of "smell" testimony after one police officer successfully justified a search by saying that he had smelled marijuana on the defendant. *Time,* Feb. 4, 1974, p. 79.

the Stanford study pointed out, the odor of burning marijuana *is* distinctive; the difficulty is that police officers sometimes claim to have smelled the odor under circumstances in which it seems improbable that they were able to do so.[64]

Search for weapons. "When an arrest is made, it is reasonable for the arresting officer to search the person arrested in order to remove any weapons that the latter might seek to use in order to resist arrest or effect his escape. Otherwise, the officer's safety might well be endangered, and the arrest itself frustrated." [65] If this rule applies without qualification to routine arrests for traffic offenses, a police officer will seldom have difficulty in creating an occasion to search a driver whom he suspects of being in possession of marijuana.[66] Recognizing this danger, some courts have held that an arrest for a minor traffic violation does not justify a search for weapons unless the arresting officer has probable cause to believe that the suspect is armed and dangerous.[67] In other jurisdictions, however, the courts have given the police greater latitude.[68]

Even when the rules are couched in restrictive terms they may allow a good deal of leeway for the subjective judgment of the officer. For example, the Minnesota court indicated that probable cause might be found where the suspect "assume[d] a hostile and threatening attitude when stopped" or when "cursory observation" gave the officer "valid reason to believe that the motorist [was] engaged in the commission of a more serious crime." [69] To the officer who regards any male with long hair as a "symbolic assailant," [70] almost any kind of gesture may suggest a "hostile attitude," while "cursory observation" may permit the officer to find marijuana "in plain view." Of course, where the officer is not primarily interested in obtaining a conviction, he can search for weapons without fear of being called to account for not having probable cause to believe that the suspect was armed.[71]

[64] Comment, *supra* note 7, at 116.
[65] Chimel v. California, 395 U.S. at 762–63; see also Terry v. Ohio, 392 U.S. 1 (1968); Adams v. Williams, 407 U.S. 143 (1972).
[66] See *supra* note 42.
[67] See, e.g., State v. Curtis, 290 Minn. 429, 190 N.W.2d 631 (1971); People v. Superior Court (Kiefer), 3 Cal. 3d 807, 478 P.2d 449, 91 Cal. Rptr. 729 (1970); Sam v. State, 500 P.2d 291 (Okla. Crim. 1972); People v. Marsh, 20 N.Y. 2d 98, 228 N.E.2d 783, 281 N.Y.S.2d 789 (1967). See Annot., 10 A.L.R.3d 314 (1966).
[68] See, e.g., State v. Gustafson, 258 So. 2d 1 (Fla. 1972), *aff'd*, 94 S. Ct. 488 (1973).
[69] State v. Curtis, 290 Minn. at 437, 190 N.W.2d at 636.
[70] See Skolnick, *supra* note 5, at 45.
[71] See *supra* pp. 104–5.

In late 1973, the United States Supreme Court ruled that the police may search the person of a traffic offender whether or not they have any grounds for thinking that he is armed or dangerous, as long as they arrest him rather than simply giving him a ticket.[72] The effect of the decision will be considered at the end of this section.

Abandonment. The courts have held that the taking of property which has been abandoned does not constitute a seizure within the meaning of the Fourth Amendment.[73] This means that if a person drops an item of property (for example, a joint or a plastic bag containing marijuana) a police officer may retrieve it, examine it, and use it as the basis for a subsequent arrest.[74] Unfortunately, recent studies suggest that in many of the cases in which an arresting officer claims that he merely picked up marijuana which a suspect dropped, the marijuana was actually found in an unconstitutional search.[75] Because there are usually no disinterested witnesses to the encounter, a judge who is not inclined to believe that a police officer might commit perjury will often take the officer's word over that of the suspect (who appears to be clearly guilty of the crime of possession).[76] The result is that overzealous policemen are encouraged to stop and illegally search persons whom they suspect of carrying marijuana. If the search proves fruitless, the officer risks nothing.[77] If the search uncovers marijuana, he will feel confident of being able to persuade a judge that the suspect dropped it when he saw the policeman approaching.[78] The "abandoned property" doctrine is thus used to circumvent the Fourth Amendment.

[72] United States v. Robinson, 94 S. Ct. 467 (1973).

[73] Abel v. United States, 362 U.S. 217, 241 (1960).

[74] Comment, "Police Perjury in Narcotics 'Dropsy' Cases," 60 *Geo. L. J.* 507, 512 (1971), and cases cited.

[75] Note, "Effect of Mapp v. Ohio on Police Search-and-Seizure Practices in Narcotics Cases," 4 *Colum. J. L. & Soc. Prob.* 87 (1968); Comment, "Police Perjury," *supra* note 74.

[76] "[I]t would be a dismal reflection on society to say that when the guardians of its security are called to testify in court under oath, their testimony must be viewed with suspicion" (Bush v. United States, 375 F.2d 602, 604 [D.C. Cir. 1967] [Burger, J.]).

[77] See *supra* pp. 104–5 and *infra* pp. 126, 144.

[78] The doctrine applies only to property that has been abandoned "voluntarily." Thus, if a defendant is forced to abandon property "as the direct result of illegal police activity" (Comment, "Police Perjury," *supra* note 74, at 512), the court is required to exclude it as evidence. Unfortunately, in deciding whether a suspect abandoned property voluntarily, the court will once again have to choose between two contradictory accounts of an unwitnessed event, one that of a police officer and the other that of an apparently guilty defendant,

The various doctrines invoked by the police in these cases are not mutually exclusive. Quite the contrary—a vehicular arrest can easily serve as the base for a pyramid of inferences and exceptions that effectively obliterates the protection against indiscriminate governmental intrusion which the Fourth Amendment was designed to insure. By way of example, in a California case police officers stopped a car which happened to be in an area where a burglary had occurred several hours before.[79] Although there was no indication that the car or its occupants had had anything to do with the burglary, the court found that the "totality of [the] circumstances" justified the officers' stopping the vehicle. Said the court: "[The officers were] in an area in the early morning hours in which a burglary had occurred shortly before [they] observed the vehicle. The vehicle with two occupants was parked in front of a closed store when it was first observed. It then moved to another location where a pedestrian approached it and entered it." Having stopped the car, the officers could request that the driver and passengers alight from it: "An important consideration was whether the men whom they were investigating for burglary were armed. In view of this possibility, it was safer for the officers if the occupants of the car were asked to alight so that they could better be observed while the investigation was in progress."

As the driver got out, he left the car door open. One of the officers looked into the car and observed, among other things, a pipe with a chrome or silver cover on the floor of the driver's side, partially covered by the floor mat.[80] Since the pipe was in plain view, he could seize it without a warrant—but only if the pipe was itself contraband or if the officers could reasonably believe that it contained contraband. The court found both possibilities to be supportable: "[T]he possession of any device . . . used for smoking marijuana is a crime. . . . [The officer] testified that from his prior experience . . . the subject pipe was of the sort in which marijuana was smoked. . . . Since the pipe itself was contraband, its contents were subject to search. [Even if the pipe was not contraband, the officer] had reasonable grounds for believing that [it] contained contraband." The officer was thus justified in searching the inside of the pipe. Upon finding what he considered to be mari-

---

[79] People v. Nickles, 9 Cal. App. 3d 986, 88 Cal. Rptr. 763 (1970).

[80] This encounter occurred at two o'clock in the morning. The court expressed no surprise at the officer's ability to see a pipe lying on the floor of a car, partially covered by the floor mat, at that time of night.

juana seeds and debris, he could arrest the driver for possession of the marijuana. Since the arrest was proper, the officer was justified in making a search of the driver's person incident to the arrest. When the search revealed additional marijuana, the officer could and did arrest the driver (again). All of the marijuana thus seized was held properly admitted into evidence against the driver.

Each step in the court's analysis might be supportable by itself, but the cumulative effect is to uphold a thorough search of the occupants of the car, without a warrant, even though the police never had probable cause (and perhaps not even "reasonable suspicion")[81] to believe them guilty of anything until after the investigation and forcible detention had begun.[82]

Although the doctrinal justifications for the various exceptions may differ, their practical effect is very much the same. In each instance the police officer has an apparently legitimate reason for stopping the driver of the vehicle. Having made a lawful arrest, the officer claims to have had probable cause to search the vehicle or the driver's person. The truthfulness of the claim cannot be easily disproved: How can the defendant show that the officer could not have reasonably believed the defendant's gesture to be "furtive"? Or that the defendant did not "assume a hostile and threatening attitude when stopped"? Or that the plastic bag or pipe was not "in plain view"? Moreover, whatever the *a priori* plausibility of the policeman's claimed observations, the fact will be that he *did* discover contraband. Although courts constantly warn against justifying a search by what is found,[83] "[t]he illegality of the search is likely to be tempered" (as Skolnick puts it) by the discovery of incriminating evidence on the suspect's person or in his vehicle.[84] Nor does this mean that the officer will necessarily be lying; rather, he may have "reconstruct[ed] a set of complex happenings in such

[81] See N.Y. Code Crim. Proc. § 180-a (the "stop and frisk" law); People v. Taggart, 20 N.Y. 2d 335, 229 N.E.2d 581, 283 N.Y.S.2d 1 (1967).

[82] It is also arguable that the officers violated the suspects' Fifth Amendment rights by failing to warn them of their right to remain silent. See Yale Kamisar, " 'Custodial Interrogation' Within the Meaning of Miranda," in *Criminal Law and the Constitution,* ed. John Reed, *et al.* (Ann Arbor, Mich., 1968), 335.

[83] See, e.g., United States v. Di Re, 332 U.S. 581, 595 (1948).

[84] Skolnick, *supra* note 5, at 221. See, e.g., People v. Meyers, 38 A.D.2d 484, 486, 330 N.Y.S.2d 625, 627 (1972): "the seizure establishes that the officer was right in believing that a crime had been committed. On the narrow question of whether that belief was reasonably engendered, the fact that it was correct should receive some recognition."

a way that, subsequent to the arrest, probable cause can be found according to appellate court standards." [85]

Thus, unless courts begin to take a much more skeptical attitude toward police accounts of probable cause in traffic-arrest cases, the police officer risks very little if he conducts an unlawful search after stopping a vehicle. "If a search yields no incriminating evidence, those who are illegally searched are usually pleased to drop the matter." If the search does uncover marijuana or narcotics, the officer has a good chance of convincing the court that the search came within one of the doctrines discussed above. Even if the court does not believe the officer, "the worst punishment he can suffer is loss of a conviction." [86] In any event he has the satisfaction of preventing the suspect from making use of the contraband.

The Robinson decision. In December, 1973, the United States Supreme Court handed down a decision significantly expanding the authority of police officers to search motorists arrested for traffic offenses.[87] The Court held that whenever an officer makes a "lawful custodial arrest" for the violation of a motor vehicle regulation, he may conduct a full search of the person of the driver even if he has no reason to believe that the search will uncover either a weapon or evidence of a crime. Three justices, in dissent, protested that the majority's approach "represents a clear and marked departure from our long tradition of case-by-case adjudication of the reasonableness of searches and seizures under the Fourth Amendment." [88] The majority insisted in equally strong terms that its decision merely reaffirmed settled principles. Each side could cite precedents in support of its position; in essence, Justice Rehnquist and Justice Marshall reached opposing conclusions because they began by asking different questions.

Justice Rehnquist and the majority began with the proposition that a search of the person incident to a lawful arrest is a traditional exception to the warrant requirement; the question for them was whether there was any reason to create "an exception to the exception," so to speak, for arrests for violation of a motor vehicle regulation. Their answer was no. The dissenters, in contrast, took the warrant requirement as their starting point. Recognizing the

[85] Skolnick, *supra* note 5, at 215.
[86] *Ibid.,* 221.
[87] United States v. Robinson, 94 S. Ct. 467 (1973).
[88] *Ibid.,* 478.

existence of the search-incident-to-arrest exception, they insisted that the courts must scrutinize each search to determine whether, under the particular circumstances, it could be justified by the purposes of that doctrine. From their perspective the majority was creating a new exception, of potentially enormous breadth, to the warrant requirement.

Because the majority's rule eliminates any need for particularized inquiry in the cases to which it applies, it is important to take note of the exact scope of the holding. The only issue settled by the decision is the validity of a search of the person of a driver following a full-custody arrest. The Court put aside any questions relating to the permissible scope of a search of the offender's vehicle.[89] Nor did the opinion address itself to possible justifications for searching anyone in the vehicle except the driver. Thus, when marijuana is found on the floor or seat of an automobile, in the glove compartment, or on the person of a passenger, the police must still rely on the special circumstances described earlier in this chapter.[90] Finally, the Court carefully confined its holding to the full-custody arrest, avoiding any discussion of the scope of police authority to search following a routine traffic stop, in which the officer simply issues a notice of violation and allows the offender to proceed.[91] In practical terms, however, this caveat may not make much difference. As the dissenters pointed out, the rules governing when an officer may effect a full arrest and when he is limited to issuing a ticket are matters of state law; in most jurisdictions and for most traffic offenses the decision is left to the discretion of the officer.[92] This means that as long as the officer can find reason to charge a motorist with one of the traffic offenses for which an arrest is permissible, he can conduct a full-scale search of the driver's person.

In a brief concurring opinion, Justice Powell advanced his own rationale for allowing such searches. "[A]n individual lawfully subjected to a custodial arrest," he argued, "retains no significant Fourth Amendment interest in the privacy of his person. . . . If the arrest is lawful, . . . [n]o reason . . . exists to frustrate law enforcement by requiring some independent justification for a search. . . . The search . . . is reasonable . . . because the pri-

[89] *Ibid.,* 471.
[90] Prosecution efforts to legitimize the discovery of marijuana in the interior of a vehicle tend to rely on three of the five doctrines: the plain view rule, the furtive gesture theory, and the odor rationale.
[91] 94 S. Ct. at 477 n. 6.
[92] *Ibid.,* 482.

vacy interest protected by [the Fourth Amendment] is legitimately abated by the fact of arrest." [93]

This argument is a non sequitur. Functionally as well as conceptually, an individual's interest in freedom of movement is quite distinct from his interest in the privacy and security of his personal effects. His freedom of movement is restrained by a custodial arrest (lawful or otherwise); he suffers a new and different intrusion when, in addition, his personal effects are probed, examined, and perhaps taken away from him. As the Court said in answer to a similar argument in an earlier search-incident-to-arrest case, there is "no reason why, simply because some interference with an individual's privacy and freedom of movement has lawfully taken place, further intrusions should automatically be allowed despite the absence of a warrant that the Fourth Amendment would otherwise require." [94] This does not mean that the search is necessarily bad; rather, it leaves us with the question of whether, as a matter of policy, a lawful custodial arrest for a traffic violation *should* carry with it the right to search the person of the individual arrested.

The policy considerations need not be pursued at great length here. In defense of the majority ruling it can be said that in large numbers of cases that ruling will eliminate the need for time-consuming and legally perplexing hearings on defense motions to suppress evidence. In those same cases the police will no longer have any reason to fabricate testimony about the circumstances of their finding marijuana on the person of a traffic offender. Moreover, the ruling will permit the police to apprehend some law violators whose offenses—usually crimes of possession—would otherwise go undetected. Against these benefits, however, must be weighed a significant detriment: the increased opportunity for police officers, lacking probable cause to obtain a search warrant, to use a traffic arrest as a pretext to conduct a search for marijuana or other contraband. As the following chapter demonstrates, such pretextual arrests are far from uncommon—even before one takes into account the searches never passed on by a court because the motorist did not, after all, have anything unlawful in his possession.[95]

[93] *Ibid.*, 494.

[94] Chimel v. California, 395 U.S. at 766 n. 12. This passage was quoted by Justice Marshall in his dissent, 94 S. Ct. at 487. The Chimel opinion was written by Justice Stewart, who voted with the majority in Robinson.

[95] Perhaps for these reasons a New York court has rejected the rule of *Robinson* as an "ignoble shortcut to decision" and has adhered to the less latitudinarian standard of People v. Marsh, 20 N.Y. 2d 98, 228 N.E.2d 783, 281 N.Y.S.2d 789 (1967). People v. Kelly, 42 U.S.L.W. 2471 (N.Y. City Crim. Ct. 1974).

PEDESTRIAN ARRESTS

Much of what has been said about vehicular arrests can be applied, *mutatis mutandis,* to pedestrian arrests.[96] Although a police officer cannot often claim that his investigation was touched off when he witnessed the violation of a traffic law,[97] he can invoke an "open sesame" that is perhaps more powerful: the stop-and-frisk doctrine laid down by the Supreme Court in *Terry* v. *Ohio* in 1968 and broadened four years later in *Adams* v. *Williams.*[98]

In the stop-and-frisk cases of 1968 the Court addressed itself to two issues. First, may a police officer make a forcible stop of a citizen on the street even though the officer lacks probable cause to make an arrest? Second, having insisted upon the encounter, may the officer then conduct a search of the suspect's person—again in the absence of probable cause? [99]

Although an affirmative answer to the first question was implicit in the 1968 decisions,[100] it was not until 1972 that the Court stated in unmistakable terms that a police officer may *forcibly* detain a citizen " 'for purposes of investigating possibly criminal behavior even though there is no probable cause to make an arrest.' " [101] The question in each case is whether a brief stop is "reasonable in light of the facts known to the officer at the time." [102] It is sufficient that the officer has observed "unusual conduct which leads him reasonably to conclude in the light of his experience that criminal activity may be afoot. . . ." [103] In the view of Justice Harlan, this standard requires less than reasonable suspicion that the person stopped "is committing, has committed or is about to commit a crime." [104]

Once an individual has been forcibly stopped, the Court con-

[96] For example, the abandonment doctrine is relied upon with great frequency. See *infra* pp. 151–54.

[97] But see cases cited at *infra* pp. 130–31, 137–38.

[98] Terry v. Ohio, 392 U.S. 1 (1968); Adams v. Williams, 407 U.S. 143 (1972). Terry was accompanied by a companion case, Sibron v. New York, 392 U.S. 40 (1968).

[99] This analysis draws upon that of Justice Harlan in his concurring opinion in Terry, 392 U.S. at 32–33.

[100] See *ibid.* and the following note.

[101] Adams v. Williams, 407 U.S. at 145, quoting Terry v. Ohio, 392 U.S. at 22. The language of the earlier case does not make clear the officer's right "to *insist* on an encounter" (392 U.S. at 32 [Harlan, J., concurring] [emphasis added]). Indeed, the court insisted that it was *not* passing upon the constitutionality of any forced stops. See 392 U.S. at 19 n. 16.

[102] Adams v. Williams, 407 U.S. at 145.

[103] Terry v. Ohio, 392 U.S. at 30.

[104] Sibron v. New York, 392 U.S. at 72 (Harlan, J., concurring).

tinued, the officer may conduct a limited search of his person: "So long as the officer is entitled to make a forcible stop and has reason to believe that the suspect is armed and dangerous" he may engage in "a limited protective search for concealed weapons." [105] In *Adams* v. *Williams,* the 1972 case, the Court held that both the stop and the frisk were lawful although the officer was acting on the basis of what the dissent persuasively characterized as "unsubstantiated, conclusory hearsay." [106]

It may plausibly be assumed that the Court's decisions have increased the readiness of police officers to engage in on-the-street questioning, often accompanied by a frisk. What is more significant, for present purposes, is that the "reasonable suspicion" test which the Court appears to adopt provides after-the-fact validation for almost any field interrogation which leads to the discovery of contraband on the suspect's person. As Chevigny states, "It is hard to know just what 'suspicions' leading to a stop and frisk are so absurd as to be unreasonable, and one is tempted to lay down a general rule that a police abuse cannot officially occur under such a vague [test]." [107] The Supreme Court's opinions appear to suggest that a stop will often be justified when a frisk is not,[108] but in practice the courts are likely to adopt the view of Justice Harlan that "[t]here is no reason why an officer, rightfully but forcibly confronting a person suspected of a serious crime, should have to ask one question and take the risk that the answer might be a bullet." [109] This view is likely to be especially persuasive when the consequence of hold-

[105] Adams v. Williams, 407 U.S. at 145.

[106] *Ibid.,* 152 (dissenting opinion). The dissenting opinion stated: "The Court explains what the officer knew about respondent before accosting him. But what is more significant is what he did not know. With respect to the scene generally, the officer had no idea how long respondent had been in the car, how long the car had been parked, or to whom the car belonged. With respect to the gun, the officer did not know if or when the informant had ever seen the gun, or whether the gun was carried legally, as Connecticut law permitted, or illegally. And with respect to the narcotics, the officer did not know what kind of narcotics respondent allegedly had, whether they were legally or illegally possessed, what the basis of the informant's knowledge was, or even whether the informant was capable of distinguishing narcotics from other substances" (*ibid.* at 153 [footnotes omitted]).

[107] Chevigny, *supra* note 2, at 193–94.

[108] A stop is justified by a "reasonable suspicion" (Sibron v. New York, 392 U.S. at 71 [Harlan, J., concurring]) that "criminal activity may be afoot" (Terry v. Ohio, 392 U.S. at 30 [1968]), while a frisk is permissible only when the officer "has reason to believe that the suspect is armed and dangerous" (Adams v. Williams, 407 U.S. at 145 [1972]).

[109] Terry v. Ohio, 392 U.S. at 33 (concurring opinion); *cf.* State v. Curtis, 290 Minn. 429, 190 N.W.2d 631 (1971).

ing the frisk unlawful is that the contraband is suppressed as evidence and the criminal goes free.

The result is that, as with the vehicular stop, a police officer who has detained a pedestrian, for whatever reason, runs very little risk if he engages in a "pat-down" while consciously or unconsciously looking for marijuana paraphernalia. If the search uncovers no contraband the officer is unlikely to suffer any adverse consequences, since the suspect will usually be happy enough to proceed on his way without seeking any redress. If marijuana is found the officer stands a good chance of being able to persuade the court that the discovery occurred in the course of a lawful frisk for weapons.[110] Even if the marijuana is suppressed, the officer has the satisfaction of taking the drug out of circulation and subjecting the suspect to the inconvenience and embarrassment of a court appearance.

The cases provide numerous examples of forcible stops and subsequent frisks on the basis of police hunches which do not meet even the latitudinarian standards of *Terry* and *Williams*. In Saint Louis, for example, three police officers detained two men sitting quietly in a parked car although the only suspicious circumstances (if they can be called such) were the fact that the car had Nevada license plates and the officers' general knowledge that the area was "highly trafficked in narcotics." [111] In Oregon two officers on routine patrol forcibly stopped four men who had just left a house and entered a van parked at the curb. Apart from the fact that the general area had a high incidence of crime, the only reasons for detaining the men were their hurried departure from the house and the fact that the officers knew that the house was "commonly known as a

110 The officer will not necessarily be lying when he states that he conducted the frisk because he feared that the suspect was "armed and dangerous" rather than because he hoped to find marijuana. First, the officer may have done no more than to "construct an ex post facto description of the preceding events so that these conform to legal arrest requirements, whether in fact the events actually did so or not at the time of the arrest" (Skolnick, *supra* note 5, at 215). Second, if the suspect is an "otherwise respectable citizen" who does not conform to the policeman's portrait of respectability—for example, an individual "with long hair, nondescriptly dressed" (State v. Henneke, 78 Wash. 147, 150, 470 P.2d 176, 179 [1970])—the policeman may regard him as a "symbolic assailant" (Skolnick, *supra* note 5, at 217–18) who *does* pose a danger.

111 Nicholas v. U.S., 448 F.2d 622 (8th Cir. 1971). The court noted that the police had no information concerning the car or its occupants, that there was no showing that the police had been informed of suspicious activities in the area at the time of the encounter, and that "the hour, 11:15 p.m., was a reasonable hour for individuals to be abroad on the streets on a June evening" (*ibid.*, 625).

commune-type crash pad. We have had runaway girls, narcotics crimes, and for awhile an arson suspect lived in the house." [112]

In a high-crime residential area which was the private property of Stanford University, a university police officer observed a man "dressed in unusual garb" who appeared to be a stranger to the neighborhood. When the man saw the uniformed officer, he turned his head away, "kind of like to avoid me." The officer stopped the man to ask for identification and "ascertain if he had business." The man showed a draft card and said that he was going to a certain residence. The officer knew that the occupant of that residence had a police record. This was enough, in the officer's mind, to warrant detaining the pedestrian while the officer checked the man's identification via police radio. [113]

Questionable stops are not limited to high-crime areas. In Los Angeles two officers stopped a pedestrian because of his "furtive actions." What the pedestrian had done was to turn toward the police car when its muffler emitted a clanging noise and to thrust his hand into his left front pants pocket. [114] A Reno officer decided to stop and question three men in a public park when from across the Truckee River, more than fifty yards away, he saw one of the men "appear to roll" and light a cigarette that burned in the dusk with a bright red glow and he observed the cigarette passing between the man and his companions, who "cupped" their hands when smoking it. The officer conceded that he could not distinguish the rolling of a marijuana cigarette from the rolling of a tobacco cigarette and that he could not identify the glow of a marijuana cigarette at a distance of fifty yards. Nor did he explain what he

[112] State v. Devine, 496 P.2d 51 (Ore. App. 1972). The court found that "the combination of circumstances" described in the text "did create in alert officers a reasonable suspicion . . . that the car or its occupants might be connected with criminal activity and thus warrant a 'routine check' of the vehicle to require that its occupants identify themselves" (*ibid.,* 52).

[113] People v. Courtney, 11 Cal. App. 3d 1185, 90 Cal. Rptr. 370 (1970). The court states that "[b]cause of the stranger's paucity of identification and his statement that he was headed for the home of one known to have a police record, the officer's decision to detain him while he ran a radio check was proper" (11 Cal. App. 3d at 1190, 90 Cal. Rptr. at 373). Why a draft card is not adequate identification the court does not explain.

[114] People v. Collins, 1 Cal. 3d 658, 463 P.2d 403, 83 Cal. Rptr. 179 (1970). Although the officers had been informed several days earlier that a grand theft auto suspect, described only as a male Negro, six feet tall and weighing 160 pounds, might be found in the area, the court pointed out that the description applied to "a substantial portion of the population of south-central Los Angeles" (1 Cal. 3d at 661, 463 P.2d at 405, 83 Cal. Rptr. at 181).

meant by "cupped" hands, although he testified that he had been taught that marijuana is often smoked in that fashion.[115]

About 9:40 on a January evening two Los Angeles police officers received a report that shots had been fired at a nearby intersection. Twenty minutes later the officers saw a man, apparently a complete stranger to them, walking towards the intersection with his left hand in his jacket pocket.[116] The officers detained the man and insisted on knowing what he had in his pocket. The court found the forcible stop to be permissible, although the officers had no information to suggest that the man had anything to do with the shots, which had been fired at least twenty minutes earlier; the man was walking towards rather than away from the intersection, and he had done nothing to call attention to himself except place his hand in his jacket pocket.[117]

Questionable frisks of persons who have been detained are also common. In a park in Tucson two officers stopped a man they believed had run from them earlier in the day. The man's fatigue jacket was draped over his left shoulder "in a manner which concealed his left arm." The officers asked him for some identification. The man asked to be left alone, but the officers persisted in their questioning. The man became "abusive in his language." [118] The officers asked the man to remove his left arm from under his jacket so that they could be sure he did not have a weapon. When the man refused to do so, the officers grabbed the jacket. Although the court conceded that the officers' initial observations would not have justified even a frisk,[119] it held that once the defendant became "abusive

[115] Schmitt v. State, 497 P.2d 891, 892 (Nev. 1972). The court stated: "[E]xcept for such suspicion as that mannerism [the cupped hands], appellant's youth, and his presence in the park might arouse, the record establishes no cause for his arrest, prior to [the officer's] warrantless search of his person. We cannot hold that the police may stop, handcuff, and search any young person in a park, and justify this action by saying they saw a cigarette smoked with 'cupped' hands" (497 P.2d at 895).

[116] People v. Woods, 6 Cal. App. 3d 832, 86 Cal. Rptr. 264 (1970). The court states that the pedestrian's hand was "concealed" in his pocket (6 Cal. App. 3d at 835, 96 Cal. Rptr. at 266). The court does not explain how "concealing" one's hand in a pocket differs from holding it there.

[117] The subsequent search was also of questionable constitutionality. See *infra* pp. 129–30.

[118] State v. Baltier, 17 Ariz. App. 441, 443, 498 P.2d 515, 517 (1972). The court states that the man's language became "abusive . . . to the point of being threatening," but the opinion does not cite any threats, and it seems clear that the man was belligerent because he wanted to be left alone, not because he wanted to tangle further with the officers.

[119] 17 Ariz. App. at 449, 498 P.2d at 523.

and belligerent in his language, . . . the seizure of the jacket was the only way in which the officers could have readily determined whether defendant did, in fact, have a weapon in his hand. . . . [T]herefore such action was not improper." [120] This reasoning seems to encourage police officers to provoke persons they have detained, for if the individual is sufficiently short-tempered, his belligerent response may permit a search which would otherwise be unlawful.

While inspecting passengers at Kennedy Airport for concealed weapons, a security agent noticed a large bulge in the left pocket of the winter overcoat worn by a passenger. The agent asked what the man had in his pocket. "A pair of gloves," the man replied. The agent then patted down the coat with his hands and requested the gloves. The passenger handed the gloves to the agent. At that point the bulge had been satisfactorily explained; the passenger displayed no unusual nervousness or suspicious mannerisms; in short, as the court held, there were no grounds even to justify reasonable suspicion. Nevertheless, the agent unrolled the gloves and found a clear plastic bag containing what appeared to be marijuana.[121]

In Los Angeles, after stopping a pedestrian on rather flimsy grounds,[122] an officer patted down the man's pocket. He felt a "little lump" which turned out to be a lid of marijuana loosely packed in a plastic bag. Although, as the court pointed out, an object that soft could hardly have felt like a weapon, the officer put his hand in the man's pocket anyway and extracted the object.[123]

In the "shots fired" case discussed earlier,[124] the pedestrian had his left hand in his jacket pocket. Upon approaching him, the officer placed his right hand on the pedestrian's left hand and asked him what he had in the pocket. The officer then reached into the pocket, placed his hand over the pedestrian's knuckles, and pulled his hand out "to discover whether [he] was holding a pistol." The man's hand was empty. Nevertheless, the officer, "without spreading the pocket or pulling it open," shone his flashlight into the pocket and found a clear plastic bag containing a green leafy substance that looked like marijuana. He seized the bag and arrested the man for possession.[125]

Several points about this case deserve comment. First, it is not

120 17 Ariz. App. at 443, 449, 498 P.2d at 517, 523.
121 People v. Erdman, 69 Misc. 2d 103, 329 N.Y.S.2d 654 (1972).
122 See *supra* p. 127.
123 People v. Collins, 1 Cal. 3d 658, 463 P.2d 403, 83 Cal. Rptr. 179 (1970).
124 See *supra* p. 128.
125 People v. Woods, 6 Cal. App. 3d 832, 86 Cal. Rptr. 264 (1970).

clear whether the court, in upholding the search, gives any weight to the pedestrian's being nervous. Who would not be nervous if, while walking down the street, he found his hand gripped by a policeman? Second, once the officer realized that the pedestrian did not have a weapon in his hand, why would it not have been sufficient, if the officer's real concern was for his safety, simply to pat down the pocket? (It must be remembered that the pedestrian was outnumbered two to one and that he had done nothing suspicious except to have his hand in his pocket.) Finally, it is hard to accept the court's apparent conclusion that by shining his flashlight into the man's pocket the officer did no more than to illuminate what was in plain view anyway.[126] The "plain view" doctrine rests on the notion that "a search implies a prying into hidden places for that which is concealed, and it is not a search to observe that which is open to view." [127] In other words, the individual cannot complain of an invasion of privacy when an officer observes something that the individual could not reasonably have expected to remain private. A man who goes outside at night, however, would surely think of his pocket as a "hidden place" and the objects in it as "concealed"; he would assume that those objects would *not* be subject to the scrutiny of a passing stranger. To say, as the court does, that the officer "illuminated the interior of defendant's pocket with his flashlight without in any way *otherwise* improving his view" [128] is therefore to beg the question, for it is the flashlight which alone makes it possible for the officer to see what he could not otherwise see and thus frustrates the reasonable expectations of the pedestrian.[129]

As with motorists, pedestrians who have been arrested are often subjected to searches which go substantially beyond the legitimate needs of law enforcement. In Los Angeles, for example, a man was arrested for starting to cross a street against a "don't walk" signal. Because he was unable to produce any identification he was transported to a police station. At the station, before any actual booking took place, the police ordered him to remove his clothes, which were then searched. There was no evidence that the police

---

[126] This reasoning is explicitly adopted in Onofre v. State, 474 S.W.2d 699, 701 (Tex Crim. App. 1972).

[127] People v. Marvin, 358 Ill. 426, 193 N.E. 202 (1934).

[128] People v. Woods, 6 Cal. App. 3d at 838, 86 Cal. Rptr. at 268 [emphasis added].

[129] The analysis in the text could be summarized by saying that shining a flashlight into a man's pocket at night violates his "reasonable expectations of privacy." See *supra* pp. 95–96.

feared possible violence. The court does not state whether the Los Angeles police ordinarily subject unidentified jaywalkers to the indignity of a strip search.[130]

While hitchhiking on U.S. Route 13 in Delaware, a young man was arrested for unlawfully soliciting a ride on the highway.[131] Although the officer conceded that he did not fear for his safety and had no reason to suspect the hitchhiker of carrying a dangerous weapon, he not only frisked the young man but also searched his two suitcases. In a separate incident,[132] three men were arrested on the same road at 5:30 A.M. for the offense of walking on the highway at night without a light. The officers were "not satisfied, under the circumstances, with [the] information [the men] furnished as to origin or destination." Pat-down searches of the three men uncovered no weapons, but before taking the men and their luggage to a magistrate, one of the officers searched a bedroll and a laundry bag belonging to one of them. The court held in both cases that the luggage searches were proper because the arrestees could have gained access to weapons. The officers had no reason to suspect that any of the arrestees were armed, but if that was really their concern it would have been easy enough, as the lower court pointed out, to place the luggage in the trunk of the police car.[133]

In many of the cases involving pedestrians, the conduct of the police seems to go so far beyond the legitimate needs of law enforcement that one can only conclude that the officer deliberately staged the encounter in the hope of finding incriminating evidence. These cases will be discussed in the following chapter.

[130] People v. Mercurio, 10 Cal. App. 3d 426, 88 Cal. Rptr. 750 (1970).

[131] State v. Culver, 288 A.2d 279 (Del. 1972). The court explains that "[i]t is the prevailing police practice in Delaware to take non-resident hitchhikers into custody when they are very young, unable to give satisfactory answers as to identification or destination, or otherwise appear to be possible runaways or fugitives" (*ibid.*, 281).

[132] The cases are decided in a single opinion (*ibid.*).

[133] The court insists that "[w]e are satisfied that the arrests in these cases were . . . not pretextual for the real purpose of searching for drugs" (288 A.2d at 285). It is worth noting, however, that the individuals stopped in the daytime were arrested for hitchhiking, while the men stopped at 5:30 A.M., when soliciting a ride would have been a rather implausible activity, were arrested for failure to have a light.

VII

Selective Enforcement
and Harassment

In its tally of the costs of laws against marijuana possession the Shafer commission includes "the distinct impression among the youth that some police may use the marijuana laws to arrest people they don't like for other reasons, whether it be their politics, their hair style or their ethnic background. Whether or not such selectivity actually exists, it is perceived to exist." [1] The commission need not have expressed the point so tentatively, for substantial evidence supports the conclusion that marijuana laws are enforced not only selectively but often in a manner that may be termed harassment.

The term *selective enforcement* can refer to a wide spectrum of law enforcement practices, depending on who makes the selection and the basis on which it is made. For example, in some jurisdictions Sunday closing laws have been enforced regularly against large discount houses and supermarkets while the smaller "ma and pa" stores are allowed to remain open. This is selective enforcement, but the distinction is arguably one which the legislature itself could have made, consistent with the Equal Protection clause.[2] In the context of marijuana laws, selective enforcement usually means something different and less admirable. As Kaplan puts it, "Since there are far too many marijuana violators for the police to arrest or even investigate more than a small fraction, the police are forced to pick and choose among possible violators." The result is that

[1] National Commission on Marihuana and Drug Abuse, *Marihuana: A Signal of Misunderstanding,* 146.
[2] See Wayne LaFave, *Arrest: The Decision to Take a Suspect into Custody* (Boston, 1965), 73, 81.

the police "arrest for marijuana violations those who they feel should be dealt with for entirely different reasons." [3]

The reasons why individuals are singled out as targets of investigation are usually grounded in political or cultural antipathy. It is difficult to avoid the conclusion that John Sinclair, Leslie Fiedler, and Lee Otis Johnson were subjected to investigation because of their political activities.[4] More often, the police focus their attention on an individual because of his appearance, his life-style, or his friends. That kind of selectivity can seldom be proved, but occasionally a policeman is candid—or naïve—enough to reveal the considerations that prompted a particular investigation.

In Fort Collins, Colorado, after arresting one juvenile for possession of marijuana, a police officer proceeded to arrest and search all eight of the other juveniles who were with him. The officer stated that the arrests were based on his conclusion that hippies were more likely to possess narcotics than other members of the public. Only one of the eight was found in possession of anything incriminating—marijuana debris scraped from the pocket of a coat that the youth was wearing but did not own. The court commented, "This mass arrest, based upon the theory that birds of a feather flock together, cannot be sustained." [5] That same discredited theory, however, must have been what prompted the investigation of a rock musician staying at a motel in Minnesota. He had not been implicated in any unlawful activity, but "some of [his] associates occupying rooms on another floor were known to have possessed and smoked marijuana." [6]

[3] John Kaplan, *Marijuana: The New Prohibition*, 41.

[4] See *supra* pp. 61–62, 80–81 (Sinclair), 63–64, 92 (Fiedler), and 62–63 (Johnson). The reader may point out that Sinclair, Fiedler, and Johnson were all convicted. What is more important is that all three convictions were ultimately reversed—and on grounds that were far from being "technicalities." Sinclair's conviction was overturned on various grounds, including a holding that he had been entrapped into giving the two joints to the undercover officer (People v. Sinclair, 387 Mich. 91, 115–23, 194 N.W.2d 878, 887–91 [1972]). Two of the six participating judges accepted the entrapment defense; the others did not pass upon it. Fiedler's conviction was reversed on the ground that "no crime was charged or proven" (People v. Fiedler, 31 N.Y. 2d 176, 178, 286 N.E.2d 878, 879, 335 N.Y.S.2d 377, 378 [1972]). Johnson was set free on habeas corpus when the federal district court found that prejudicial publicity had made impossible for him to have a fair trial (Johnson v. Beto, 337 F. Supp. 1371 [S.D. Tex. 1972]). Moreover, we have no way of knowing whether other unpopular political figures may have been subjected to investigations which uncovered no evidence of marijuana use.

[5] People v. Feltch, 483 P.2d 1335, 1337 (Colo. 1971).

[6] State v. Buchwald, 293 Minn. 74, 83–84, 196 N.W.2d 445, 451 (1972) (Otis, J., dissenting).

In Wyoming, police officers entered a house and found marijuana plants. "It [was] . . . freely admitted," the court notes, that "the officers had no reason to suspect that a crime had been committed or was being committed. The only reason given for having defendant under surveillance was the manner in which he wore his hair and the kind of motor vehicle he drove." The court then adds, in what one hopes was intended as an understatement, "This would not constitute reasonable cause for entering and searching defendant's home without a warrant." [7]

Sometimes the thrust behind an investigation is not admitted but can be inferred from the conduct of the police. Paul Chevigny, who investigated many narcotics arrests as a staff attorney for the New York Civil Liberties Union, describes a case in which the police shouldered their way into an apartment just as a guest was leaving. They arrested the householder and two of his guests for possession of marijuana, but released a third guest after searching him and made no attempt to arrest a fourth. Chevigny was puzzled about what had prompted the police raid, since there was no way in which the officers could have seen what was going on inside the apartment. He learned that "White [the householder] was known as a hippie in the neighborhood, and his apartment was likely to be identified as a place where narcotics users hung out. Everyone thought that the police had been waiting for the chance to arrest White, and this appeared to be correct since other people in the apartment had been so casually released." [8]

The evils of using the marijuana laws as a device for persecuting unpopular political figures need hardly be spelled out. Scarcely less obvious are the evils of investigating individuals for marijuana violations because of their long hair or their pot-smoking friends. Under either of these rationales the police are proceeding on a theory of guilt by association.

From the standpoint of efficient law enforcement, guilt by association appears to make a good deal of sense. Experience tells us that if the police hope to find and apprehend persons who violate the marijuana laws, they do better to look for them in rock bands and hippie communes than in Rotary clubs and old-age homes. Similarly (although the conclusion is more tenuous), an individual whose friends are known to use marijuana is probably more likely to be found in possession of *Cannabis* than someone whose friends'

[7] Goddard v. State, 481 P.2d 343, 344 (Wyo. 1971).
[8] Paul Chevigny, *Police Power: Police Abuses in New York City,* 183–86.

only social drugs are alcohol and tobacco. Moving still further into the realm of inference, the police would sensibly go to greater lengths to search a man with long hair parking a flashy motorcycle in front of a "head shop" than a businessman with a crew cut leaving an expensive restaurant.

The flaw in this method of operation is twofold. First, the net sweeps far too wide. For every person in the various suspect categories who might be found to have violated the drug laws, there will be ten or a hundred others who will be innocent of any such offense. To condemn these law-abiding citizens to the loss of security and privacy which befalls anyone who becomes the target of police investigatory tactics is to pay a high price for apprehending the few who are guilty; yet that is the inevitable consequence of encouraging the police to investigate people on the basis of their recreations, their companions, or their styles of living. At the same time, we know from the Shafer commission's studies and from other reports that hundreds of thousands of people who use marijuana do not fit the various stereotypes. Housewives, businessmen, and even policemen turn on safely in their homes and at quiet parties;[9] unless they become careless or fall victim to some kind of freak occurrence they will never be apprehended at all. By virtue of their conventional appearance and life-styles they have been "selected out" from the enforcement of the marijuana laws.

Selective enforcement of the marijuana laws is bad enough. Some policemen go further: they investigate or arrest people for other crimes—often misdemeanors—in the hope of discovering that the individual has violated the more serious marijuana laws. It is this practice that I have termed *harassment*.[10]

Police officers seldom acknowledge that the ostensible reason for stopping or arresting a person was no more than a pretext to permit a search for marijuana, but every now and then the harassment is conceded. In Oklahoma, for example, a narcotics officer testified that he asked a policeman from a neighboring city to stop a car for speeding so that the narcotics officer could search the vehicle for marijuana.[11]

[9] See Nancy Mayer, "How the Middle Class Turns On," *New York,* Oct. 20, 1969, p. 42.

[10] In other words, "selective enforcement" refers to the way in which the police enforce the marijuana laws; harassment refers to the use of other laws in order to obtain marijuana convictions. The terminology used here differs from that used by Chevigny, *supra* note 8, at 219.

[11] Sam v. State, 500 P.2d 291 (Okla. Crim. 1972).

Sometimes the harassment is not admitted but the facts leave no room for any other conclusion. In reversing a court-martial conviction, the Court of Military Appeals commented, "One cannot read the testimony of the Government's witnesses . . . without gaining the abiding impression that the entire proceedings were designed to apprehend the accused in the apartment ostensibly for unauthorized absence and thereby to gain a pretext for making an otherwise unauthorized search for narcotics." [12] The New Jersey court, in the "noisy party" case described earlier, said, "We have here a classic example of a search grounded on mere suspicion, a suspicion which the officers hoped would turn up some incriminating evidence. . . . In our view, the noise abatement reason for the entry and search served as nothing more than a smoke screen." [13] In several cases courts have concluded that police officers arrested drivers for minor traffic violations only as a pretext to enable the officer to search for marijuana on the driver's person or in his car.[14]

In Milwaukee three officers from the narcotics division visited an apartment at 10:30 one night, supposedly to arrest Melvin Dodd on an assault and battery warrant. When they arrived, they found that Dodd had been living with a woman, not his wife, for about a month. The officers arrested Dodd for lewd and lascivious conduct and then searched the apartment. In a small closet one of the officers found a sweater belonging to Dodd. Upon going through its pockets he found two seeds of marijuana. Dodd was arrested and convicted for possession. The state claimed that because Dodd was wearing pajamas, the officers were entitled to search his clothing to make sure that he obtained no weapons while dressing. It was also claimed that the officers might lawfully search for "evidence and fruits" of the crime of lewd and lascivious behavior, such as clothing, rent receipts, and keys. The Wisconsin Supreme Court rejected these contentions and reversed the conviction. Justice Hallows remarked,

[T]he search seems . . . [to have been] an exploratory search for narcotics without a search warrant. . . .

It seems rather strange that three police officers of the narcotics

[12] United States v. Santo, 20 U.S.C.M.A. 294, 295, 43 C.M.R. 134, 135 (1971).
[13] State v. Allen, 113 N.J. Super. 245, 250–51, 273 A.2d 587, 590–91 (1970), *supra* pp. 91–92.
[14] See, e.g., Blazek v. Eyman, 339 F. Supp. 40 (D. Ariz. 1971); Taglavore v. United States, 291 F.2d 262 (9th Cir. 1961); Amador-Gonzales v. United States, 391 F.2d 308 (5th Cir. 1968).

division of the vice squad were necessary to arrest an ordinary citizen at 10:30 at night for a battery if that was all that was involved. A search for weapons in the clothing to be worn by Dodd would hardly include such a minute search of a pocket in a shirt as would disclose two seeds of marijuana. . . . Not much more can be said for the search for evidence or fruits of the crime of lewd and lascivious behavior. . . .[15]

When the police are less candid or the evidence more ambiguous, harassment cannot be proved. In Seattle, for example, two plainclothesmen saw "an individual with long hair, nondescriptly clothed," jaywalking through traffic. The officers got out of their unmarked patrol car and asked the man, whose name was James Henneke, to produce identifying indicia so that they could prepare a citation. Henneke failed to produce any identification. When asked about his place of employment and residence, he replied that he traveled for a California corporation and lived "all over." One of the officers then told him that it would be necessary to arrest him and take him to police headquarters for booking. Before placing Henneke in the police car the officer "asked permission" (as the courts puts it) to search him. Henneke removed his hands from his jacket pockets, saying nothing. During the ensuing search the officer placed his hands in the jacket pockets, where he found a wad of tissue paper containing marijuana. Henneke was then arrested for unlawful possession.[16]

In sustaining Henneke's conviction, the Washington Supreme Court said, "There is no evidence in the record indicating, or which would sustain an inference to the effect that the officers were utilizing the misdemeanor involved as a ruse to conduct a search for narcotics. . . . On the contrary, the evidence indicates the discovery of the marijuana involved was fortuitous." Perhaps so. One would have to know whether Seattle plainclothesmen ordinarily arrest short-haired businessmen wearing suits and ties for jaywalking before one could conclude that the jaywalking arrest in this case was "a ruse to conduct a search for narcotics." Nevertheless, it is worth pointing out that Henneke was searched only because he could not, or would not, produce "identifying indicia"; the businessman is unlikely to be placed in that position. Even if one ac-

[15] State v. Dodd, 28 Wis. 2d 643, 646–47, 137 N.W.2d 465, 467 (1965).
[16] State v. Henneke, 78 Wash. 2d 147, 470 P.2d 176 (1970). As noted in the text, Henneke did not object to the search, but the court does not hold that his silence implied consent.

cepts the *a priori* legitimacy of the arrest, the fact that the officer then searched *inside* Henneke's jacket pocket raises some questions about his motives. The court found the search to be justifiable on the ground that Henneke might have been carrying a weapon, but as a Connecticut court pointed out in a very similar case, it will ordinarily be sufficient to pat down the suspect in order to search for weapons.[17] If the officer feels nothing which resembles a concealed weapon but continues with the search anyway, there is a strong implication that he was looking for something else.

In Brunswick, Georgia, a police officer virtually admitted that he stopped and questioned a young pedestrian, whose conduct was not otherwise suspicious, because of his long hair.[18] He then subjected the youth to a meticulous and humiliating search,[19] in the course of which a "very small bag" of marijuana was found. The court does not state whether it considered the initial stop to have been a subterfuge, but the opinion reversing the conviction emphasizes the obvious hostility of the officer toward the pedestrian. Unlike his counterpart in Seattle, the Georgia officer did not even claim that he was looking for weapons. In the light of these facts, it seems more than likely that he was searching for marijuana.

Similarly, in many of the cases in which marijuana is found after a vehicle has been stopped for a traffic offense, harassment cannot be *proved*, although the facts may strongly suggest it. In Houston, for example, a police officer detained a motorist supposedly because the latter had failed to signal before making a right turn into a private driveway from an otherwise deserted street at eleven o'clock at night. Nothing is said about the driver's hair or appearance, but one wonders if Houston policemen ordinarily arrest drivers who neglect to signal their turns under those circumstances. The Texas

[17] State v. Anonymous, 6 Conn. Cir. 583, 280 A.2d 816 (1971).

[18] Holtzendorf v. State, 125 Ga. App. 747, 188 S.E.2d 879 (1972). The cross-examination is revealing:

Q. But also, the fact that the boy had long hair had something to do with it, too, didn't it?

A. Possibly. Anytime you see a long hair, you got a, it goes along with the rest of them.

Q. I mean, you and I are human beings that are normal, and long hair is not, it's indicative of something, a movement other than what you and I may agree with?

A. That's the way I see it. . . . You can see how I believe.

[19] "The defendant was ordered to stand with his back to the officer and hands against the roof of the police car and was subjected to a minute search, in the course of which his pants came unbuttoned and he was forced to remove his shoes" (125 Ga. App. at 748, 188 S.E.2d at 880).

court apparently thought not, for it reversed the driver's conviction for possession, saying that "[t]here are no facts . . . shown which would warrant the detaining of the appellant. . . ." [20]

A police officer in Kansas City, Missouri, stopped a motorist for parking too far from the curb, in violation of a city ordinance, at ten o'clock at night. The officer went to the front of the vehicle to obtain the city license number printed on a sticker affixed to the windshield. He shone his flashlight on the sticker; while doing so, he observed on the front seat of the car a hand-rolled cigarette which he "reasonably believed" to contain marijuana. The court upheld the subsequent arrest, but again one wonders if Kansas City policemen ordinarily write citations for drivers who park too far from the curb at 10 P.M.[21]

In Carrollton, Georgia, a man parked his car, and he and his companions started walking down the street. After walking about 150 feet, they were stopped by policemen and ordered to get into the police car. The only reason given for the detention was that "the city police had been earlier notified by the campus police of West Georgia College to be on the lookout for a car fitting the description of defendant's because a college parking ticket had been placed on the car as it was not registered on campus and the campus police wanted to advise the defendant that he would have to pay the parking fine." After the campus police were informed that the driver had been found, he and his car were searched.[22]

It may be argued that cases like these, no matter how numerous, do not support the conclusion that harassment is taking place. After all, are not the police justified in stopping a driver who has failed to signal his turn or whose headlights are not functioning? Has not the Supreme Court upheld the right of the police to stop

---

[20] Willett v. State, 454 S.W.2d 398, 400 (Tex. Crim. App. 1970). The court may also have been skeptical about the officer's claim as to how the marijuana was found. After pulling into the driveway, the officer ordered the motorist and his two passengers to get into the back seat of his patrol car. The officer then drove two blocks to a service station to check the motorist's identification by phone. After completing the call, the officer returned to the patrol car and asked one of the men—not the driver—to step out. At that time, according to his testimony, he saw the driver reach down as if placing something on the floor. The officer then asked the driver to step out. He looked on the floor where the driver had been sitting and found a penny matchbox which appeared to contain marijuana. What may have puzzled the Court of Criminal Appeals is why, if the motorist was carrying contraband, he waited until the officer was returning from the phone to dispose of it, rather than doing so while the officer was making the call.

[21] State v. Hawkins, 482 S.W.2d 477 (Mo. 1972).

[22] Davidson v. State, 125 Ga. App. 502, 188 S.E.2d 124 (1972).

suspicious persons on the street and frisk them for weapons? [23] And is it not possible that many police officers routinely engage in unlawful searches of all pedestrians or persons arrested for traffic violations but that the courts see only those found in possession of marijuana or other illegal drugs? [24] In short, the argument goes, the evidence proves only that the police are sometimes overzealous in enforcing traffic laws, in anticipating mischief on the streets, and in seeking to ferret out evidence of possessory crimes.

The difficulty with this line of argument is that the harassment lies not so much in the search as in the initial arrest or stop. As a Missouri judge has pointed out, "[f]ew drivers . . . can drive any considerable distance without violating some traffic law or ordinance." [25] But the police do not stop every driver who violates a traffic law; they are more likely to stop a driver whose long hair or "nondescript" clothing suggests to them that he may be carrying marijuana. Similarly, when observing pedestrians on the street, the policeman may focus his attention on "hippy type[s]" [26] or on young people with long hair, and behavior which would ordinarily go unnoticed—someone's keeping his hand in his pocket [27] or turning away from the policeman's glance [28]—takes on an aura of suspicion that may trigger an investigatory stop. These predilections—regardless of whether the officer consciously hopes to find marijuana—can appropriately be called harassment.

In December, 1970, the American Civil Liberties Union filed suit against the New Jersey State Police, charging that the police were pursuing a systematic policy of illegally searching long-haired persons traveling the major highways of the state.[29] The plaintiffs were thirty-seven persons who had been stopped and searched within the preceding two years. The thirty-seven cases produced ten arrests, about half of them for marijuana possession. According to the complaint, the police often arrested drivers for alleged motor

[23] Terry v. Ohio, 392 U.S. 1 (1968), *supra* pp. 124–26.

[24] See People v. Lingo, 3 Cal. App. 3d 661, 664, 83 Cal. Rptr. 755, 757 (1970): "It was admitted that these officers 'routinely' questioned all persons detained for any reason if they had narcotics." Would the officers put those questions to a conservatively dressed businessman or housewife?

[25] State v. Robinson, 447 S.W.2d 71, 74 (Mo. 1969) (concurring opinion).

[26] Holtzendorf v. State, 125 Ga. App. at 750, 188 S.E.2d at 881, *supra* p. 138.

[27] People v. Woods, 6 Cal. App. 3d 832, 86 Cal. Rptr. 264 (1970), *supra* pp. 128 and 129–30.

[28] People v. Courtney, 11 Cal. App. 3d 1185, 90 Cal. Rptr. 370 (1970), *supra* p. 127.

[29] *N.Y. Times,* Dec. 12, 1970, p. 25, col. 3.

vehicle violations, then used the arrest as an excuse to search the car. Although the police denied the charges at the time, one and one-half years later a sergeant assigned to the New Jersey Turnpike admitted that "[s]ome of the men were stopping long-haired motorists a few years ago because they were confident of coming up with narcotics." (He added that the practice stopped when "everyone began wearing long hair, and [the police] were stopping lawyers and teachers.") [30] More recently, in Long Island, New York, police indiscriminately stopped and searched dozens of cars as they exited from a parkway onto access roads leading to Nassau Coliseum, where a rock concert was to be held. The tactic was abandoned for later concerts when observers from the American Civil Liberties Union stood by to protect against illegal searches.[31]

New opportunities for harassment are provided by the airport searches instituted in the 1970's to foil hijackers. Some government officials have conceded privately that there are agents who have searched passengers on the pretext of looking for weapons "when they actually suspected that the passenger carried contraband." [32]

The effects of harassment on its victims—or on those who by virtue of their age [33] or hair length or manner of dress are potential victims—need not be belabored. Kaplan's comments about selective enforcement apply even more strongly to harassment: it "heightens the sense of differential treatment . . . which contributes to the hostility of three groups that we might most wish to bring into the mainstream of our society: the alienated middle-class drug user, the high-school youth, and the inhabitants of our urban Negro and Spanish-American ghettos." [34] If a black man, a teenager, or a man with long hair cannot take a walk or drive a car without the fear that he may be stopped at any time by a police officer hoping to find marijuana, his estrangement from the dominant culture may understandably turn into rage and even rebellion.

It should not be thought, however, that widespread harassment is bad only for the victims; the adverse effects also extend to the police themselves, and through them to society. It is hardly conducive to effective law enforcement if large numbers of policemen

---

[30] *N.Y. Times,* July 7, 1972, p. 33, col. 8.

[31] *N.Y. Times,* May 15, 1973, p. 41, col. 1.

[32] *N.Y. Times,* Nov. 26, 1972, § 1, p. 1, col. 1; p. 81, col. 3.

[33] See Reich, "Police Questioning of Law Abiding Citizens," 75 *Yale L. J.* 1161, 1165 (1966).

[34] Kaplan, *supra* note 3, at 43.

feel that they ought to investigate anyone who drives through town with long hair or hippie clothing on the chance that he may be carrying marijuana. To begin with, the policeman who is constantly on the lookout for possible drug law violators will probably not be able to devote as much attention as he should to detecting other behavior that may more immediately threaten society. Beyond this, a policeman cannot function effectively in a nontotalitarian country if he regards anyone with long hair or nondescript clothes as a "symbolic assailant" [35] to be combatted rather than as a constituent to be aided and, if need be, called upon to give aid. The nightstick and the gun are powerful weapons, but in a free society the authority of the police depends ultimately on the moral support and cooperation of the citizenry—as recent incidents in and out of ghetto areas have reminded us.[36]

It may be argued that if so many policemen are truly intent on harassing longhairs or hippies they will find a way to do so, and the repeal of the marijuana laws will not make a difference. For example, one writer contends that "[i]f Jerry Rubin had not been arrested three times for marijuana violations, he, like many of us, could probably have been arrested for something else." [37] This may be true for Jerry Rubin, but it is not necessarily true for less notorious members of the counterculture. Policemen, Jerome Skolnick has observed, "tend to polarize the population between respectable people and criminals." [38] Under present laws, anyone who uses marijuana is a criminal. The policeman, however, does not ordinarily see people using marijuana. What he does see are individuals who share traits which he associates with marijuana use—long hair, for example, or hippie clothing, or residence in a commune. By a process of transference he begins to assume that men with long hair or persons who live in a commune are more likely to be criminals than "respectable people." As Skolnick puts it, "If the policeman's job is to observe [and investigate] deviations from 'normality,' a more rigid definition of normality will make him more watchful and suspicious." [39] When marijuana use is proclaimed to be a deviation from normality, and that deviation is

---

[35] Jerome Skolnick, *Justice without Trial,* 45.

[36] See President's Commission on Law Enforcement and Administration of Justice, *Task Force Report: The Police* (Washington, D.C., 1967), 224.

[37] Schneyer, "Problems in the Cost-Benefit Analysis of Marijuana Legislation," 24 *Stan. L. Rev.* 200, 205 (1971).

[38] Skolnick, *supra* note 35, at 218.

[39] *Ibid.,* 206–7.

commonly found among persons with long hair or nondescript clothing, then it is only natural for policemen to be watchful for and suspicious of longhairs or hippies.

Of course, neither "normality" nor the parameters of police suspicion are defined solely by the penal system, but the fact of criminality is crucial in two contexts: the policeman's relationship to his superiors, and his relationship to the public. Within the police organization the laws are important because they tend to legitimize the harassment I have described. As long as commonplace transactions in marijuana are against the law, large numbers of policemen will feel justified in using the investigation of other offenses as a pretext to apprehend persons who they suspect are guilty of marijuana crimes. If the investigation uncovers evidence confirming their suspicions, they—and their superiors—will tend to feel that the pretext was justified.[40] If there were no marijuana laws, so that the policeman could not expect to uncover evidence of a more serious crime, it would be much harder to justify the harassment.[41]

The law's definition of normality also affects the relationship between the policeman and the public. As Chevigny suggests, "Policemen are clever enough to know that the impulse to control morality through punishment runs directly against the increasingly rigid protection of due process of law by the courts, and they recognize that any lingering public demand for due process, as compared with the demand for a crime cleanup, must be largely hypocritical." [42] Thus, the criminalization of marijuana tends to persuade the policeman that anything goes in detecting violators of the marijuana laws. By the same token, if the laws are repealed the police would have less reason to think that the public supports the use of any means that are effective in apprehending marijuana users. Harassment of the kind I have described would lose much of its aura of legitimacy.

[40] *Cf. ibid.,* 221, 223.

[41] Of course, the policeman might still engage in harassment in the hope of finding other illegal drugs, but the temptation would be substantially reduced. First, because the incidence of use is relatively low, the odds that the person stopped will be in possession of these other drugs will be much smaller. Stopping people in the hope of finding pills or powders will seldom be worth the effort. Second, because other drugs are much more compact and do not require bulky paraphernalia, it will usually be impossible for the officer who finds them to plausibly claim that he was looking for something else—for example, a weapon. This means that it will be difficult for the policeman to persuade either a judge or his superior officer that the search was made in good faith.

[42] Chevigny, *supra* note 8, at 234.

The considerations just advanced suggest that under the commission's partial prohibition scheme police behavior might remain pretty much as it is today. Outside of the home, possession or distribution of marijuana would be no less illegal—except possession of one ounce or less; and that ounce would be contraband. The laws would thus continue to give legitimacy to the harassment of individuals who the police think are likely to be carrying marijuana. The fact that possession of one ounce or less would no longer be a crime is of little significance; as Chevigny has suggested, the police will often be content "to obtain the contraband and get it out of circulation, while making life difficult for those who possessed it." [43]

[43] *Ibid.*, 209.

VIII

Chance and Stupidity

The preceding chapters have emphasized that a high proportion of marijuana arrests result from police misbehavior or from investigatory tactics that significantly infringe individual privacy, whether or not they fail to comport with current constitutional standards.[1] Indeed, because marijuana is ordinarily used and distributed in private among individuals who are not likely to tell outsiders about their activities, such a conclusion might well be justified in the vast majority of cases. Occasionally, however, arrests result from chance discoveries of marijuana or from foolhardy behavior that seems to invite the attention of the police. In neither of these situations do the marijuana laws emerge with flying colors.

Marijuana is often discovered under unforeseen, even bizarre, circumstances. Indeed, Kaplan suggests that for the middle-class user, arrests *usually* occur because of some "freak occurrence."[2] Consider the following examples: A woman in Florida was taken to a hospital after being injured in an auto accident. While she was being prepared for the physical examination by a hospital attendant, a bottle of marijuana fell from her brassiere.[3] In California hospital attendants found marijuana while searching for identification in the clothing of a man brought to the hospital unconscious as the result of a severe knife wound.[4] Firemen extinguishing a blaze in a

[1] It must be emphasized again that tactics which are constitutional may nevertheless invade individual privacy and security. See *infra* pp. 163–64.
[2] Kaplan, "Forward, Marijuana Laws: An Empirical Study of Enforcement and Administration in Los Angeles County," 15 *U.C.L.A. L. Rev.* 1501, 1505 (1968).
[3] Adams v. State, 240 So. 2d 529 (Fla. App. 1970).
[4] People v. Gonzales, 182 Cal. App. 2d 276, 5 Cal. Rptr. 920 (1960).

home in New York became suspicious about large quantities of dry vegetable material in the kitchen. They told the police, who found 722 pounds of marijuana on the premises.[5] A girl arriving at the Cincinnati airport mistakenly picked up a suitcase containing 50 pounds of the drug. She called the sheriff, and with the girl's help a trap was set for the owner.[6]

Even if the police were to abandon all questionable tactics so that the majority of marijuana arrests resulted from chance discoveries such as these, the marijuana laws would still not be put in a very good light. Those arrested would tend, as Kaplan suggests, "neither to respect the majesty of the law which has caught them, nor to realize that, after all, they did take their chances. Rather, they [would] tend to chalk it up as a very bad break." [7] More important, it is hardly a recommendation for a law that its enforcement depends in a significant part on the bad luck of those who violate it.

Whether chance actually plays an important role in the enforcement of marijuana laws is difficult to say. The reason is that discoveries of marijuana that appear on the surface to be fortuitous may in fact result from encounters deliberately staged by the police—or even by private citizens [8]—in the hope of finding incriminating evidence. In Oklahoma, for example, two police officers stopped a pedestrian to ask if he knew the whereabouts of his girlfriend, who had just escaped from a state mental institution. The officers "detected the strong odor of marijuana" on the man's person. They took him into custody, searched him, and found two partially smoked joints and a matchbox containing marijuana. The trial court found that "there was absolutely no subterfuge here," but it is worth noting that the officers had previously been informed that the man they stopped had been in possession of marijuana. Can the arrest be laid to chance? Only the officers know.[9]

Many of the cases described in the preceding chapters point up the difficulty of attempting to distinguish between chance discoveries of marijuana and those resulting from harassment. A particular incident may be fortuitous in the sense that the individual has done

---

[5] *N.Y. Times,* July 4, 1972, p. 7, col. 2.
[6] *N.Y. Times,* May 30, 1972, p. 46, col. 8.
[7] Kaplan, *supra* note 2, at 1505.
[8] See *supra* pp. 74–75.
[9] Ellis v. State, 476 P.2d 352 (Okla. Crim. 1970).

something (often quite innocent) to bring him to the attention of the wrong policeman at the wrong time.[10] At the same time, the policeman may have focused his attention on the individual because of the latter's dress, hairstyle, or general appearance. Even the officer himself may not be able to separate the elements of chance and purposefulness in his actions. Indeed, it may well be that until large numbers of policemen cease to regard the counterculture as a hostile force, individuals who appear to be part of that group will continue to have more than their share of fortuitous encounters with police officers. Decriminalization of marijuana will not alone change police attitudes, but together with the growing acceptance and use of marijuana by social groups with whom the policeman identifies, it can be expected to provide a powerful impetus for change.

Sometimes marijuana arrests result from behavior by users that seems to invite apprehension. In Hawaii a group of people sat around a picnic table in a public park passing from hand to hand a pipe containing marijuana. Three police officers were watching them as they smoked.[11] A Stanford University student kept thirty-eight small plastic bags of marijuana in his locker in a university library. The bags also contained a preservative that permeated the room with a smell described variously as resembling that of sweet applies, sour wine, and vomit.[12] Two men in Los Angeles squatted down behind an automobile in the parking lot of a taco stand at six o'clock one morning, passing a joint back and forth between them.[13] A man in Milwaukee offered to sell some marijuana to a drugstore clerk whom he had never met (though the clerk did know the girl who accompanied the man).[14] In Fort Collins, Colorado, a man went to the police department to help a friend who had been arrested for the alleged theft of a bicycle. In his shirt pocket he

[10] For example, an individual may find himself subjected to police scrutiny because he has smoked a cigarette in a particular way (see Schmitt v. State, 497 P.2d 891 [Nev. 1972]); because he happens to be in an area where a crime has been committed (see People v. Nickles, 9 Cal. App. 3d 986, 88 Cal. Rptr. 763 [1970]); because he is carrying bulky gloves in his pocket (see People v. Erdman, 69 Misc. 2d 103, 329 N.Y.S.2d 654 [1972]); or for an infinite variety of other reasons.

[11] State v. Hogue, 486 P.2d 403 (Hawaii 1971).

[12] People v. Lanthier, 5 Cal. 3d 751, 488 P.2d 625, 97 Cal. Rptr. 297 (1971).

[13] People v. Beal, 268 Cal. App. 2d 481, 73 Cal. Rptr. 787 (1969).

[14] State v. Paszek, 50 Wis. 2d 619, 184 N.W.2d 836 (1971).

was carrying a small aluminum foil–wrapped package containing hashish.[15]

The reader may not have much sympathy for people who smoke marijuana out in the open or who offer to sell the drug to a stranger. Nevertheless, however foolish such behavior might be, the fact that it can continue in the face of active and widely publicized efforts by law enforcement officials to control marijuana may suggest a significant point about American society. In spite of the ever-increasing use of surveillance, wiretapping, and other intrusive practices by police and FBI agents, most people—even those who have great reason to be secretive about some of their activities—continue to think of America as an open society. They assume that their neighbors and acquaintances will not turn informer. They assume that they are not being watched by police officers ready to arrest them at the slightest hint of a misdemeanor. They trust strangers. The reader who believes that marijuana presents a significant danger to society might well ask whether the attempt to suppress it is worth the price of destroying this sense of openness and trust.

It may be suggested that society is hardly benefited if a sense of openness or trust leads people to believe that they can violate the law in the sight of witnesses without fearing that someone will inform the police of their activities. Would it be desirable for the mugger or burglar to feel free to commit his crime, confident that his fellow men will not betray him? [16] The difference, I suggest, lies in the nature of the crime involved. While the term *victimless crime* may be criticized as question-begging,[17] it seems clear that if society is harmed at all by the use of marijuana, the harm is of a much lower order of magnitude than the harm resulting from a mugging or a burglary. The harm is indirect; it is impersonal (one cannot point to an identifiable individual victim); it is intangible.[18] Even the most passionate opponents of marijuana use would be

---

[15] People v. Ware, 484 P.2d 103 (Colo. 1971). This is another case in which the arrest may not have been as fortuitous as it seems. The bicycle which Ware's friend had been accused of stealing belonged to Ware, and Ware came to the police station to explain that he had given his friend permission to use it. How often do the police arrest someone for the theft of a bicycle that has not been reported as stolen? (It is perhaps worth noting that Ware was arrested by a narcotics detective who had third-hand information that Ware's name had in some unexplained manner been related to narcotics activities.)

[16] Cf. Abe Rosenthal, *Thirty-Eight Witnesses* (New York, 1964) (a woman was murdered as neighbors failed to respond to her screams for help).

[17] Cf. Herbert Packer, *The Limits of the Criminal Sanction*, 267.

[18] See *supra* pp. 6–9.

hard pressed to point to the harm resulting from the smoking of a single joint or the sale of a single lid.

Crimes against persons and property differ from marijuana offenses in a second relevant respect: the extent to which a consensus exists in society that the activity is wrong. Conduct like mugging or burglary or drunken driving is recognized by virtually everyone— including most of the individuals who commit such acts—to be wrong.[19] Thus, the would-be burglar who is reported to the police by an observant neighbor will probably curse his luck, but he is not likely to question the propriety of the neighbor's action.[20] No such agreement exists about marijuana. Further, many persons who believe that the use of marijuana is highly undesirable may nevertheless conclude that the use or distribution of the drug should not be criminalized.

In the light of these differences, it can be seen that the marijuana user's sense of trust is not and will not be shared by the burglar or the mugger. The naïveté that permits a person to smoke marijuana out in the open or offer to sell the drug to a stranger does not extend to the rapist or the thief. To preserve—or restore—the marijuana user's sense of openness will not encourage criminals to believe that they can violate the law in the sight of witnesses without fear of being reported.

[19] See Gusfield, "Moral Passage: The Symbolic Process in Public Designations of Deviance," 15 *Social Problems* 175, 178.

[20] The difference cannot be explained simply by the fact of personal contact between the would-be marijuana seller and the person who reports him. A man who offered a bribe to an Internal Revenue Service agent would not, I think, feel a sense of betrayal if the agent should report him (unless the agent had given him particular reason to believe that the bribe would be accepted).

IX

Police Perjury

Alan Watts, the philosopher, wrote recently that "our police forces are being corrupted . . . by being required to serve as armed clergymen enforcing sumptuary laws against 'crimes' without complaining victims." [1] *Corrupted* is a strong word, but not too strong to describe police officers who commit perjury in court in order to justify an arrest or search which results in a prosecution for violation of the marijuana laws. Unfortunately, researchers have compiled substantial evidence to suggest that many policemen do just that. This kind of corruption will continue as long as legislators demand enforcement of laws against marijuana and the Supreme Court requires lower courts to follow the Exclusionary Rule.

The high incidence of police perjury in marijuana trials stems from a conflict described by John Kaplan: "The policeman, caught between society's demands that, on the one hand, he enforce the laws against crimes for which no witnesses exist and, on the other hand, that he respect the constitutional imperative of probable cause before search may take the easy way out and simply make the arrest and lie about the probable cause." [2] The officer may "fudge" the evidence to justify either the search that uncovers the marijuana or the forcible stop that precedes the search. [3]

[1] Alan Watts, "Letter," *Harper's*, June, 1972, p. 10.
[2] Kaplan, "Forward, Marijuana Laws: An Empirical Study of Enforcement and Administration in Los Angeles County," 15 *U.C.L.A. L. Rev.* 1501, 1504 (1968).
[3] I use the term *forcible stop* to characterize any situation in which "a police officer accosts an individual and restrains his freedom to walk [or drive] away" (Terry v. Ohio, 392 U.S. 1, 16 [1968]).

As stated earlier, the "most basic constitutional rule" of search-and-seizure law is that "searches conducted outside the judicial process, without prior approval by judge or magistrate, are *per se* unreasonable under the Fourth Amendment—subject only to a few specifically established and well-delineated exceptions." [4] Some policemen lie on the witness stand in order to establish that marijuana was found in a search falling within one of those exceptions. Perjury may also follow as a consequence of the harassment or selective enforcement described earlier in this volume. A police officer is not likely to admit that he stopped a pedestrian because of his long hair or that he pursued a vehicle with a defective taillight because he thought the driver might be carrying marijuana. Instead, he misrepresents the circumstances of the forcible stop.

Sometimes *perjury* will be too strong a word to describe what the police witness has done. The policeman may not be a liar; rather, he may "construct an ex post facto description of the preceding events so that those conform to legal arrest [or search] requirements, whether in fact the events actually did so or not at the time of the arrest." [5] For example, government officials have admitted that some airport security agents who have searched passengers on the pretext of looking for weapons when they were actually looking for contraband "may have tailored their court testimony to conform with guidelines of . . . earlier court decisions." [6] At some point, however, the act of "reconstructing a set of complex happenings" in such a way that an appellate court will uphold the search becomes indistinguishable from actual perjury. Indeed, it is hard to say which presents a greater danger to the integrity of the police force: deliberate misstatements, or repeated reconstruction of events to the point that the officer himself may not always know where invention ends and reality begins.

Several patterns of police testimony commonly heard in marijuana cases are tantamount to perjury by anyone's standards. Three of these patterns have recently been subjected to judicial scrutiny. In New York, Criminal Court Judge Irving Younger focused on what has come to be known as "dropsy" testimony. The case,

---

[4] Coolidge v. New Hampshire, 403 U.S. 443, 454 (1971); Katz v. United States, 389 U.S. 347, 357 (1967); but see Telford Taylor, *Two Studies in Constitutional Interpretation* (Columbus, Ohio, 1969), 23–24. It is questionable whether the exceptions can accurately be said to be "well-delineated." See *supra* p. 90.

[5] Jerome Skolnick, *Justice without Trial*, 215.

[6] *N.Y. Times,* Nov. 26, 1972, § 1, p. 1, col. 1; p. 81, col. 3.

People v. *McMurty*,[7] was a paradigm of the genre. The police officer, Frisina, testified as follows:

> At 8:30 P.M. on July 23, 1970, I was on duty driving a patrol car. While stopped for a light at West 3rd Street and Broadway, I observed two men in a doorway of the building at 677 Broadway. One of these men—James McMurty, as I later learned—saw the patrol car and stepped out of the doorway. From his right hand he let drop a small plastic container. I got out of the patrol car and retrieved it. In my opinion, based upon a fair amount of experience, its contents were marijuana. I approached McMurty, who had begun to walk away, and asked him if the container was his. He said no. I said that I had seen him drop it and placed him under arrest.

The defendant told a completely different story: "On July 23, 1970, at 8:30 P.M., I was walking on Broadway near West 3rd Street when I saw Patrolman Frisina coming toward me. I knew that I had a container of marijuana in my pocket. I also knew, after twelve years of involvement with drugs and four or five prior convictions, that illegal-search-and-seizure was my only defense. The last thing I would do is drop the marijuana to the ground. I simply left it in my pocket. Frisina told me to get into a doorway. I obeyed, hoping that he would search me. He did just that, found the marijuana and arrested me." Cases virtually identical in their relevant facts could have been found in other jurisdictions.[8]

If the officer was telling the truth, the marijuana was lawfully seized after the defendant had abandoned it.[9] If the defendant was telling the truth, the marijuana was found in an unlawful search and could not be used as evidence against him. Judge Younger noted that if this were the first time a policeman had testified that a defendant dropped a packet of drugs to the ground, "the matter would be unremarkable. The extraordinary thing is that each year in our criminal courts policemen give such testimony in hundreds, perhaps thousands, of cases. . . . 'Usually the very language of the testimony is identical from one case to another.'" The judge concluded: "'Surely . . . not in *every* case was the defendant unlucky enough to drop his narcotics at the feet of a policeman. It follows that at least in some of these cases the police are lying.'" To com-

[7] 64 Misc. 2d 63, 314 N.Y.S.2d 194 (N.Y. City Crim. Ct. 1970). The court quotes the testimony of the officer and the suspect in "condensed but substantially verbatim form."
[8] See, e.g., State v. Boykins, 434 S.W.2d 484 (Mo. 1968).
[9] See *supra* p. 118.

bat the problem, Judge Younger proposed that dropsy testimony be "scrutinized with special caution" and rejected if there is "[t]he slightest independent contradiction of the policeman's testimony or corroboration of the defendant's testimony." [10]

In support of his conclusion Judge Younger cited Sally Barlow's study of police testimony in Manhattan narcotics cases before and after the Supreme Court's decision in *Mapp* v. *Ohio,* which required state courts to exclude evidence obtained as the result of an illegal search or seizure.[11] According to that study, the number (and proportion) of complaints alleging that the suspect dropped the contraband increased sharply for all groups of officers in the period immediately after *Mapp*. For uniform and plainclothes officers the percentage rose still further in 1966. The overall increases between 1960–61 and 1966 were striking: from 14 to 41 percent for the uniformed officers; from 10.6 to 33 percent for plainclothesmen. Similar increases were reported in the incidence of allegations that the suspect had the contraband in general view either "in hand" or "openly exposed in the premises." Conversely, allegations that the contraband was found hidden on the suspect's person, which were common in the period before *Mapp,* virtually disappeared.

The only practical conclusion to be drawn from these figures is the one stated by Paul Chevigny and implicitly accepted by Judge Younger: "[T]he proportion of abandonment cases rose because the police could no longer admit that they had made searches for narcotics without probable cause, but they were not inclined to forgo the practice entirely." [12] Less than a year after Judge Younger's decision, District Attorney Frank Hogan of New York County, one of the nation's most respected law enforcement officials, acknowledged in a brief submitted to the New York Court of Appeals that dropsy testimony is often perjured: "For the last ten years [since *Mapp* v. *Ohio*] participants in the system of justice . . . have privately and publicly expressed the belief that in some substantial but indeterminable percentage of dropsy cases, the testi-

[10] 64 Misc. 2d at 65, 67, 314 N.Y.S.2d at 195–96, 197–98. Judge Younger quoted from an article he had written a few years earlier, "The Perjury Routine," *The Nation,* May 8, 1967, p. 596.

[11] Mapp v. Ohio, 367 U.S. 643 (1961). The article cited by Judge Younger is Barlow, "Patterns of Arrest for Misdemeanor Narcotics Possession: Manhattan Police Practices 1960–62," 4 *Crim. L. Bull.* 549 (1968). The figures in the text are also drawn from a more comprehensive paper based on the same study, Note, "Effect of Mapp v. Ohio on Police Search-and-Seizure Practices in Narcotics Cases," 4 *Colum. J. L. & Soc. Problems* 87 (1968).

[12] Paul Chevigny, *Police Power: Police Abuses in New York City,* 188.

mony is tailored to meet the requirements of search-and-seizure rulings. . . . [I]t is very difficult in many such cases to distinguish between fact and fiction." [13] Mr. Hogan's concern was shared by three members of the court of appeals. Unfortunately, the majority rejected the prosecutor's suggestion that "the burden of proving the lawfulness of a search or seizure . . . be cast on the People in all narcotics and gambling cases when the search or seizure has been effected without a warrant." [14] Although the court urged trial judges and police departments to take measures to curtail "the alleged abuses," the majority refused to believe that "the police are systematically evading the mandate of Mapp by fabricating their testimony." [15] As the preceding paragraphs have suggested, the evidence is otherwise.[16]

Police perjury is also common in the "furtive gesture" cases,[17] as the California Supreme Court appeared to acknowledge in the *Kiefer* case in 1970. "[P]olice reliance on so-called 'furtive movements,' " the court suggested, "has on occasion been little short of a subterfuge. . . . [I]n order to conduct a search on the basis of mere suspicion or intuition, guilty significance has been claimed for gestures or surrounding circumstances that were equally or more likely to be wholly innocent." [18] The court cited an empirical study of marijuana law enforcement in Los Angeles County which commented on the "'almost total uniformity of the arrest reports." The study concluded: "The traffic officer appears to be aware that if he tailors his report to a certain style with certain facts, he will almost certainly have it accepted by the court." [19] A later study offered further basis for the court's skepticism.[20]

Perjured testimony claiming furtive gestures is far more difficult to detect than is perjured dropsy testimony. For one thing, the line

---

[13] Quoted in People v. Berrios, 28 N.Y. 2d 361, 370, 270 N.E.2d 709, 714, 321 N.Y.S.2d 884, 890–91 (1971) (dissenting opinion).

[14] 28 N.Y. 2d at 372, 270 N.E.2d at 716, 321 N.Y.S.2d at 893 (dissenting opinion).

[15] 28 N.Y. 2d at 368, 270 N.E.2d at 713, 321 N.Y.S.2d at 889.

[16] See, in addition to the authorities cited in the preceding notes, Comment, "Police Perjury in Narcotics 'Dropsy' Cases," 60 *Geo. L. J.* 507 (1971); Note, "Marijuana Laws: An Empirical Study of Enforcement and Administration in Los Angeles County," 15 *U.C.L.A. L. Rev.* 1501 (1968); Comment, "Possession of Marijuana in San Mateo County: Some Social Costs of Criminalization," 22 *Stan. L. Rev.* 101 (1969).

[17] See *supra* p. 116.

[18] People v. Superior Court of Yolo County (Kiefer), 3 Cal. 3d 807, 827, 478 P.2d 449, 462, 91 Cal. Rptr. 729, 742 (1970).

[19] Note, "Marijuana Laws," *supra* note 16, at 1534 n. 95.

[20] Comment, "Possession of Marijuana," *supra* note 16, at 116–17.

between fact and fiction is much dimmer: "[When] an officer searches a car without pausing to puzzle about constitutional probable cause and finds what he thought he might find, he may not have much trouble 'recalling' a furtive gesture." [21] Moreover, it will usually be extremely difficult to contradict the policeman's testimony: although "some [defense] attorneys have successfully gone to great lengths to prove that the officer could not have seen inside the car from his vantage point," [22] the want of a disinterested witness will usually foreclose the effective use of the remedial measures suggested by Judge Younger. As a result, unless furtive gesture testimony is to be rejected out of hand, policemen will continue to report such gestures as the justification for their searches.[23]

The "plain view" doctrine provides another fertile field for police perjury. As stated earlier, the theory is that no search takes place when an officer observes an object in plain view from a position where he has a right to be; if the officer sees an item that is contraband, he may seize it without a warrant. The problem is that police officers repeatedly claim to have seen incriminating objects in plain view under circumstances in which it seems extremely difficult to believe that they could have done so.

In Oregon, for example, an undercover agent claimed that while visiting a home in his "drug culture" manner of dress he saw a plastic bag of marijuana on a low table twelve to fifteen feet away on the other side of a room divider, the shelves of which were cluttered with books, stereo equipment, a large aquarium, a house plant, and other personal belongings. The only light in the room came from a single overhead bulb near the door; the far side of the room, where the table was located, was in shadow. The trial judge did not believe this feat of observation to have been possible.[24] In Minnesota, an officer testified that he could discern, from a distance of six or seven feet, that six cigarettes protruding from an open cigarette box were hand-rolled and therefore "probably contained marijuana." [25] In New York police officers claimed that

[21] *Ibid.*

[22] Note, "Marijuana Laws," *supra* note 16, at 1534 n. 96.

[23] *Cf.* People v. McMurty, 64 Misc. 2d at 66, 314 N.Y.S.2d at 198: "One is tempted to deal with [dropsy testimony] by suppressing 'dropsy' evidence out of hand; yet I cannot. Reason and settled rules of law lead the other way. . . ."

[24] State v. Alexander, 495 P.2d 41 (Ore. App. 1972). The circumstances of the agent's entry are discussed at *supra* pp. 66–67.

[25] State v. Buchwald, 293 Minn. 74, 77, 196 N.W.2d 445, 447 (1972). Other aspects of the case are discussed at *supra* p. 107. Otis, J., dissenting, forcefully questioned the assumption that a hand-rolled cigarette must contain marijuana (293 Minn. at 83, 196 N.W.2d at 450–51). See, in this connection, *supra* pp. 114–15.

they saw a youth standing outside a parked car at night pass four small envelopes to the driver of the car. Judge Keating, speaking for the New York Court of Appeals, commented that "it would seem impossible that these small envelopes [about the size of pay envelopes] could have been seen in daytime, let alone at night, from a car parked across the street." [26]

An extraordinary feat of visual acuity was reported by a sheriff's deputy in Jasper County, Missouri. He testified that while standing about fifty feet from a house at night he could see, through an "unobstructed kitchen window," a boy smoking "a small corncob pipe which had a piece of aluminum foil pulled down over the bowl, depressed in the center, with a rubber band tightly around it to hold the foil in place." [27] Natty Bumppo could hardly have done better.[28]

Judicial concern about police perjury was expressed in another context in a recent California case. The defendant had been arrested at Los Angeles International Airport by a U.S. marshal after a search of his carry-on luggage revealed a plastic bag containing marijuana. The marshal testified that the defendant had consented to the search; the defendant insisted that he had not. In support of his testimony, the defendant offered to introduce into evidence the result of a polygraph (lie detector) examination purporting to show that he had been telling the truth. The court held the evidence admissible and granted the defendant's motion to exclude the marijuana. The court did not state that the marshal must have been lying, although the implicit finding that the defendant was telling the truth leaves no room for any other conclusion.[29]

The evils of repeated police perjury need hardly be spelled out, but several points merit emphasis. First, we are dealing here not with the acts of a few overambitious officers but, as Skolnick has shown, with a practice that has become institutionalized and, indeed, a part of the police ethos.[30] Awareness of this development can only intensify the mistrust that many segments of the community have towards policemen.

[26] People v. Corrado, 22 N.Y. 2d 308, 313 n. 3, 239 N.E.2d 526, 528, 292 N.Y.S.2d 648, 651 (1968).

[27] State v. Erwin, 473 S.W.2d 394, 395 (Mo. 1971). Since the episode took place in March, with snow covering the ground, one may doubt that the window was open.

[28] Cf. Mark Twain, "Fenimore Cooper's Literary Offenses," in A Subtreasury of American Humor, ed. E. B. White and Katherine White (New York, 1941), 519.

[29] People v. Cutter, 12 Crim. L. Rptr. 2134 (Cal. Super. Ct. 1972).

[30] Skolnick, supra note 5, at 212–15.

Second, even if no one else knows with certainty that a police officer has perjured himself, the defendant will be aware of it.[31] To the alienation that results from his arrest for an act that he believes no more pernicious than drinking a cocktail or selling a bottle of liquor must be added the bitterness of the realization that his conviction has been accomplished through the unlawful conduct and false testimony of an agent of the government which convicted him.

Finally, the effect on the policeman himself must be considered. The fact that an officer repeatedly reconstructs the circumstances of a search for the benefit of a court does not necessarily mean that he will become generally less truthful or honest; as Kaplan has suggested, "police officers who would not dream of fabricating evidence to make the defendant look more guilty, take a very different attitude toward 'fudging a little' on a search and seizure point." [32] Nevertheless, the difference is one of degree, and the purpose is the same: to insure the conviction of a suspect who the policeman believes is guilty. Once a policeman has crossed the line, he may be less reluctant to take a longer step, especially when the cause appears equally worthy.

It is difficult to predict whether adoption of the Shafer commission's partial prohibition scheme would lead to a lower incidence of police perjury. If fewer individuals are prosecuted for marijuana offenses, there will presumably be fewer hearings on motions to suppress and fewer occasions for the police to reconstruct the events of an arrest or search; but one should not be too quick to assume that the number of prosecutions will decrease.[33] In the cases that do come before courts on motions to suppress there is little reason to expect significant change. When the issue is the constitutionality of the forcible stop preceding a search, the situation would remain exactly what it is today, for the officer rarely claims that he detained the individual because he suspected him of having committed a marijuana offense. Searches and seizures would raise more complicated problems. Would an officer be justified in searching an individual who "dropped" one or two joints when possession of such a small quantity would not be unlawful but the marijuana would be contraband? How would the courts react to a claim by the officer that he saw in plain view a quantity of marijuana that looked like more than an ounce but in fact was less?

---

[31] Kaplan, *supra* note 2, at 1504.
[32] *Ibid.*
[33] *Cf. infra* p. 193.

It might be thought that the easiest way to eliminate police perjury on search-and-seizure issues would be to abandon the Exclusionary Rule rather than revise the substantive law of crimes. This suggestion is unrealistic. Even Chief Justice Burger, who has long been an opponent of the rule, agrees that it should not be discarded "until some meaningful alternative can be developed." [34] Prosecutors have expressed similar caveats.[35] Any meaningful alternative, however, will be just as much an invitation to police perjury as is the Exclusionary Rule.

For example, the chief justice has suggested that "Congress should develop an administrative or quasi-judicial remedy against the government itself to afford compensation and restitution for persons whose Fourth Amendment rights have been violated." The proposed remedy is "the creation of a cause of action for damages sustained by any person aggrieved by conduct of governmental agents in violation of the Fourth Amendment. . . ." [36] Thus, in order to recover damages under this scheme the plaintiff would have to prove exactly what he would have to show today in support of a motion to suppress: that the police officer violated his constitutional rights. Presumably a state or municipality will not look with favor on an officer whose conduct is held to warrant awarding damages against it. An officer who persistently violates the constitutional rights of citizens will not (one hopes) remain long on the force. The result is that police officers will have the same incentive as they do today to reconstruct events in order to bring the arrest or search within the bounds of constitutionality. Indeed, enactment of the proposed statutory remedy might actually increase the frequency of police perjury. For one thing, the policeman's career, not just the conviction of a single defendant, might be at stake. For another, the civil remedy would be available to the innocent persons whose cases would otherwise never come before the courts.

[34] Bivens v. Six Unknown Named Agents of Federal Bureau of Narcotics, 403 U.S. 388, 415 (1971) (dissenting opinion).

[35] See *N.Y. Times,* Mar. 27, 1972, p. 31, col. 1 (remarks of Queens County, N.Y., Dist. Atty. Thomas Mackell).

[36] 403 U.S. at 422–23.

X

The Police, the Courts, and Law Reform

SOME GENERALIZATIONS FROM THE CASES

At this point it is hardly necessary to say anything more about the evils of repeated surveillance, snooping, infiltration, and harassment. Nevertheless, several general observations suggested by the narratives in the preceding sections bear relevance to the central question of how society is affected by the techniques used by the police to enforce the marijuana laws.

First, in case after case the police display an extreme reluctance to apply for search warrants, even though they have no reason to believe that the contraband is likely to disappear if they seek judicial authorization before attempting to seize it. Instead, they proceed directly to the home of the suspect, hoping, apparently, that when they get there they will "inadvertently" find something that will justify a warrantless entry—the odor of burning marijuana, perhaps, or a group of people sitting in front of an open window sharing a pipe.

Occasionally a court comments on the failure to apply for a warrant. In Rockland County, New York, when the police raided an apartment on the basis of an informant's tip, the court ordered the evidence seized at the apartment to be suppressed, saying, "The informer told Detective Krassow that she had been suspicious about the apartment for several days. The apartment had only recently been rented. The defendants were not fleeing, nor should the officers have been in hot pursuit. They might have applied for a search warrant that evening. Or, in view of the stated suspicious circumstances for several days, a further investigation could have been begun and a search made with a warrant at the opportune repetition of the event." [1] In Tennessee a car was impounded in a wrecker's garage after an accident. The garage operator found a bag of marijuana in the car and summoned the deputy sheriff, who, with the aid of a state investigation agent, conducted an extensive search of the car. He made no attempt to obtain a warrant. The court commented: "The sheriff had proper custody, through Rainey, of the appellant's automobile. Furthermore, the sheriff had cause to arrest and detain the owner for the offense of permitting an unlicensed driver to operate a vehicle had appellant attempted to claim his car prior to the issuance of a warrant. Under these circumstances, it is not reasonable to assert that the opportunity to search the car was 'fleeting.' " [2]

Other courts have been more tolerant of the police proclivity for acting without judicial authorization. In Great Falls, Montana, detectives had accumulated information from various sources indicating that drugs were being used in a particular apartment. Instead of applying to a magistrate for a search warrant, they went to the apartment house to conduct an investigation. When they reached the apartment in question, they found the door open and smelled burning marijuana. The detectives entered the apartment, walked up a short flight of stairs, and saw two women and a man sitting around a table with marijuana on it. Although the court appears to acknowledge that the officers did not have probable cause to make a warrantless arrest until after they had intruded upon a "constitutionally protected area," [3] the arrest was nevertheless upheld.[4]

From the summary provided by the court it is not clear whether, under the prevailing federal constitutional standards, the officers could have obtained a search warrant on the basis of the information they had accumulated.[5] What is reasonably certain is that police officers in Montana will have little incentive to apply for a

[1] People v. Madow, 60 Misc. 2d 742, 745, 303 N.Y.S.2d 974, 977 (Justice Court, Village of Spring Valley, 1969).

[2] Cash v. Williams, 455 F.2d 1227, 1231 (6th Cir. 1972).

[3] State v. Bennett, 493 P.2d 1077, 1080 (Mont. 1972).

[4] See also State v. Wetteland, 496 P.2d 27 (Ore. App. 1972) (police were excused from obtaining a warrant because the undercover agent was negotiating to purchase "a far larger amount" than he had previously observed on the premises); State v. Speed, 458 S.W.2d 301 (Mo. 1970) (police placed an apartment under surveillance for a week rather than attempting to obtain a warrrant on the basis of an informer's tip).

[5] Compare Aguilar v. Texas, 378 U.S. 108 (1964), and Spinelli v. United States, 393 U.S. 410 (1969), with United States v. Harris, 403 U.S. 573 (1971).

warrant on future occasions when they have received tips from informers. If the warrantless investigation proves fruitless, the officers can always come back. If they smell or see marijuana, they will enter, confident that any contraband they seize will not be suppressed.

No one would deny that "exigent circumstances" may sometimes justify the police in making an arrest or search without a warrant. What is striking is that in so many cases the police do not even act immediately upon receiving the informer's tip, thus giving a hollow ring to any claim of "exigent circumstances." Moreover, other cases indicate that warrants can be obtained with great speed when the occasion requires it.[6] These facts suggest either that the police feel that seeking judicial authorization is too much of a bother, or that they fear that a "neutral and detached magistrate" will find their affidavits to be insufficient. Which conclusion is correct will ordinarily be a matter for speculation. In either event, the citizen loses the benefits of the warrant requirement, as explained in the classic opinion by Justice Jackson:

> The point of the Fourth Amendment, which often is not grasped by zealous officers, is not that it denies law enforcement the support of the usual inferences which reasonable men draw from evidence. Its protection consists in requiring that those inferences be drawn by a neutral and detached magistrate instead of being judged by the officer engaged in the often competitive enterprise of ferreting out crime. Any assumption that evidence sufficient to support a magistrate's disinterested determination to issue a search warrant will justify the officers in making a search without a warrant would reduce the Amendment to a nullity and leave the people's homes secure only in the discretion of police officers.[7]

Second, in an alarming number of cases the courts seem to bend over backwards to sustain police conduct that even in the most favorable light stretches the Fourth Amendment to the breaking point. Sometimes this disposition manifests itself in the refusal to suppress evidence that has been obtained through a pyramiding of

[6] See, e.g., Commonwealth v. Tirpack, 216 Pa. Super. 310, 263 A.2d 917 (1970) (police, informed that a "pot party" was in progress, obtained a warrant while the party was still going on); State v. McGee, 473 S.W.2d 686 (Mo. 1971) (officers secured a warrant on the same day that application was made); State v. Thacker, 496 P.2d 729 (Ore. App. 1972) (a warrant was obtained within twenty-four hours of an informant's tip that a sale was to take place).

[7] Johnson v. United States, 333 U.S. 10, 13–14 (1948).

questionable procedures.[8] In other cases the courts rely on far-fetched comparisons which liken the use of marijuana to trafficking in hard drugs or operating a brothel.[9] In giving their imprimatur to the police in cases like these, the courts ignore the often-quoted warning of Justice Jackson, himself a former prosecutor: "[T]o the extent of any privilege of search and seizure without warrant which we sustain, the officers interpret and apply themselves and will push to the limit. . . . [T]he authority which we concede to conduct searches and seizures without a warrant may be exercised by the most unfit and ruthless officers as well as by the fit and responsible, and resorted to in cases of petty misdemeanors as well as in the case of the gravest felonies." [10]

Third, the practices I have described are not aberrations; they are the practices routinely used by the police to ferret out violators of the marijuana laws. Undercover agents and informers are not deployed only to incriminate large-scale dealers or political activists; their use is the standard operating procedure when the police attempt to control the marijuana subculture.[11] Snooping and surveillance are not limited to the "big cases"; the police may set up watch on a house or an individual on the basis of a tip suggesting any kind of marijuana activity, however minimal. Traffic arrests and pedestrian stops that are no more than a pretext for a warrantless search; pat-downs for weapons that continue after it is obvious that the suspect is not carrying a weapon—these are not the occasional acts of a few overzealous officers; they are the everyday acts that are responsible for a high proportion of all marijuana convictions.

Finally, and most important, whether the police are candidly seeking to enforce the marijuana laws or engaging in harassment in the hope of finding violators, they rely on practices which inevitably intrude on the privacy and security of the innocent as well as the guilty. Any law-abiding citizen with long hair or nondescript clothing may be stopped on the street or the sidewalk, while driving on a highway, or while waiting to board an airplane. Any law-abiding citizen who goes to a party where some guests are smoking marijuana may be arrested and searched, even though he was in another room and unaware that the law was being violated. Any law-abiding person whose companions or associates have been found in possession of marijuana may be searched on the theory that "birds

8 See *supra* pp. 101 and 119–20.
9 See *supra* pp. 70 and 111–12.
10 Brinegar v. United States, 338 U.S. 160, 182 (1949) (dissenting opinion).
11 *Cf. supra*, chap. 4, note 4.

of a feather flock together." Any law-abiding citizen who chats with a person who is the target of an undercover agent may have his movements watched and his conversation monitored. Any law-abiding citizen who visits a house that has been placed under surveillance will be subjected to scrutiny and possibly a search. The victims of these practices are not only the "heads" and the "hippies"; they are all of us.

Intrusion upon the innocent cannot be avoided as long as the police take seriously the job of enforcing the marijuana laws. The reason is this: marijuana is used and distributed in private. Unless the police are tipped off by an informer,[12] they have no way of knowing, with any high degree of confidence, who is violating the laws. What they do know (or what they believe) is that the violators are likely to be found within various larger groups—teenagers with long hair, friends or associates of known users, guests at a party where some people have smoked marijuana, and so forth. The policeman's response is to investigate, with more or less thoroughness, everyone who falls within the larger group. But not everyone in the larger group uses marijuana. The result is that many innocent people are subjected to the effects of police scrutiny.

The police approach to marijuana law enforcement thus exemplifies par excellence what Tussman and tenBroek, in their classic article on equal protection, term *over-inclusiveness:* it "imposes a burden upon a wider range of individuals than are included in the class of those tainted with the mischief at which the law aims." [13] That burden is the loss of privacy and security. The crucial question is whether our society can tolerate imposing that burden on large numbers of law-abiding citizens in order to apprehend the few who are violating the law. That is the choice; we cannot ask the police to detect the guilty without requiring them to violate the rights of the innocent.

ALTERNATIVES TO TOTAL DECRIMINALIZATION

Before one can conclude that the undesirable police practices I have described can be ended only by a total decriminalization of marijuana, two other possible solutions must be considered.

First, it may be suggested that to the extent the police use improper means to enforce the marijuana laws, their excesses can be

[12] Of course informers' tips are not always reliable either. See *supra,* chap. 4, note 45.

[13] Tussman and tenBroek, "The Equal Protection of the Laws," 37 *Cal. L. Rev.* 341, 351 (1949).

restrained by the courts. This argument fails for several reasons. To begin with, as I have already suggested, the courts see no more than a small fraction of the instances of police misbehavior; in particular, improper police tactics which uncover no evidence of wrongdoing will never come before a court.[14] Second, even in the cases which come before them, the courts exercise a very circumscribed function. All they can do is to hold that particular investigatory tactics overstepped legislative or constitutional bounds. The limitations imposed by the legislature and the Constitution, however, cannot be expected to do more than provide a check on the worst police excesses.

In an era when crime has become the major concern of so many of their constituents, legislators tend to expand, not contract, the powers of the police. The Constitution, though it protects certain rights, does not guarantee the values which underlie them, for these values must be balanced against countervailing interests.[15] A distinguished scholar has reminded us that "it is no great compliment to a statute to say that it is constitutional." Similarly, to say that a particular example of police investigatory work did not violate the Fourth Amendment is not to say that it is a practice to be encouraged; it simply means that in the judgment of the court the conduct of the police was not "unreasonable." In this connection it must be remembered that the courts do not write search-and-seizure law only for marijuana cases; they must consider as well the interest of society in apprehending murderers, rapists, and burglars.[16] Thus, in any Fourth Amendment case the court must balance society's interest in individual privacy and security against its interest in apprehending criminals generally. The judgment that the interest in privacy must be subordinated does not mean that the intrusion is not substantial. Nor does it mean that repeated intrusions of a similar kind might not be too high a price to pay for the enforcement of particular laws.[17]

[14] See Brinegar v. United States, 338 U.S. at 181 (Jackson, J., dissenting).

[15] Even the late Justice Black, who is usually thought of as the archenemy of "balancing," accepted this point. Although he set great store by the values of privacy and free expression, he was not willing to hold unconstitutional every governmental action that interfered with the realization of those values. See, e.g., Griswold v. Connecticut, 381 U.S. 479, 507 (1965) (dissenting opinion) (privacy); Adderley v. Florida, 385 U.S. 39 (1966) (free speech).

[16] See, e.g., Coolidge v. New Hampshire, 403 U.S. 443 (1971) (murder); Davis v. Mississippi, 394 U.S. 721 (1969) (rape); Chimel v. California, 395 U.S. 752 (1969) (burglary).

[17] Cf. Jackson, J., dissenting in Brinegar, 338 U.S. at 183: "[I]f we are to make judicial exceptions to the Fourth Amendment . . . it seems to me they should

Certainly the courts could do more than they are doing today to safeguard the values of privacy and security that underlie the Fourth Amendment. The preceding pages have amply demonstrated the willingness of some courts to sustain police practices which could easily have been held to violate the letter and the spirit of the constitutional provision. But expansive interpretations of constitutional protections are not in fashion today,[18] and it would be unrealistic to look to the courts for significant restraints on the excesses of the police.

Finally, there remains the alternative of partial decriminalization—that is, legalizing possession for personal use but retaining penalties for distribution. This, of course, is the thrust of the Shafer commission's proposal; it is also the recommendation of the LeDain commission in Canada.[19] Nevertheless, as I have tried to show throughout these pages, replacing total prohibition by what the Shafer commission terms partial prohibition could be expected to have very little effect on the practices of the police. Further support —perhaps the strongest support—for this argument is found in the history of Prohibition.

What the Shafer commission appears to forget is that the Volstead Act—the enforcement legislation for the Eighteenth Amendment—expressly exempted from its penalties the possession of liquor in a private dwelling for personal use.[20] In other words, Prohibition was not very different, in its essentials, from what the commission today calls partial prohibition. Nevertheless, the Vol-

depend somewhat upon the gravity of the offense. If we assume, for example, that a child is kidnapped and the officers throw a roadblock about the neighborhood and search every outgoing car, it would be a drastic and undiscriminating use of the search. The officers might be unable to show probable cause for searching any particular car. However, I should candidly strive hard to sustain such an action, executed fairly and in good faith, because it might be reasonable to subject travelers to that indignity if it was the only way to save a threatened life and detect a vicious crime. But I should not strain to sustain such a roadblock and universal search to salvage a few bottles of bourbon and catch a bootlegger." See also United States v. Soyka, 394 F.2d 443, 451 (2d Cir. 1968) (Friendly, J., dissenting).

[18] See, e.g., Kirby v. Illinois, 406 U.S. 682 (1972) (6th Amendment); Kastigar v. United States, 406 U.S. 441 (1972) (5th Amendment); Branzburg v. Hayes, 408 U.S. 665 (1972) (1st Amendment).

[19] *N.Y. Times,* May 21, 1972, p. 12, col. 1.

[20] 27 U.S.C. § 50 (repealed). The consultants who prepared the commission's working paper on "Models and Statutory Schemes for Controlling Marijuana" were well aware that the Volstead Act embodied only a "partial prohibition" scheme. See National Commission on Marihuana and Drug Abuse, *Marihuana: A Signal of Misunderstanding, Appendix,* 1184.

stead Act was responsible for police misconduct on a scale which dwarfs anything that is happening today.[21] In particular, the Fourth Amendment, which for most people had become a "dim thing of history, seldom asserted or even examined because so seldom encroached upon," [22] became almost a dead letter. Professor Howard McBain of Columbia University Law School commented in 1928: "Of a certainty, . . . so far as searches and seizures are being made upon mere suspicion for the purpose, not of prosecuting the guilty, but of seizing and destroying liquor, the guarantee of the fourth amendment is being swept blithely into the discard." [23] In 1931 the Wickersham commission condemned law enforcement practices in language which strikingly anticipates the words of the Shafer commission forty years later: "High-handed methods, unreasonable searches and seizures, lawless interference with personal and property rights, have had a bad effect on the work of prosecution at a time when the general condition of American administration of justice was imperatively demanding improvement." [24]

The lesson of Prohibition, then, is that a ban on the sale and distribution of a widely used commodity cannot be enforced without resort to the same undesirable police practices that the commission agrees are a consequence of laws proscribing marijuana possession for personal use.[25] Decriminalizing possession while retaining criminal sanctions against distribution will continue to expose the innocent as well as the guilty to snooping, surveillance, and other intrusions on privacy and security. These consequences can be avoided only by removing *all* marijuana transactions from the purview of the criminal law.

---

[21] Indeed, Fourth Amendment litigation was quite rare until the adoption of Prohibition. See Jacob Landynski, *Search and Seizure and the Supreme Court* (Baltimore, 1966), 87–88.

[22] Howard McBain, *Prohibition: Legal and Illegal* (New York, 1928), 168.

[23] *Ibid.*, 105.

[24] National Commission on Law Observance and Enforcement, *Report on the Enforcement of the Prohibition Laws of the United States* (Washington, D.C., 1931), p. 57. Compare National Commission on Marihuana and Drug Abuse, *Marihuana: A Signal of Misunderstanding,* 145: "Arrests without probable cause, illegal searches and selective enforcement occur often enough to arouse concern about the integrity of the criminal process."

[25] Professor Michael Rosenthal, who in 1969 advocated "significant (though not inordinate) sanctions" for "commercial trafficking," conceded that "[a]s long as sales are unlawful, use of informants and undercover agents is necessary, and practices approaching the borderline of entrapment are likely to occur." Rosenthal, "A Plea for the Amelioration of the Marihuana Laws," 47 *Tex. L. Rev.* 1359, 1372 n. 55, 1373 (1969).

PART THREE

XI

The Futility of
Partial Prohibition

In the preceding chapters of this volume I have discussed some of the most significant costs of marijuana criminalization and have indicated why these costs are likely to remain largely unchanged under the partial prohibition scheme recommended by the National Commission on Marihuana and Drug Abuse. Turning to the other side of the ledger, I suggest that partial prohibition would not achieve the benefits sought by the commission, while the minimal effectiveness that present laws have would probably be lost.

The purpose of the partial prohibition scheme is to "discourage marijuana use, while concentrating primarily on the prevention of heavy and very heavy use." The commission asserts that the legal system can assist this objective in three ways: "first, by deterring people from use; second, by symbolizing social opposition to use; and finally, by cutting off supply of the drug." [1] This conclusion rests on inaccurate assumptions about patterns of marijuana use and implausible projections of smokers' behavior.

DETERRING USE

The commission states first that the legal system can deter people from using marijuana. But it agrees that present laws, under which the mere possession of marijuana is illegal, have had no more than a minimal effect.[2] Why, then, does the commission believe

[1] National Commission on Marihuana and Drug Abuse, *Marihuana: A Signal of Misunderstanding*, 134, 143 [hereinafter cited as *Signal of Misunderstanding*].
[2] *Ibid.*, 143.

that a partial prohibition scheme will have any greater success? It would be difficult to discover how many individuals now refrain from using marijuana solely because they would have to violate the law in order to do so, but however large that group might be, the commission's plan would allow them to satisfy their curiosity.[3] Present nonusers who have no interest in getting high or who fear that marijuana will be harmful to their health will not change their behavior. This means that at best partial prohibition would be no more of a deterrent than are present laws; more likely, it would be less of one.

A recurring theme in the commission's report is that marijuana use is probably a fad which if not institutionalized "will recede substantially in time." This argument is made to support "discouragement" instead of "neutrality" and again in defense of partial prohibition rather than regulation;[4] unfortunately or otherwise, it is no more than wishful thinking. Every survey indicates that marijuana use continues to expand dramatically, with no falloff in prospect.

In the same week that the commission issued its report, the Gallup poll released figures indicating that the percentage of adults who had tried marijuana had risen from 4 percent in October, 1969, to 11 percent in March, 1972—an increase of nearly 300 percent. Gallup found that almost three persons in ten in the 18–29 age group had used the drug at least once.[5] A report prepared for the commission by Professor Erich Goode of the State University of New York at Stony Brook, author of the comprehensive study *The Marijuana Smokers,* predicted that the number of Americans smoking marijuana at least once a week might double by 1976 to a figure of 10 million.[6] By that year, 50 million Americans will have tried marijuana, according to a forecast by the Bureau of Narcotics and Dangerous Drugs.[7] A 1972 report by the Secretary of Health, Education, and Welfare found "every indication that use has increased and is very widespread. In teenage and young adult groups use is very extensive—in some groups as high as 90 percent have used marijuana at some time." [8] A Gallup poll released in early

[3] Compare the behavior of writer William F. Buckley, Jr., who admitted that he had smoked marijuana but emphasized that he had done so while on a boat outside the three-mile limit (*N.Y. Times,* Nov. 29, 1972, p. 27, col. 1).

[4] *Signal of Misunderstanding,* 131–32, 147.

[5] *N.Y. Times,* Mar. 26, 1972, p. 45, col. 2.

[6] See *N.Y. Times,* Feb. 14, 1972, p. 24, col. 2.

[7] *N.Y. Times,* Dec. 3, 1972, § 4, p. 2, col. 5.

[8] Subcommittee on Alcoholism and Narcotics of the Senate Committee on Labor and Public Welfare, *Marihuana and Health: Second Annual Report to*

1971 indicated that the proportion of college students who had tried marijuana doubled between 1969 and 1971 to 42 percent.[9] A year later the figure rose again, this time to 51 percent.[10]

In the months since the Shafer commission published its first report, the evidence has pointed to a continuation of these trends. A Gallup poll taken in early 1973 indicated that 12 percent of American adults, including 36 percent of those between the ages of 18 and 29, had experimented with marijuana.[11] In late 1972 the commission itself conducted a survey which found that 25.9 million Americans (16 percent of all adults) had tried the drug at least once, 2 million more than the figure suggested by the commission's first survey a year earlier. Perhaps more important, the survey indicated that 13 million Americans considered themselves to be present users of *Cannabis.* "What this shows," the commission's executive director concluded, "is that there are three recreational drugs in this country: alcohol, tobacco, and marijuana." [12]

Substantial evidence indicates that marijuana use is not only more widespread but also more broadly based; it is no longer confined to a single narrow segment of society. Even in 1969 and 1970 reports showed that *Cannabis* was being used fairly extensively by professional people and other middle-class adults.[13] The commission's first survey, taken in 1971, found that "[t]he stereotype of the marijuana user as a marginal citizen has given way to a composite picture of large segments of American youth, children of the dominant majority and very much a part of the mainstream of American life." Moreover, said the commission, use is found "in all socioeconomic groups and occupations. . . . [T]he use of the drug among adults is by no means confined to college students. . . . Nonstudent users now span social class, income level, and occupational classification." [14] More recently, police in the Wash-

Congress from the Secretary of Health, Education, and Welfare, 92d Cong., 2d Sess., (Comm. Print, 1972), p. 7; see also *ibid.,* 22–29.

[9] *N.Y. Times,* Jan. 17, 1971, p. 52, col. 4. The 42 percent figure coincided with the estimate for mid-1971 made in a report for the U.S. Bureau of Narcotics and Dangerous Drugs. See Subcommittee on Alcoholism and Narcotics, *supra* note 8, at 24.

[10] *N.Y. Times,* Feb. 6, 1972, § 1, p. 36, col. 4. The commission's second survey, taken at about the same time, estimated the figure at 58 percent. National Commission on Marihuana and Drug Abuse, *Drug Use in America: Problem in Perspective,* 66 [hereinafter cited as *Drug Use in America*].

[11] *N.Y. Times,* Feb. 22, 1973, p. 9, col. 1.

[12] *N.Y. Times,* Mar. 18, 1973, § 1, p. 57, col. 5.

[13] Sam Blum, "Marijuana Clouds the Generation Gap," *N.Y. Times Magazine,* Aug. 23, 1970, pp. 28, 45; Nancy Mayer, "How the Middle Class Turns On," *New York,* Oct. 20, 1969, p. 42.

[14] *Signal of Misunderstanding,* 7, 32–34.

ington, D.C., area reported that although the bulk of those arrested on marijuana charges continue to be young men between the ages of eighteen and twenty-five, many more persons in their late twenties and thirties are also being arrested.[15] The most dramatic data, however, are those which emerge from the commission's second survey, taken in late 1972. It might not be surprising that 37 percent of the adult student respondents reported that they were present users of marijuana. But a similar response was made by 10 percent of the salesmen, 11 percent of those with annual incomes of $15,000 or more, and 14 percent of those in professional or technical occupations.[16] These developments were pungently summarized by a suburban police captain: "You don't have to be a creep any more to be using dope." [17]

The fact that marijuana is most widely used by persons under thirty has obvious significance for the future of the drug. As these persons become older, the percentage of the total population that has "ever used" marijuana will increase; so, perhaps, will the proportion of persons who continue to use it. Indeed, there is evidence that these phenomena have already begun. By early 1973 the Gallup poll could report that 36 percent of persons between the ages of 18 and 29 had tried *Cannabis,* compared with 29 percent a year earlier.[18] In Portland, Oregon, the senior deputy district attorney commented in late 1973 that "[m]arijuana use had become so common that the grand jury just wouldn't indict and when they did, the juries wouldn't convict." [19] And although the commission's second report asserted that the 1972 commission survey supported its speculation "that use may have reached its peak and begun levelling off," survey figures printed on the same page suggested otherwise: the proportion of *present* users among adults had increased from 5 percent to 8 percent between the first survey and the second.[20] What this means is that in 1971 only one respondent in twenty considered himself to be a present user; a year later the figure was one

15 *Washington Post,* Aug. 20, 1973, p. C-1, col. 6.
16 *Drug Use in America,* 66.
17 *Washington Post,* Aug. 20, 1973, p. C-1, col. 6.
18 *N.Y. Times,* Feb. 22, 1973, p. 9, col. 1.
19 *N.Y. Times,* Dec. 18, 1973, p. 29, col. 3. Similarly, in the District of Columbia, the chief of the U.S. attorney's superior court division commented in late 1974 that when marijuana cases go to trial, "we're not all that successful. . . . Juries don't seem to show that much interest." The number of acquittals, he reported, is quite high (*Washington Post,* Nov. 16, 1974, p. A-1, col. 6; p. A-5, col. 1).
20 *Drug Use in America,* 64.

in twelve. This development hardly suggests a "levelling off." At the same time, use continues to expand among those at the youngest end of the age spectrum; as the *New York Times* reported in 1971, "Today's college freshman, unlike his counterpart of a few years ago, was probably exposed to a wide range of drugs in high school." [21] The result will be a further broadening of the incidence of marijuana use.

The commission also urges that we "deglorify, demythologize and deemphasize the use of marijuana and other drugs" and suggests that the present interest in marijuana "will diminish . . . once the major symbolic aspects of use are deemphasized." [22] Once again, the commissioners' hopes have given them a distorted view of reality. For a large segment of the population—probably the people most likely to become regular users if the drug were legal—marijuana has already been demythologized. Early in 1971 the *New York Times* reported that on many campuses drugs are now used "with an increasing degree of discretion, sophistication and nonchalance." Marijuana "has become a staple on almost every college campus. . . . [U]sers have grown to include virtually all segments of the student population." The drug has become the common denominator among such disparate groups as fraternity members, athletes, and "freaks." [23]

What is perhaps most significant about the demythologizing of marijuana is that, as one writer put it in 1970, use "can no longer be interpreted as a sign of alienation." [24] With so many users it "has lost some of its value as a symbol of rebellion and communal bond among its early smokers." [25] In late 1972 the *New York Times* could report that on college campuses in the tristate New York area the use of marijuana had become "common, casual and virtually institutionalized." [26] A similarly casual attitude was reported in the Washington, D.C., area a year later.[27]

A vivid manifestation of changing attitudes can be found in patterns of behavior at social gatherings. Only a few years ago the marijuana smokers at a campus party tended to segregate themselves from the other partygoers. Typically, those who wanted to

[21] *N.Y. Times,* Jan. 17, 1971, p. 52, col. 6.
[22] *Signal of Misunderstanding,* 91, 147.
[23] *N.Y. Times,* Jan. 17, 1971, p. 52, cols. 4, 6.
[24] Blum, *supra* note 13, at 45.
[25] *N.Y. Times,* Jan. 17, 1971, p. 52, col. 6.
[26] *N.Y. Times,* Nov. 20, 1972, p. 1, col. 5.
[27] *Washington Post,* Aug. 20, 1973, p. C-1, col. 6.

turn on made their way unobtrusively to a back room, where they would share a joint or a pipe, paying as little attention to the rest of the gathering as the nonparticipants paid to them. This behavior stemmed in part from the recognition that they were doing something unlawful and perhaps risky, and in part from the sense of belonging to a small band of different and special people—almost a secular cult. Rolling a joint, passing it from hand to hand and smoking it, or inhaling from a hookah tended to be solemn, almost ritualistic procedures. Today if someone feels the desire to smoke some marijuana he is likely to roll a joint or fill a pipe without elaborate preparation or particular concern about who is in the room. When guests pass around a joint or pipe they are apt to do so casually rather than ceremonially. Those who happen to be within reach may take a toke or not, as the spirit moves them; no one is likely to pay much attention either way. In short, smoking marijuana has become, among more and more people, no more a matter of moment than drinking beer.

These developments are significant because they undermine the principal justification for the Shafer commission's go-slow policy. The commission expresses its concern that "even neutrality toward use as a matter of policy could invest an otherwise transient phenomenon with the status of an accepted behavior," but concedes that "[i]f marijuana smoking were an already ingrained part of our culture, this objection would be dispelled." [28] Contrary to the commission's belief, marijuana *is* now an ingrained part of the culture, at least in those segments of society where marijuana is most likely to be used regularly after decriminalization.

It is worth emphasizing again that the widespread experimentation with marijuana that would probably occur after criminal laws are repealed is extremely unlikely to produce a significant public health problem. Indeed, the commission concedes as much but goes on to express the fear that "social influences might cause those who would not otherwise use the drug to be exposed to . . . the potential escalation of drug-using patterns." [29] "Social influences" are varied and unpredictable enough that no one could say with confidence that the commission is wrong, but the experience of Prohibition teaches us that outlawing the sale and distribution (but not the

[28] *Signal of Misunderstanding,* 147.

[29] *Ibid.,* 91. The full quotation is: "We are concerned that social influences might cause those who would not otherwise use the drug to be exposed to this minimal risk [that is, the risk from experimental or intermittent use] and the potential escalation of drug-using patterns."

possession or use) of a popular social drug may help to create a social climate that actually fosters increased use. It was during Prohibition that the carrying of liquor became "almost a badge of respectability." In New York City, fifteen thousand saloons were closed by the law, only to be replaced by an estimated thirty-two thousand speakeasies. Women, who seldom frequented saloons in the days before Prohibition, "took to drink and speakeasies in large numbers." And while it is hardly possible to adduce exact figures, historians have concluded that per capita consumption of liquor actually increased during the nation's supposedly dry years, reaching a level even higher than that reported today.[30]

Moreover, at least one important direction for the potential escalation of drug-using patterns is likely to be cut off under a licensing scheme. As long as the distribution of marijuana is unlawful, persons wishing to purchase it will often deal with a seller who is equally willing and able to sell them "harder" drugs. Indeed, the commission's statutory scheme would give the seller a strong incentive to add barbiturates or other addictive drugs to his wares: "tabs" and pills are less bulky, more easily concealed and transported, and usually more profitable than marijuana. If the seller faces severe penalties for selling *Cannabis,* as he would under the commission's plan, he may well decide to sell these other drugs or even encourage his marijuana customers to try them, thus enabling him to attain greater profits with no significant increase in risk. If, on the other hand, marijuana can be purchased legally at the corner liquor store, persons buying it will not have this opportunity to escalate to more dangerous drugs.

In the light of what has been said, it seems unlikely that partial prohibition will serve any significant function in deterring marijuana use, especially the heavy use that may be of special concern to the legislator. To the extent that deterring heavy use is the benefit sought from the laws, the legislator would do better to vote for a licensing scheme that would avoid the social costs which accompany the attempt to enforce any kind of prohibition.

SYMBOLIC FUNCTIONS

A major attraction of the present law, according to the commission, has been its value in symbolizing social opposition to marijuana

[30] The facts and quotations in this paragraph are taken from Andrew Sinclair, *Era of Excess* (New York, Harper Colophon ed., 1964), 230–38; and *N.Y. Times,*

use. One reason for the commission's rejection of even a "tightly controlled regulatory scheme" is that such a change would instead symbolize approval of use, or at least a position of neutrality." [31]

Symbolism is a tricky thing; as Justice Jackson pointed out, "A person gets from a symbol the meaning he puts into it." [32] Certainly there are some people who would regard decriminalization of marijuana as symbolizing approval of use, but that can hardly be the end of the matter. Even if one assumes that symbolism is a proper function of the law,[33] the commission's conclusions ignore a number of important questions. Would significant numbers of people in fact interpret decriminalization as symbolizing approval? If so, what would be the consequences of this response? Would those who oppose the use of marijuana become inflamed at the apparent betrayal by their elected representatives? Would other people experiment with the drug on the ground that the legislature has given the go-ahead? Indeed, it is hardly meaningful to say that decriminalization would symbolize approval without considering the behavioral consequences of the belief.

On the simplest level it is by no means clear that decriminalization of marijuana, coupled with the enactment of a strict regulatory scheme, would be widely regarded as symbolizing approval of marijuana use. Legislative action of such significance will not occur in a vacuum; the matter will be extensively debated. If the prohibition is repealed "not [because] the drug is good but [because] the costs of criminalization are out of proportion to the benefits of this policy," [34] the legislators' constituents will be made aware of this fact. Further, as Kaplan points out, several states have repealed prohibitions against various kinds of private sexual behavior by consenting adults "despite the argument that repeal constituted an approval of the conduct in question." [35]

The commission argues that "[a]ny attempt to adopt a regulatory approach now" would "maintain the debate at a highly emotional level and would perpetuate the tendency to perceive marijuana use as a symbol of the struggle between two conflicting philosophies." [36]

Oct. 27, 1969, p. 47, cols. 5–8 (review of Prohibition fifty years after the Volstead Act by writer Joseph G. Herzberg).

[31] *Signal of Misunderstanding*, 143, 147.

[32] West Virginia State Board of Education v. Barnette, 319 U.S. 624, 632–33 (1942).

[33] See *supra* pp. 21–27.

[34] John Kaplan, *Marijuana: The New Prohibition*, 326.

[35] *Ibid.*

[36] *Signal of Misunderstanding*, 148.

Standing alone, this statement makes little sense, for it is hard to imagine the debate being carried on at a higher emotional level than it is at present. Recall, for example, the outcry that arose when it was reported that Senator George McGovern, then a candidate for the presidency, had endorsed the legalization of marijuana. Perhaps the commission is referring to a point made earlier in the report—the fear that the "larger segment of our population which supports the implications of the existing social policy" might "lose respect for a policy making establishment which appear[s] to bend so easily to the wishes of a 'lawless' and highly vocal minority." [37]

In the first place, as I have already suggested, if legislatures vote to decriminalize marijuana, the principal impetus will come not from pot lovers, to paraphrase one writer, but from "protector[s] of a beleaguered legal system." [38] The architects of reform will not be John Sinclair or Allen Ginsburg, but men like John Kaplan and organizations like Consumers Union.[39] Kaplan, as his book reveals, has a strong Puritan impulse,[40] while Consumers Union's sober approach to cars, toys, and other products belies any notion that its call for decriminalization stems from a desire to encourage the use of mood-altering drugs.

Second, the commission's reference to a "lawless" minority is either meaningless or misleading. If the commission is saying only that the minority opposes an existing law, this is true of any group seeking legislative reform. If the commission is suggesting that the minority is urging repeal simply to ratify its own widespread violations of the law, it seriously misunderstands the thrust of the argument. The point is not that the law should be abandoned because so many people violate it; the point is that the law should be abandoned because its enforcement is too costly to society in relation to its benefits.[41]

[37] *Ibid.*, 133.

[38] Schneyer, "Problems in the Cost-Benefit Analysis of Marijuana Legislation," 24 *Stan. L. Rev.* 200, 201 (1971).

[39] Edward M. Brecher, *The Consumers Union Report on Licit and Illicit Drugs* (Mount Vernon, N.Y., 1972). See generally Patrick Anderson, "The Pot Lobby," *N.Y. Times Magazine*, Jan. 21, 1973, p. 8; Tim Cahill, "The New Pot Advocates," *Rolling Stone,* Jan. 3, 1974, p. 53.

[40] See *infra* pp. 196, 200.

[41] The number of people violating the law is relevant, but for subsidiary reasons. The greater the extent of actual or suspected use, the greater the incentive for unsympathetic police officers to engage in harassment in order to apprehend violators. See *supra,* chap. 7, note 41. Second, the fact that twenty-four million Americans have used marijuana with little apparent harm to themselves (or to society) is relevant in evaluating the benefits of the present laws. Third, the fact

Finally, it would be disingenuous to say that a legislature which votes for decriminalization in 1975 or 1976 is bending "easily" to the wishes of any group. Writers have been advocating decriminalization for at least six years.[42] During that time the issue has been debated at great length. Research has added to our knowledge of marijuana but has done little to contradict the statement made in 1970 that "the dangers of marijuana are largely hypothetical," at least where use is moderate.[43] Meanwhile, the cause of total decriminalization (accompanied by enactment of a licensing system) has been embraced by such disparate groups as the Consumers Union and the one-hundred-year-old Public Health Association.[44] Under these circumstances it could hardly be said that the change would come about "easily"; rather, it would be the product of steadily mounting pressure from a broadly based coalition of advocates.

I also question whether the antimarijuana forces whose reaction concerns the commission would regard legislative acceptance of the use of marijuana as significantly less objectionable than a total decriminalization of the drug. As the commission recognizes, the threats that are perceived to flow from marijuana use often have little relation to reality. Persons who continue to believe the myths which the commission so skillfully deflates are likely to be affronted by any liberalization of the laws, except perhaps the most minimal.[45] For that segment of the population partial prohibition would not, as the commission suggests, "symboliz[e] a continuing societal discouragement of use." [46] Indeed, that group would perceive the commission's scheme not as one of partial prohibition but as one

that marijuana is used so widely by individuals who believe that their behavior is legitimate indicates that the law is not supported by a consensus. *Cf.* Herbert Packer, *The Limits of the Criminal Sanction,* 296; and see *supra,* p. 29.

[42] See, e.g., Comment, "The Legalization of Marihuana: A Realistic Approach, Part I," 21 *Vand. L. Rev.* 517 (1968); Arthur Hellman, "The Time Has Come to Legalize Marijuana," *Hennepin Lawyer,* Feb., 1970, p. 10.

[43] See Hellman, *supra* note 42, at 11. For a review of the medical literature as of the end of 1974, see Richard Christie, "Attention: Smoking Grass May Be Good for Your Health," *New Times,* Dec. 13, 1974, p. 24.

[44] *N.Y. Times,* May 19, 1972, p. 7, col. 1. Late in 1974 the *Washington Post* endorsed the repeal of criminal sanctions against the possession of marijuana, adding, "If there is merit in relaxing the rules on possession, simple logic dictates that it makes sense eventually to legalize its sale and use and control its quality" (*Washington Post,* Nov. 18, 1974, p. A-22, cols. 1-2).

[45] Conversely, reforms mild enough to meet with the approval of staunch opponents of marijuana would do nothing to mitigate the worst evils of criminalization.

[46] *Signal of Misunderstanding,* 150.

of partial legalization—and even partial legalization would be regarded as a surrender to hostile and deviant forces. To the extent that the symbolic value which the commission is attempting to preserve rests on the attitude of that group, little more would be lost by replacing total prohibition with a licensing system instead of partial prohibition.[47]

The other aspect of the symbolic approval argument centers on the fear that decriminalization would serve as a sort of go-ahead signal to many nonusers to try marijuana. The weakness of this argument is that it overestimates the influence of the law as a determinant of human behavior. In 1961 the Illinois legislature voted to repeal all criminal penalties for homosexual acts committed in private by consenting adults.[48] No one has reported an upsurge in homosexuality in Illinois as a result. Of course, the taboo against homosexuality is far stronger than the social deterrents to marijuana use, but the point is that citizens do not ordinarily regard repeal of a criminal prohibition as an invitation to taste thitherto forbidden fruit.

Perhaps the best evidence now available of what could be expected to happen if marijuana were decriminalized comes from Oregon. In December, 1973, that state became the first to eliminate criminal penalties for the possession of up to one ounce of the drug. One year later, a survey by the independent Drug Abuse Council found that there had been no significant increase in marijuana use. On the contrary, 52 percent of the "current users" interviewed showed no change in how much they smoked, and 40 percent reported a decrease in usage. Moreover, of those who stopped using marijuana or who never used it, 23 percent cited a possible health danger as a reason, while only 4 percent mentioned the possibility of legal prosecution. By far the most common explanation—given by 53 percent of the current nonusers—was "lack of interest." The survey data confirmed earlier estimates by Oregon law enforcement authorities. Thus, while the new Oregon statute falls far short of

[47] The analysis in the text is supported by the response of anti-abortion forces to proposals to liberalize abortion laws. In Pennsylvania, for example, supporters of a bill which would have prohibited abortions in virtually all circumstances refused to accept a compromise which would have permitted abortions in cases of rape or of incest. See *N.Y. Times*, Dec. 1, 1972, p. 17, col. 1. Much the same thing happened in Connecticut. While there are obvious and significant differences between the two issues, they are similar in that they arouse great extremes of emotion and commitment. Those who oppose liberalized laws tend to regard *any* change in that direction as intolerable.

[48] Ill. Rev. Stat. c. 38, § 11–3 (1961).

complete decriminalization, the subsequent events lend support to the conclusion that the law is only one factor, and probably not the most important one, in influencing individual decisions on whether or not to smoke marijuana.[49]

The symbolic value argument is no more persuasive if it is made in the context of the patterned evasion theories of Gusfield and Williams. Those who strongly support the existing norm are likely to regard even partial prohibition as a capitulation to the "enemy deviant." Those who proclaim a new norm are not likely to be satisfied by laws which seriously restrict their ability "to pursue the behavior they find legitimate."

CUTTING OFF THE SUPPLY

The Shafer commission suggests, finally, that the legal system can discourage the use of marijuana by "cutting off supply of the drug." Later, in defending the partial prohibition approach, the commission states that "an increase in marijuana use may be prevented by a concerted effort to eliminate major trafficking." The commission concedes that it will not be possible to eliminate the supply of marijuana but insists that "an intensive effort to eliminate *commercial criminal enterprise* should have some impact on the extent of use." [50] These variant statements suggest that the commission did not decide just how much it could expect from intensive efforts to eliminate "commercial criminal enterprise," but repetition of the point suggests a certain amount of optimism. Unfortunately, this optimism rests on a series of incorrect assumptions.

The commission's reference to "commercial criminal enterprise" reflects a fundamental misapprehension about the way marijuana is distributed. Even Commissioners Javits and Hughes, who recommend that all not-for-profit sales be excluded from the criminal sanction, urge that there be a "clear separation between the serious, commercial, profit-making seller, or 'pusher,' as he is known, and the individual who merely splits the cost of a reasonable supply of the drug with his friends or acquaintances." [51]

[49] Drug Abuse Council, *Marijuana Survey—State of Oregon* (Washington, D.C., 1974); *N.Y. Times,* Dec. 25, 1974, p. 19, col. 6. For earlier estimates by Oregon law enforcement officials, see California Legislature Select Senate Committee on Control of Marijuana, *Marijuana: Beyond Misunderstanding,* 43–47. For further details on the new Oregon law, see *infra* p. 194.

[50] *Signal of Misunderstanding,* 143, 164 [emphasis added].

[51] *Ibid.,* 156n.

In the real world of marijuana use, no such clear separation exists. Probably the most comprehensive study of marijuana distribution that has yet appeared is that of Erich Goode. Goode discovered that "the user and the seller are largely indistinguishable; there is no clear-cut boundary between them." The line is fuzzy in several respects. First, except at the very highest levels of the distributional pyramid the *roles* of seller and buyer are not constant; "it may be an arbitrary decision as to who is the buyer and who the seller on a specific transaction." A person may sell occasionally or frequently, with every shade of variation between. Second, no clear distinctions can be made in terms of the quantity of marijuana involved in a sale, with sales taking place at the level of the ounce, the pound, the kilogram, and larger quantities. Third, no clear line can be drawn in terms of whether or not the transaction is for profit. A person who has bought a kilogram of marijuana may give some of it away, sell some of it to close friends at cost, sell some to less intimate friends at less than the standard prices, and sell some to strangers or near-strangers at the full "retail" price. Characterization of the transaction becomes even more complicated when marijuana is given away or sold at cost to cancel debts or otherwise used as a kind of "tribal barter currency." At what point in this spectrum can one say that the distributor is selling for profit or that he has engaged in a "commercial criminal enterprise"? [52]

Even if the legislature were able to devise a law aimed only at major trafficking in marijuana, recent experience gives no reason to believe that the prohibition could be successfully enforced. Most of the marijuana used in the United States is smuggled from Mexico. A remarkable television report broadcast by CBS in June, 1972, pointed up some of the difficulties of trying to break the "Mexican connection." Marijuana is grown in hundreds of small patches scattered in hidden mountain valleys. Detection is hampered by the lack of adequate law enforcement resources and by widespread official corruption. Large quantities of marijuana are brought across the Mexican-American border by air. The border is 1,900 miles long and largely unpatrolled. As the CBS report made clear, it is virtually impossible to catch smugglers except through a chance mishap or a tip from an informant.[53] Once marijuana has crossed the border, detection becomes even more difficult.

[52] This analysis is based on Erich Goode, *The Marijuana Smokers*, 249–55.
[53] Columbia Broadcasting System, "CBS Reports: The Mexican Connection," broadcast, June 25, 1972, transcript p. 6 and *passim*.

The failure of Operation Intercept in September, 1969, was not a consequence of poor planning or inadequate execution; it was symptomatic of the impossibility of cutting off the flow of drugs across the border.[54]

Finally, in pinning its hopes on "an intensive effort to eliminate commercial criminal enterprise" in marijuana, the commission ignores the phenomenon referred to by Packer as the "crime tariff." Packer points out that when the law attaches criminal sanctions to "transactions between willing buyers and willing sellers, each of whom gets what he wants from the deal," the effect is to increase the risk to the seller, thereby driving up the price of what he sells. The "tariff" is the premium which the buyer pays in order to compensate the seller for that risk.

The crime tariff comes into play in its most extreme form when the demand for a commodity is inelastic—that is, when people want it so badly that they are willing to pay any price for it. Few commodities fall into that category; the most obvious are narcotic drugs. Packer writes:

> [W]hen we make it illegal to traffic in commodities for which there is an inelastic demand, the effect is to secure a kind of monopoly profit to the entrepreneur who is willing to break the law. In effect, we say to him: "We will set up a barrier to entry into this line of commerce by making it illegal and, therefore, risky; if you are willing to take the risk, you will be sheltered from the competition of those who are unwilling to do so. Of course, if we catch you, you may possibly (although not necessarily) be put out of business; but meanwhile you are free to gather the fruits that grow in the hothouse atmosphere we are providing for you." [55]

Marijuana is not a narcotic (that is, it is not addictive), and the demand for it is not inelastic. If the price were to double or triple, many potential purchasers would refrain from buying; they would turn to other mood-altering drugs or perhaps abandon drugs altogether.[56] The elasticity of the demand, however, does not preclude the operation of the crime tariff. In the northeast part of the country, the "retail" price of marijuana in late 1972 ranged from fifteen

[54] See Kaplan, *supra* note 34, at 373–76; Brecher, *supra* note 39, at 434–50.
[55] Packer, *supra* note 41, at 277–79.
[56] See *N.Y. Times*, Nov. 5, 1972, § 1, p. 99, col. 4 (teenagers in New Mexico use toxic jimsonweed seeds as a hallucinatory drug; official sees a possible link to a shortage of marijuana).

dollars to fifty dollars an ounce.[57] By far the largest proportion of the buyer's cost could be attributed to the illegality of the drug; if it were not for the fact that every person in the chain of distribution must be compensated for the risk he takes, marijuana could probably be sold profitably at one dollar an ounce or less.

In the light of this analysis, the absurdity of decriminalizing possession while retaining sanctions against distribution becomes plain. Sellers (except for those toward the bottom end of the chain who distribute small amounts for small or insignificant remuneration) would continue to risk arrest and conviction, while the number of potential buyers would probably increase.[58] If the supply were to remain constant, the result would be that the price would rise. This rise, in turn, would increase the incentive for entrepreneurs to enter the market and find ways of bringing more marijuana into the United States. More likely the supply would keep pace with the demand. In either event, partial prohibition would continue to insure "a kind of monopoly profit to the entrepreneur who is willing to break the law." [59]

The commission might argue that because the demand for marijuana is elastic, "a concerted effort to eliminate major trafficking" would drive the price up enough to discourage use, even if the effort did not succeed in cutting off the supply entirely. To accomplish even this limited function, however, would require resources which would not be available and border controls which would not be feasible.[60] The more likely result of partial decriminalization would be to encourage venturesome entrepreneurs to seek their share of the monopoly profit awaiting those who could satisfy the demand for a product whose use would now be lawful. By contrast, if distribution as well as possession were legal, the sums which

[57] *N.Y. Times*, Nov. 20, 1972, p. 1, col. 5.

[58] It is possible that the number of potential buyers (that is, the number of persons interested in using marijuana more than occasionally) would remain the same; the effect then would probably be to maintain the sellers' profits at their present level.

[59] Packer, *supra* note 41, at 279. When New York State imposed severe new penalties for drug dealing, the number of sellers who "dropped out of action" as a result of the law was at least partly offset by the number who set up business "in an attempt to fill the void and 'get rich quick.' " One addict commented, "Uptown, downtown, in Chinatown—more places than before are opening up. Everybody's thinking, 'If this law's so tough, others will stop; so I'll start. I'll run with the chance.' And that's what they're doing" (*N.Y. Times*, Oct. 8, 1973, p. 46, cols. 4, 8).

[60] See *supra* pp. 43, 181–82. A further problem, as indicated earlier, is that if marijuana becomes too expensive some users may turn to more dangerous drugs.

the buyer pays in excess of the product's cost could be diverted from the entrepreneur to the public treasury in the form of taxes.[61]

In short, partial decriminalization would re-create for marijuana exactly the situation that prevailed for alcohol during Prohibition,[62] and Prohibition was the classic example of the operation of the crime tariff.[63] The commission acknowledges that Prohibition "failed to achieve its avowed purpose of eliminating the use of intoxicating liquors from American life," but it suggests that "two reasons were essentially responsible for this failure: the unwillingness of a substantial minority, and probably a majority, of the American public to discard a habit deeply ingrained in their lives; and the inability of the law enforcement community to eliminate the bootlegging traffic which catered to this continuing demand." [64] The commission thus falls back on its beliefs that the social interest in marijuana is "only transient" and that "a concerted effort to eliminate major trafficking" could be successful. As the preceding pages have demonstrated, these beliefs are not supported by the facts.[65]

The commission may well be correct in endorsing "a social control policy seeking to discourage marijuana use," but there is little reason to believe that a scheme of partial prohibition would be successful in achieving this goal. A licensing scheme could be almost as effective without the heavy social costs which must result from the effort to enforce *any* prohibition.

[61] I include in the product's "cost" a reasonable profit for the producers and distributors.

[62] See Henry Johnston, *What Rights Are Left* (New York, 1930), ch. 1.

[63] Packer, *supra* note 41, at 279.

[64] *Signal of Misunderstanding,* 164.

[65] As suggested in Part Two, the analogy to Prohibition cuts against the commission's proposal for a second reason: it strongly supports the argument that even a partial prohibition cannot be enforced without undesirable police practices.

XII

Alternatives
for the Legislature

REGULATION VERSUS PARTIAL PROHIBITION

The Shafer commission rejects the regulation approach—the licensing model—for a number of reasons, several of which have already been considered.[1] The others withstand scrutiny no better.

The commission finds that the regulatory approaches which the United States has used for alcohol and tobacco "have failed to accomplish two of their most important objectives: the minimization of excessive use and the limitation of accessibility to the young."[2] Since, as most people would agree, the young user and the chronic user would probably present the most serious public health problems if marijuana were easily available, it is understandable that the commission takes a wary attitude toward establishing a licensing system for the drug. Further study, however, indicates that the commission may be unnecessarily pessimistic about the effects of such a system on the two risk groups.

John Kaplan has painstakingly examined the problem of marijuana use by minors under a licensing system permitting sales only to adults. He agrees that there would be a certain amount of leak-

[1] The commission believes that marijuana use is "a fad which, if not institutionalized, will recede substantially in time" (National Commission on Marihuana and Drug Abuse, *Marihuana: A Signal of Misunderstanding* 165 [hereinafter cited as *Signal of Misunderstanding*]; see *supra* pp. 170–74). The commission apparently believes that the institution of a governmental licensing scheme would necessarily connote a policy of neutrality rather than discouragement (*ibid.*, 165–66; see *supra* pp. 43–44). The Commission fears the impact of decriminalization on those who support the present policy (*ibid.*, 167; see *supra* pp. 176–79).

[2] *Ibid.*, 148.

age to minors but suggests that the high resale price will be a "serious obstacle to heavy use," at least for some.[3] If Kaplan is correct in thinking that the price of legal marijuana can be maintained at a figure comparable to the "street price" of marijuana today, then his conclusion about leakage to minors is probably also correct. If, as I believe, the legal price will have to be substantially lower than Kaplan's projected price,[4] then the amount of leakage will probably be greater. Unfortunately, a significant amount of leakage is probably inevitable under any licensing system that will not encourage bootlegging.

The commission is probably correct, then, in thinking that substantial amounts of marijuana are likely to reach children under a licensing system. Nevertheless, as Kaplan has pointed out, "there is reason to believe that the problem of marijuana use [by minors] could be better controlled under a licensing system." Children would be more likely to experiment with marijuana under adult supervision rather than "within the peer group under conditions that tend to increase the thrill of doing what their parents are afraid to do." A reduction in abuse of more dangerous drugs might be expected.[5] Finally, it must be remembered that the relevant question is not how much leakage is likely to occur under a licensing system, but how much of an increase in use by minors could be expected. Surveys during the past four years have consistently shown that the incidence of use in high schools and even junior high schools has been rising.[6] As early as 1968 the *New York Times* reported that many freshmen arrive at college "already smoking marijuana or taking it for granted that it is part of the college experience."[7] Since then, the level of use has increased further. In short, prohibitory laws may be no more effective in deterring use by the young than they are in deterring use by anyone else.

These reports have also emphasized that for youths, as for adults, the law is only one factor—and probably not the most important one—in determining the extent and depth of drug use. When the dangers of "acid" (the hallucinogen LSD) were widely publicized, both in newspapers and through word of mouth, after the summer of 1967, the use of that drug fell off rapidly.[8] Similarly, after a brief

[3] John Kaplan, *Marijuana: The New Prohibition,* 349–54, 357.

[4] See *infra* pp. 198–99.

[5] Kaplan, *supra* note 3, at 357.

[6] See *supra* pp. 170–71.

[7] *N.Y. Times,* Jan. 11, 1968, p. 18, col. 2.

[8] Joseph Brenner, "Medical Care without a Hassle," *N.Y. Times Magazine,* Oct. 11, 1970, pp. 30, 110 (a doctor who directed a medical clinic for "street

upsurge in the use of hard drugs at the end of the 1960's, the demand for those drugs on college campuses virtually disappeared. One reason was "[b]ad experience with [those] substances in high school." [9] The commission appears to assume that prohibitory laws are the only barriers preventing the nation's youths from falling victim to the "maladjustment" that the commission fears will result from extensive marijuana use. Happily, as the reports I have cited suggest, most Americans—including the young—have internalized values which keep them from such excesses regardless of what the law permits or forbids. It cannot be assumed, therefore, that use by the young would increase more under a regulatory scheme than it would under partial prohibition.

The commission also expresses concern about the "minimization of excessive use" under a licensing system.[10] Here again, it is unlikely that partial prohibition would serve as significantly more of a deterrent than would regulation. Although the point cannot be proved, it seems very likely that the vast majority of those persons who are most likely to use marijuana in excess are already doing so. In most of the population centers of the country marijuana is easily available, although usually at a higher price than it would probably command under a licensing system. If a person is reasonably careful about where he smokes and from whom he buys, the odds are extremely high that he will not be caught. The only reason for not using marijuana may be the simple fact of its illegality. But surely those persons who are most likely to use marijuana in excess are those who are least likely to be deterred from doing so simply because they would thereby be breaking the law.[11]

These circumstances cast serious doubt on the commission's hypothesis that if prohibition were replaced by a regulatory system the prevalence of heavy use would remain the same in relation to total use.[12] On the contrary, the extent of heavy use would probably decrease in relation to total use, while remaining roughly the same in absolute terms. Thus, the public health problem which the commission envisions as a result of "a larger incidence of long-term

people" in Cambridge, Massachusetts, notes that "when the news first broke that there was some evidence that acid could cause genetic damage, there was a significant falling off in the use of LSD"); *N.Y. Times,* Jan. 11, 1968, p. 18, col. 4; Feb. 26, 1970, p. 1, col. 2; p. 69, col. 1.

[9] *N.Y. Times,* Nov. 20, 1972, p. 1, col. 5; p. 47, col. 1; see also *ibid.,* Jan. 17, 1971, § 1, p. 52, col. 6.

[10] *Signal of Misunderstanding,* 148.

[11] See Kaplan, *supra* note 3, at 355–56.

[12] *Signal of Misunderstanding,* 90.

heavy and very heavy use of potent preparations" [13] is not likely to materialize under a regulatory scheme.

Even if it is assumed that easier availability would increase the extent of excessive use, the commission's approach is hardly a satisfactory solution. Under the partial prohibition scheme both stigma and risk would be virtually eliminated for the user. For those whose inclinations lie in the direction of excessive use, partial prohibition would present no more than a nominal barrier. Certainly the Volstead Act's ban on the sale and distribution of liquor did not prevent widespread drunkenness.[14] What is worse, the partial prohibition scheme precludes all of the various controls that could be imposed under a regulatory system. Again, the experience of the Volstead Act is illuminating. The fact that all sales of liquor were unlawful meant that bootleggers and moonshiners made their own untrammeled decisions about the purity and potency of the liquor they put into the hands of their customers. The result was widespread consumption of liquor that was strong and often poisonous.[15] Similarly, under the commission's scheme marijuana sellers might mix more potent drugs in with *Cannabis* to give it a particular "kick." The kick may be accompanied by an addictive substance which the user did not ask for and does not want. (Sometimes the seller may be deliberately attempting to build a market for more profitable hard drugs.)

In support of its conclusion the commission points to the "failure" of alcohol regulation: "Despite the warning and restraints on distribution and consumption, . . . more than nine million Americans are 'problem' drinkers." [16] This may be true, but as Kaplan points out, the situation was no better, and probably was worse, during Prohibition.[17] Moreover, the very fact that marijuana has only recently become popular as a social drug increases the likelihood that abuse can be dealt with successfully. Alcohol has been used to excess for so many decades that it is hardly surprising that belated efforts to deal with it on the basis of modern knowledge and public health techniques have had only limited success. In short, the acknowledged failure of a regulatory approach to control alcohol abuse does not mean that regulation will be unsuccessful in controlling marijuana abuse.

[13] *Ibid.*, 148.
[14] Andrew Sinclair, *Era of Excess,* 233–38.
[15] *Ibid.*
[16] *Signal of Misunderstanding,* 148–49.
[17] Kaplan, *supra* note 3, at 356.

The commission rejects the argument that a licensing system would permit regulation of the quantity and quality of marijuana available to users. *Cannabis* can be grown so easily in this country that "many persons would choose to ignore the legitimate source and grow their own." The commission notes too that "intensive regulation of alcoholic beverage production has not eliminated illicit production." [18]

It is true that *Cannabis* "can be grown easily almost anywhere in the United States with little or no human assistance." Harvesting the *Cannabis,* however, does require effort, and so does preparing it for smoking: the plant must be dried, broken up, and sifted. Further effort is required in rolling the joint. Even in a nation of do-it-yourself enthusiasts, most people would probably prefer to avoid this effort and purchase already-rolled joints at the corner drugstore or liquor store. (Tobacco smokers can save a substantial amount of money by rolling their own cigarettes, but only a tiny proportion of the nation's smokers do so.)

The likelihood that home-grown marijuana would threaten the regulatory scheme in a significant way is further reduced by the fact that marijuana grown in this country tends to be much less potent than marijuana grown in Mexico, the principal source for today's users.[19] Even if some American marijuana occasionally equals the potency of the Mexican product, the bootlegger, or the one who buys from him, will never be sure of what he is getting. If ready-rolled joints containing marijuana of a known and uniform potency are available at a reasonable price from a licensed dealer, most users will patronize the licensed dealer rather than resort to the black market.[20]

In noting that illicit production of alcoholic beverages has continued despite intensive regulation, the commission cites the fact that in 1971 the number of illegal stills destroyed was 3,327, and 5,512 persons were arrested.[21] If these statistics are relevant at all, they cut the other way. Moonshining has been declining steadily in

[18] *Signal of Misunderstanding,* 149.

[19] Erich Goode, *The Marijuana Smokers,* 247.

[20] Kaplan suggests other reasons why "the great majority of consumers are willing to pay a considerable premium to obtain [marijuana] from one legally licensed to sell it. . . ." It will usually be more convenient "to go to a regular place of business . . . than [to] hunt up one's 'connection.' " And most people would probably prefer not to cooperate in an illegality, even though they can save a small amount of money by so doing, "if they can have their desires satisfied with complete legality" (Kaplan, *supra* note 3, at 349).

[21] *Signal of Misunderstanding,* 149.

recent years. That number of illegal stills destroyed in 1971 is little more than one-third of the 9,225 destroyed only twelve years earlier, in 1959.[22] Even the 1959 figure is trivial in comparison to the total production of alcoholic beverages in this country.[23]

The commission expresses doubt that a licensing scheme would succeed in limiting the potency of the marijuana that would be available.[24] This skepticism rests in part on the commission's belief that marijuana would be sold extensively on the black market, an assumption that has already been found dubious. The commission also fears that a regulatory scheme would lead to the increased use of hashish.[25] A more plausible hypothesis is that there would be less incentive to use hashish if marijuana were easily and legally available. As Kaplan points out, "So long as marijuana of sufficient potency is available, even though it is not perhaps so strong as desired, the preference for legal and convenient drug purchasing will incline users towards the use of the more available rather than the stronger drug. . . . Indeed, once we see the issue as to which is the better way to arrest the spread of hashish—licensing or forbidding its principal and most logical competitor—the answer becomes fairly clear." [26]

What seems to underlie the commission's fears about the efficacy of potency controls and the possible spread of hashish use is a fundamental distrust of the marijuana smoker. The commission concedes that "few of the 24 million Americans who have tried marijuana use it, or have used it, irresponsibly." In the commission's view, this is because the vast majority of users have internalized a "preference for individual productivity." [27] No reason is given to

[22] *Time*, May 1, 1972, p. 24.

[23] It might be thought that the comparison is irrelevant, for distilling alcoholic beverages is a much more cumbersome and complicated process than raising and preparing marijuana. Nevertheless, the Wickersham commission reported that "[f]ew things are more easily made than alcohol. A home-made apparatus will suffice, and with the variety of materials available and the ease of procuring those materials, any one may carry on home distilling on a small scale" (National Commission on Law Observance and Enforcement, *Report on the Enforcement of the Prohibition Laws* [Washington, D.C., 1931], 33). It must be conceded that the difference between homemade liquor and commercially distilled liquor is much greater than the probable difference between home-grown marijuana and commercially processed marijuana. It may also be relevant that the Wickersham commission was writing at a time when home distillation probably seemed less onerous to most Americans than it would today.

[24] *Signal of Misunderstanding*, 149.

[25] *Ibid.*

[26] Kaplan, *supra* note 3, at 348.

[27] *Signal of Misunderstanding*, 136.

suggest that this internalized value might disappear as the result of a change in the law. Nevertheless, the commission seems to assume that substantial numbers of users would not be satisfied with a legal joint but would insist upon smoking marijuana of higher potency or even hashish, turning to channels outside the regulatory system in order to obtain them. This assumption, in turn, seems to rest on the unstated premise that individuals who use marijuana are motivated primarily by the desire to defy authority or to boost their egos or "to do something daring and dangerous." [28]

"The simple fact," as the commission's consultant Erich Goode concluded after an extensive study of marijuana smokers, is that "marijuana is fun to smoke. . . . [P]leasure emerge[s] as the dominant motive for continued use." [29] Nothing in Goode's survey (or in the commission's report) suggests that users who find pleasure in smoking the marijuana of variable potency which they now obtain illegally would not find satisfaction in smoking legal joints of known, standard potency. After all, if one joint is not enough, it is always possible to smoke another. In short, if marijuana smokers today are, for the most part, responsible individuals seeking pleasure, there is no reason to believe that a regulatory system would turn them into irresponsible individuals seeking a thrill.

REDUCING PENALTIES: HALF A LOAF
MAY NOT BE BETTER THAN NONE

I have tried to show that the commission's partial prohibition scheme will do little to reduce the most serious costs of present marijuana laws, that the scheme is unlikely to achieve the purposes which the commission envisions for it, and that the commission's objections to a regulatory system do not withstand analysis. The next step is to consider what kinds of controls might be appropriate under a regulatory system. Before doing so, I shall discuss another frequently-heard suggestion for dealing with the marijuana problem.

Many persons who acknowledge the injustice of sending people to prison for five to twenty years (and more) for using a drug that is probably less harmful than alcohol nevertheless remain opposed to the decriminalization of marijuana. They suggest that as an alternative (and perhaps interim) measure the penalties for possession of marijuana should be reduced. (Often this proposal is coupled

[28] Erich Goode, "Turning On for Fun," *N.Y. Times,* Jan. 9, 1971, p. 27, col. 1.
[29] *Ibid.*

with the suggestion that penalties for distribution and sale be retained or even increased. For reasons already discussed, any such distinctions are likely to rest on arbitrary and unrealistic characterizations.)

In New York, for example, a state commission recommended that a first offense of simple possession of less than a quarter of an ounce of marijuana be treated as a noncriminal violation, with a maximum penalty of fifteen days in jail. The New York commission also urged that the legislature reduce penalties for possession of larger quantities and suggested four categories of offenses involving the sale of marijuana, with penalties ranging from one to fifteen years.[30] Similar proposals have been endorsed by the National Commission on the Reform of Federal Criminal Laws, the American Medical Association, and the Canadian government.[31]

At first glance, reducing penalties for possession may appear to be an attractive compromise between broad reform of the marijuana laws and retention of the status quo. The principal argument, of course, is that violators, especially young offenders, would no longer be subject to long prison terms, not to mention all of the other deprivations resulting from a felony conviction, for having in their possession a small quantity of marijuana.[32] It is hard to quarrel with this result, but reducing penalties may have other consequences that are less desirable.

With penalties reduced, enforcement is likely to become even more capricious than it is today. In some communities law enforcement officials might decide that it is no longer worthwhile to go after marijuana law violators. In other communities enforcement efforts might continue unabated. Within a single community each policeman or precinct captain would have wider discretion to enforce the law—or not enforce it—in accordance with his own attitudes toward marijuana: an officer who closed his eyes at a felony might be regarded as derelict in his duty, while it is expected that the police will exercise a range of discretion in dealing with misdemeanors. Selective enforcement and harassment could become even more common than they are now.

[30] *N.Y. Times,* Jan. 26, 1971, p. 67, col. 4.

[31] *N.Y. Times,* Jan. 8, 1971, p. 1, col. 6 (National Commission on Reform of Federal Criminal Laws); June 21, 1972, p. 56, col. 1 (A.M.A.); Aug. 1, 1972, p. 1, col. 5 (Canadian government). The American Bar Association, which initially took a similar position, has now urged that criminal penalties for simple possession should be eliminated. See 59 *A.B.A.J.* 1134–35 (1973).

[32] Under most proposals for reducing penalties for simple possession, a person possessing a large quantity could probably be convicted of a more serious offense —for example, possession with intent to sell.

Reducing penalties might actually increase the number of convictions for marijuana offenses. Packer observes that "[g]iven the devastating consequences of a criminal conviction to a middle-class person and the growing ambivalence among law enforcement officers about the severe marijuana laws, every avenue of discretion is used to minimize the impact of the law." [33] If a prosecutor need no longer fear that a young arrestee will have to suffer the consequences of a felony conviction, he may feel less of an impetus to "wash out" cases at the pretrial stage. Judges who feel a similar sensitivity would have less reason to look for a search-and-seizure flaw or other technicality as a basis for dismissing charges. Defense attorneys would have less leeway (and perhaps less incentive) to engage in plea bargaining.

The principal difficulty with simply reducing penalties for possession (and even casual distribution) is that the most serious consequences of marijuana criminalization would remain unabated. The user would still be labeled a criminal. Drug education efforts would continue to suffer. Law enforcement resources would still be diverted, though perhaps to a lesser extent, from more pressing problems. Most important, the police would continue to use questionable practices to ferret out violators; modifying the penalties for the same conduct would have no effect on the tactics needed to enforce the prohibition.

It may be argued that once simple possession is reduced to the status of a misdeameanor police would no longer be interested in hunting down offenders. Studies of police behavior suggest otherwise. If policemen tended to be neutral toward marijuana use, the legislature's action in reducing penalties might convey to them the message that they need not be so zealous in seeking out violators. But policemen tend to be quite conservative in their "political and emotional persuasion"; in particular, they are vehemently opposed to marijuana and narcotics.[34] One result of this attitude is that a policeman may be relatively indifferent to the outcome of judicial proceedings against users if he can make life difficult for them on the street or in their homes—by engaging in harassment or by seizing marijuana in searches that he knows may not stand up in court.[35] Moreover, proposals for reducing penalties often define simple possession very narrowly, retain heavy sanctions for many other kinds of marijuana transactions, and preserve the unrealistic

[33] Herbert Packer, *The Limits of the Criminal Sanction,* 340.
[34] Jerome Skolnick, *Justice without Trial,* 61, 208.
[35] See *supra* p. 105.

distinction between users and sellers. Even a policeman who was relatively neutral toward marijuana might feel justified in continuing his enforcement practices pretty much without change.

These difficulties are illustrated by the new Oregon marijuana law, which has been described as the most lenient in the country. Under legislation enacted late in 1973, possession of one ounce or less of *Cannabis* remains illegal, but violation of the law is treated more like a traffic offense than a crime. A citation is issued, and the maximum penalty on conviction is a one-hundred-dollar fine, regardless of the number of previous convictions. No criminal record results from a conviction. The law made no change, however, in the penalties for cultivating, transporting, or furnishing marijuana to another (whatever the quantity and whether or not any money changes hands); these remain Class B felonies, for which sentences of up to ten years' imprisonment may be imposed.[36]

In the first two months under the new law, police in Multnomah County (Portland) issued about forty citations—"mostly to teen-agers, street people, hippies, the ones who smoke in public places," according to the county prosecutor. Virtually all of those who received citations pleaded guilty and accepted a penalty, usually a light one. Even in the immediate aftermath of the new legislation, however, the problems inherent in any such approach could be discerned. Some police officers and district attorneys expressed strong opposition to the new law; where such attitudes prevail, the undesirable enforcement practices described earlier can be expected to continue. Indeed, unsympathetic officers may even have intensified their pursuit of chimerical "pushers." In the state as a whole, the prohibitions may be unequally enforced, depending on local attitudes.

In spite of the lurking problems, however, the new law represents an important advance, not so much for itself as for the cumulative effect that it may have when taken together with other legislative steps in the same direction. As more and more jurisdictions move further toward decriminalization, without any of the untoward consequences that have been feared, it will become increasingly difficult to maintain that criminal sanctions for marijuana use and distribution serve any useful purpose at all. The anomaly of retaining laws that can be enforced only through practices which themselves injure society will become more and more apparent. Ultimately, if half-way reforms come fast and promi-

[36] Ore. Laws 1973, ch. 680, amending Ore. Rev. Stat. § 167.217. The account in the text also draws upon *N.Y. Times,* Dec. 18, 1973, p. 29, col. 1.

nently enough they may result in ad hoc decriminalization in many jurisdictions—at the trial level because juries will not convict, and at the enforcement level because the goal of ferreting out users and "getting marijuana off the streets" will no longer legitimize harassment and invasions of privacy, even in the eyes of many police officers. That is, grudging reforms by legislators, reinforced by the increasing acceptance of *Cannabis* use among respectable people, will make it harder and harder for some of the participants in the criminal justice system to deal with marijuana users and distributors as criminals. At the same time, other jurors and other officers will find no reason to change either their attitudes or their practices. One consequence will be to make enforcement even more haphazard and uneven than it is today. Another will be to create a sort of schizophrenia in the minds of many officers. Indeed, in jurisdictions where police policy (stated or tacit) deemphasizes enforcement of the marijuana laws, this schizophrenia already exists. A Washington, D.C., area police officer put it this way: "There's so much marijuana on the street now that either we're going to have to have strict penalties and enforce the law and try to get rid of it, or we're going to have to legalize the stuff. Now we're going both ways, and it's not worth two cents." [37]

MAKING REGULATION WORK

The leading advocate of a licensing system for marijuana has been John Kaplan, who outlined his proposals first in a widely reviewed

[37] *Washington Post,* Aug. 20, 1973, p. C-4, col. 8. The tensions that may be created by partial reforms are also illustrated by the dispute that arose when Earl J. Silbert, U.S. attorney for the District of Columbia, sought to implement a policy under which his office would no longer file court charges against persons arrested in Washington with five or fewer marijuana cigarettes or up to a gram of the drug in any form. Silbert thought he had reached an agreement with the police department, but when the plan was announced police officials attacked it, and their protests were instrumental in forcing Silbert to cancel his no-prosecution order. Although the motivations behind the quarrel were complex, news reports suggested that two of the factors were the reluctance of the police to let the city of Washington become "a haven for anyone to come in and smoke marijuana," as the acting police chief put it, and the fact that marijuana arrests constitute an easy way for police officers to build up a good record. To the extent that such attitudes prevail, statutory reforms that abrogate some marijuana offenses while retaining others will have that much less effect on police enforcement practices. (As suggested in the text, these attitudes also tend to limit the effectiveness of "de facto" decriminalization.) For details on the Silbert initiative and its demise, see *Washington Post,* Nov. 16, 1974, p. A-1, col. 6; p. A-5, col. 3; Nov. 19, 1974, p. 1, col. 4; Nov. 20, 1974, p. C-13, col. 1; Nov. 30, 1974, p. A-1, col. 3; *Newsweek,* Dec. 2, 1974, p. 113; *Washingtonian,* January, 1975, p. 51.

book *Marijuana: The New Prohibition* and later in a law review article.[38] Kaplan takes as his model the licensing system presently used for alcohol. This model is an attractive one in many respects, but some of the restrictions which Kaplan advocates may not be necessary to achieve his goals, or even those of the Shafer commission.

In devising a system of regulation, the legislator must never lose sight of the reasons for regulating the commodity in question. Whatever restrictions are to be imposed on the use and distribution of marijuana through a licensing scheme, they should be justified as a means of averting particular evils associated with that drug. Kaplan agrees with the Shafer commission that if marijuana poses any danger at all to society, the danger lies in two kinds of behavior: use by the young and excessive use. The restrictions imposed through a licensing scheme, then, should focus on two objectives: "the minimization of excessive use and the limitation of accessibility to the young." [39] Any restrictions which do not relate to these two objectives should be regarded with skepticism.

This last point deserves elaboration, for it is repudiated explicitly by the commission and perhaps implicitly by Kaplan. The commission states: "In the case of marijuana, there is no fundamental principle supporting the use of the drug, and society is not compelled to approve *or be neutral* toward it. The opinion of the majority is entitled to greater weight [than in the case of desegregation]." [40] I have disavowed any reliance in my argument on the philosophy of government associated with John Stuart Mill, but one would expect the commission to recognize that Mill's "harm to others" formula constitutes an important strain in American political thought.[41] Under that philosophy, society is compelled to be neutral toward the use of marijuana unless it has a good reason to restrict it.

Kaplan acknowledges the relevance of these considerations: "In our society, we have a tradition of freedom and autonomy that holds that a competent adult may undertake a wide range of actions in which he may damage himself. The fact that such damage may lead him to become a public charge may justify some types of pre-

38 Kaplan, "The Role of the Law in Drug Control," 1971 *Duke L. J.* 1065 (1971).

39 *Signal of Misunderstanding,* 148.

40 *Ibid.,* 133 [emphasis added].

41 See, e.g., State v. Sinclair, 387 Mich. 91, 194 N.W.2d 878, 895 (1972) (T. G. Kavanagh, J., concurring).

ventive action, but such action is generally taken only where the need is most clear. . . . In Anglo-American law, protecting the individual from himself has clearly been the exception rather than the rule." [42] In discussing alternatives to the criminalization of marijuana, however, Kaplan appears to take a more protective attitude. He finds "a unique social reason" for the control of marijuana in that "the use of any kind of psychoactive drug, including marijuana, can turn its user away from solving the societal problems responsible for his dissatisfaction. Even though this type of user by no means becomes a public charge, he may fail to realize his full value to society or to himself." [43] This statement strikes a jarring note in Kaplan's analysis: given our "tradition of freedom and autonomy," it is hardly self-evident, even for those who reject Mill's philosophy, that an individual's liberty to gratify his desires may be restricted by a democratic government on the ground that he may otherwise "fail to realize his full value to society or to himself." The other dangers which Kaplan associates with marijuana involve harm principally to the user.[44] Thus, given Kaplan's premise and his conclusions about the dangers of *Cannabis,* one is surprised that he finds it *"clear* . . . that we should treat marijuana considerably more respectfully than we do sugar candy." [45] If marijuana is dangerous principally to the user, then perhaps we *should* treat it like sugar candy, for even sugar candy can rot the teeth and contribute to obesity—the latter, at least, a major health problem in this country.

Notwithstanding these other concerns, Kaplan, like the commission, focuses primarily on means of avoiding excessive use of marijuana and use by the young. Many of the restrictions he proposes, however, seem unrelated to these goals. This is hardly surprising, since the licensing system for alcoholic beverages, which Kaplan takes as his model, typically includes many restrictions that are designed to serve very different purposes. I suggest that the principal goals of a marijuana licensing system can be best attained by a scheme that borrows from both the alcohol model and the tobacco model.

Kaplan's proposal may be summarized as follows. Marijuana of a standard potency would be sold only in liquor stores at a price of

[42] Kaplan, *New Prohibition, supra* note 3, at 147–48.
[43] *Ibid.,* 329.
[44] See Kaplan, *New Prohibition, supra* note 3, at ch. 5, *passim.*
[45] *Ibid.,* 329 [emphasis added].

about eighteen dollars an ounce, including a tax of twelve dollars. "All advertising would be forbidden except that which is done within the liquor store. . . . Sales to those under age would be prohibited under exactly the same type of regulations that now apply to hard liquor," except that the age for consumption of marijuana would be eighteen instead of twenty-one.[46]

An important aspect of Kaplan's proposal is the principle that the government should adjust the tax rate on marijuana so that the price is as high as it can be without bringing into existence an illegal market. It is by no means clear that such price controls will contribute significantly to achieving the goals of the regulatory system. Since the sale of marijuana to minors is forbidden at any price, presumably the purpose of keeping the price high is to discourage excessive use by adults.[47] One cannot assume, however, that a high price will cut down on consumption by persons prone to overuse. A person who wants to use marijuana to such excess that he becomes a public health problem may be willing to give up other commodities so that he can obtain it. For ordinary users, the high price would result in consumption at a lower-than-moderate level rather than a moderate level. Further, the high price will have no effect at all on overuse by the well-to-do.

Although Kaplan's proposed price would be somewhat lower than the street price in the eastern part of the country in recent years, it would be substantially higher than the price in the west, where a one-ounce lid can often be bought for ten dollars. I agree with Kaplan that "the majority of consumers are willing to pay a considerable premium to obtain the commodity from one legally licensed to sell it," [48] but there are limits to the premium that people will pay, and I suggest that a price of eighteen dollars is far too high. Kaplan states that the cost of producing an ounce of marijuana is about one cent.[49] Even if that figure is off by a factor of ten, it is unlikely that the retail price of an ounce in an unregulated,

[46] Kaplan, "Role of the Law," *supra* note 38, at 1101.
[47] Kaplan does rely to some extent on the high price to restrict the availability of marijuana to minors (Kaplan, *New Prohibition, supra* note 3, at 351). He assumes, however, that the regulated price will be roughly the same as the street price today, so that the price to minors would have to be even higher to compensate the seller for the risks involved. For reasons to be stated, I think that the legal price will have to be substantially lower than Kaplan does. In short, if the price is set high enough to be a significant deterrent to "leakage," it will probably be so high that it will encourage the development of a black market.
[48] Kaplan, *New Prohibition, supra* note 3, at 349.
[49] Kaplan, "Role of the Law," *supra* note 38, at 1101.

untaxed market would be more than two or three dollars. Maintaining the price at a figure six or nine times as great would almost certainly create a black market which could not be controlled without raising all of the problems that make the present system unacceptable.

Since the United States has long taxed its major legal social drugs —alcohol and tobacco—at a rate usually applied to luxuries, one cannot object to imposing a similar tax on marijuana. Clearly the tax should not be so high that it will encourage the development of a black market, but once that point is accepted it becomes difficult to find other principles bearing on the appropriate rate of taxation. If one looks to the fact that an evening of alcoholic recreation can be had at a cost of a few dollars, perhaps marijuana ought to be taxed at a rate that would bring the cost of an evening's recreation to a comparable figure. Or, if one focuses on the fact that a person who smokes one pack of tobacco cigarettes a day pays two or three dollars each week in cigarette taxes, a somewhat lower rate might be suggested. In any event, the most important consideration is to keep the tax rate low enough so that users would not be encouraged to grow their own marijuana or to engage in black-market dealings with a "Mexican connection." Otherwise, the police would turn once again to questionable tactics, this time to find violators of the revenue laws.

In *Marijuana: The New Prohibition* Kaplan considers the issue of whether marijuana should be sold under a state monopoly or by private retailers licensed by the state. He opts for the former method. His later article, however, proposes that marijuana be sold "in any store licensed to sell hard liquor." [50] This is a sensible modification, but Kaplan goes on to say that "we would incorporate by reference all of the many restrictions on liquor stores—from the moral character of the seller to the spatial distance between schools and churches."

It is difficult to understand the purpose behind this suggestion, unless it be to appease the antimarijuana forces. In most states the

[50] *Ibid.* A working paper prepared for the commission suggests that the preferable marketing system for marijuana "would be the utilization of retail pharmacies which are already licensed by the Federal Government to dispense drugs and, after meeting any necessary prerequisites, could be licensed as retail marijuana distributors." This system would probably provide the maximum convenience while making the purchaser "more conscious of the fact that he is consuming a potentially harmful drug" (*Signal of Misunderstanding, Appendix,* 1182).

sale of liquor is hedged about with a hodgepodge of restrictions that is probably unique in regulatory schemes. Some of these restrictions appear to be designed to placate temperance or prohibitionist sentiment. Others protect one segment or another of the liquor industry. Some legislation results from the combined pressure of prohibitionists and distillers or prohibitionists and small retailers. With few exceptions, these restrictions do not serve any discernable social purpose; their principal effect is to throw a series of petty and annoying hurdles in the way of those who enjoy drinking without significantly limiting access to children or preventing excessive use by adults.[51]

Whether or not similar restrictions are imposed on the sale of marijuana is hardly significant in the wider context of decriminalization versus continued prohibition. What is significant is the fact that Kaplan is untroubled by the pointlessness of most of these restrictions. His position is made explicit in a parenthetical remark: "[T]here is no purpose served by making access to the drug too convenient. . . ." [52] Surely this is the wrong way to approach the question. Restrictions that would impede access to the drug should be justified by particular evils which the legislature seeks to avoid. For example, given the uncertainties about the effects of marijuana on children, it would be reasonable not to permit the sale of marijuana in vending machines. It might be reasonable also to limit the number of outlets in which marijuana can be sold in order to make policing more feasible. But prohibiting sales at certain hours or on certain days will have no effect on limiting access to minors and little effect in preventing overuse.

Although most of the restrictions proposed by Kaplan (except those designed to restrict access to children) are likely to do little more than annoy users, such restrictions may nevertheless be justifiable because of their symbolic function. Just as today's liquor laws, absurd though they may seem to the rationalist, give some reassurance to temperance and prohibition forces, similar restrictions may serve to persuade groups opposing marijuana that the government has not capitulated entirely to the minority advocating a new norm. This kind of compromise might achieve the purpose which Gusfield and Williams attribute to some examples of patterned evasion: reduction of conflicts between social groups.[53]

[51] See Distilled Spirits Institute, *Summary of State Laws and Regulations Relating to Distilled Spirits* (Washington, D.C., 1972).
[52] Kaplan, *New Prohibition, supra* note 3, at 360.
[53] See *supra* pp. 22–24.

I have made no attempt in these pages to outline a comprehensive plan for regulating the distribution of marijuana after decriminalization. What is crucial is the perception that most Americans are not irresponsible and that the kind of irresponsibility that permits an individual to use marijuana to excess cannot be significantly counteracted by any plausible legal controls. When the problem is seen in this light, the selection of particular features for a regulatory scheme diminishes in importance. As long as *Cannabis* is neither so expensive nor so inconvenient to obtain that a black market develops, and as long as reasonable precautions are taken to minimize use by juveniles, there is no reason not to allow the states a good deal of leeway to develop regulatory schemes drawing upon the experience and social habits of their own citizens.

Conclusion

In 1928 Professor Howard McBain of Columbia University Law School published a book attacking the prohibition of liquor for some of the same reasons that I have put forth in urging the decriminalization of marijuana. Before describing the ways in which the enforcement of Prohibition had infringed the Bill of Rights, McBain commented, "Political prophecies are perilous; but it is highly improbable that the eighteenth amendment will ever be ripped from the side of the constitution or even be substantially altered by . . . amendment." [1]

It was not long, of course, before the perils of political prophecy were forcefully (though happily) brought home to Professor McBain. Within five years of his gloomy forecast Congress had submitted to the states a constitutional amendment repealing national prohibition, and less than ten months later the Twenty-First Amendment became law.

As of March, 1974, anyone proposing that criminal sanctions against the use and distribution of marijuana be replaced by a licensing system must admit that such a reform seems even more distant than repeal of the Eighteenth Amendment appeared to McBain in 1928. Nevertheless, several recent developments suggest that history may yet repeat itself. Several state court judges have expressed the opinion that marijuana laws are unconstitutional. Some courts have struck down marijuana laws on equal protection grounds which, as I have suggested in an earlier chapter, really implicate substantive due process. Most important, the widely

[1] Howard McBain, *Prohibition: Legal and Illegal*, 17.

respected Consumers Union has expressed its support for a licensing system much like the one proposed by Kaplan.

Of course, most of the other organizations that have taken a position on marijuana have called for more moderate reforms. Some have urged no more than a reduction in the penalties for simple possession; and indeed, within the last three or four years legislatures in several states have taken that step. A few groups have followed in the path of the Shafer commission, calling for the decriminalization of possession and use but not of sale and distribution. At best, however, these halfway measures would adopt for marijuana the unworkable solution that the Eighteenth Amendment legislated for the alcohol problem.[2]

If the question were only whether people who want to smoke marijuana should be permitted to indulge their desires, I would not have written a book of this size to argue the case on their behalf. As I have tried to show in these pages, however, the question cuts far deeper than that, for the marijuana laws have played an important part in creating the crisis of confidence in our legal institutions which confronts us today. It is this aspect of the marijuana laws that should be of special concern to members of the bar, quite apart from the debate about the medical or moral justification of the laws.

All too often we forget that the criminal law is a crude tool—a blunt instrument, so to speak—for dealing with social problems. The use of the criminal law to achieve ends for which it is not appropriate is—to borrow a phrase from H. G. Wells—like "a magnificent but painful hippopotamus," [3] resolved at any cost upon picking up a pea that is hidden somewhere in the jungle. The hippopotamus may conceivably succeed in its quest; more likely, it will fail. What is certain is that in the attempt it will knock down many innocent victims and will give up much of its dignity. Much the same thing has happened as a result of the attempt to control marijuana use through the processes of the criminal law: the rights of the innocent have been violated and the law has lost much of its dignity.

[2] In December, 1974, the *New York Times* noted a "clear and growing trend toward decriminalizing" marijuana, but added: "Significantly, none of the proposed state and federal statute changes goes beyond the elimination of penalties for private use and possession of marijuana. The sale and distribution of marijuana would still be illegal" (*N.Y. Times,* Dec. 8, 1974, § 4, p. 11, col. 4).

[3] H. G. Wells, *Boon,* quoted in *The Antic Muse,* ed. R. P. Falk (Evergreen ed., 1956), 133.

No constitutional amendment is needed to put an end to these depredations. The models for reform are at hand. The way to control marijuana is not through unenforceable prohibitions, but through regulation and licensing. Any other course of action will further debase the quality of justice and law enforcement and alienate from society many of its most valuable constituents.

Index